CBT for Depression:

AN INTEGRATED APPROACH

Sara Miller McCune founded SAGE Publishing in 1965 to support the dissemination of usable knowledge and educate a global community. SAGE publishes more than 1000 journals and over 800 new books each year, spanning a wide range of subject areas. Our growing selection of library products includes archives, data, case studies and video. SAGE remains majority owned by our founder and after her lifetime will become owned by a charitable trust that secures the company's continued independence.

Los Angeles | London | New Delhi | Singapore | Washington DC | Melbourne

CBT for Depression:
AN INTEGRATED APPROACH

Stephen Barton
Peter Armstrong

Los Angeles | London | New Delhi
Singapore | Washington DC | Melbourne

Los Angeles | London | New Delhi
Singapore | Washington DC | Melbourne

SAGE Publications Ltd
1 Oliver's Yard
55 City Road
London EC1Y 1SP

SAGE Publications Inc.
2455 Teller Road
Thousand Oaks, California 91320

SAGE Publications India Pvt Ltd
B 1/I 1 Mohan Cooperative Industrial Area
Mathura Road
New Delhi 110 044

SAGE Publications Asia-Pacific Pte Ltd
3 Church Street
#10-04 Samsung Hub
Singapore 049483

Editor: Susannah Trefgarne
Assistant editor: Talulah Hall
Production editor: Thea Watson
Copyeditor: Elaine Leek
Proofreader: Mary Dalton
Indexer: Silvia Benvenuto
Marketing manager: Camille Richmond
Cover design: Sheila Tong
Typeset by: C&M Digitals (P) Ltd, Chennai, India

Library of Congress Control Number: 2018937449

British Library Cataloguing in Publication data

A catalogue record for this book is available from
the British Library

ISBN 978-1-5264-0273-8
ISBN 978-1-5264-0274-5 (pbk)

In memory of Jo Stace

Contents

About the Authors

Stephen Barton is Head of Training at the Newcastle CBT Centre and former director of the Newcastle CBT Diploma. He has doctorates in cognitive science (Glasgow) and clinical psychology (Leeds), and has lectured in clinical psychology at the Universities of Leeds and Newcastle. An experienced therapist, supervisor, trainer and researcher, for the past twenty years he has specialized in providing CBT to people with complex mood disorders. He is a staunch advocate of the need to integrate evidence, theory and practice in clinical interventions, CBT in particular. His work is devoted to developing therapies for problems that are not currently treatable, with a strong emphasis on personalized healthcare. His method of development is to 'shuttle' between single case analysis in the clinic and basic studies of psychological processes in the lab or field. His other clinical interests include training models, interpersonal processes, personal and spiritual development. He is married with three sons and lives in the North East of England.

Peter Armstrong read Philosophy and English before training as a teacher and qualifying as a mental health nurse in the 1980s, then as a cognitive therapist, under Ivy Blackburn, in the early 1990s. He worked in in-patient psychiatry services, and the Newcastle CBT Centre as therapist, supervisor and teacher, finishing his NHS career as head of training there. He was an associate of the group that developed the revised cognitive therapy rating scale, CTSR, and with Mark Freeston and colleagues helped develop the Newcastle 'Cakestand' model of clinical supervision as well as models of training and interpersonal processes in CBT. He is also a poet, publishing in magazines and anthologies since 1978 with five solo collections to his name.

Preface

We want to extend our thanks to a large number of people who have contributed, directly and indirectly, to the development of this book. It is a large number, because the approach introduced in this book has evolved over a twenty-year period: the learning curve has never flattened, and we are indebted to many people who have shared their knowledge and skills with us. Our development strategy, which emerged more by accident than design, has been to engage in a broad range of activities around the treatment of depression: offering CBT to depressed clients, supervising colleagues, providing training courses and conducting research projects. We have conducted several hundred courses of therapy, supervision, training and research, and we have learned something new from each one. This book is the culmination of that learning.

We did not set out with the aim of integration; it emerged out of our exploration in the field and attempts to work with difficult-to-treat clinical presentations. In the late 1990s, it was becoming apparent that depression would one day be the leading source of disability worldwide, so the need for more potent psychological therapies was obvious. That day has now arrived. At that time, CBT for depression was dominated by Aaron Beck's Cognitive Therapy (CT). It was a revolutionary development in psychotherapy, and the cornerstone for the expansion of CBT for numerous other psychological and emotional problems. We had expected, and hoped for, a process of model refinement in CBT for depression, gradually increasing its specification and treatment potency. This R&D strategy had brought success in other fields, most notably CBT for anxiety disorders.

The depression field has developed a lot, but not as we expected. Instead of a scientifically driven process of model refinement, Beck's model has remained largely unchanged, at least in the way it is understood and used in clinical practice. It has spawned a large corpus of research, so a great deal is known about it and the associated therapy. But with relatively few exceptions, this new knowledge has not been fed back into model refinements and treatment updates. Working therapists are largely unaffected by the subsequent evidence, other than to know that CT is empirically supported and evidence-based, which it certainly is. Instead, we have witnessed the expansion of competitor therapies such as Behavioural Activation

(BA), Rumination-Focused CBT (RFCBT), Mindfulness-Based Cognitive Therapy (MBCT) and other third-wave approaches such as Compassion Focused Therapy (CFT) and Acceptance and Commitment Therapy (ACT). To different degrees these sit within the broad therapeutic school of CBT (although that is now questionable for CFT), but they are clearly distinguished from Beck's CT.

Of course, these therapies embody new models which are to be welcomed and celebrated. The field is rich and diverse, which is a good thing, but it is also hotly contested and somewhat disjointed, which is not necessarily a good thing, particularly if the same psychological processes are duplicated with different names in different CBT therapies. It is also not good if the primary effect of head-to-head contests, such as randomized controlled trials, is to produce a winner, rather than discover how depression is maintained and how best it can be overcome. The real winners in psychotherapy research are clients, assuming researchers have the humility to admit we know much less than we would like, and there is a great deal still to be learned.

As the title suggests, this book proposes an integrated approach that incorporates elements of all the above therapies. Our suggestion is simple: we believe it is time to integrate CBT therapies, not proliferate them. This is not anti-developmental, nor is it anti-innovation. It makes the simple point that after a long period of diversification, the depression field needs a period of integration to find out whether these therapies embody differences of kind, nomenclature or marketing. We suspect it is a combination of all three. This book is a contribution to that agenda: it proposes a place to start, but it is certainly not the final statement. Integration will have a long arc. To that end, the approach introduced in this book is already the result of hundreds of iterations of model refinement, research and development. Consequently, there are a lot of people to thank.

First and foremost, we want to thank our main teachers: our clients. Eleven of them have agreed for their therapy to be described in detail in this book. Without their openness, generosity and willingness to support it, the book would be a much less colourful text. There are hundreds of other clients with whom we have learned a great deal: their feedback and response to therapy has been precious. There would have been no book to write without their contribution: thank you all.

There is a large number of colleagues who have influenced us greatly, too many to mention all by name. Tony Sanford and Stephen Morley have, very sadly, both passed away in recent years. Tony had a mercurial intellect and passion for psychology and cognitive science; it was a great fortune and privilege to be supervised by him over many years. Being with Tony expanded one's mind. Stephen had an exceptionally hard head, matched only by his soft heart. His humanity and compassion marked him out as an exceptional researcher, educator and mentor. Both were big thinkers, unafraid to question the status quo, and huge personal supports in the genesis of this work.

In Newcastle, Mark Freeston has provided outstanding academic leadership since 2000 and he, like many others in the North East of England, shares our passion for CBT. His approach to refining models of OCD and GAD has been an inspiration for our parallel interest in depression. He has been generous with his time and made creative inputs at several key junctures. Lots of other colleagues have contributed indirectly, not least our fellow therapists at the Newcastle CBT Centre and its former service lead, Vivien Twaddle. Vivien supported this work as a long-term development, in an era when quick-wins were more in fashion. We are very grateful to her and all the founding and early members of the CBT Centre, particularly Ivy Blackburn, who helped to form the tradition of mood disorder research in the North East. Several other colleagues in the Centre have created lots of learning opportunities: particularly Jackie Harrison, Dominique Keegan, Cate Moorhead, Val Speed, Tracy Thorne and Margaret Whittaker.

A number of colleagues have worked closely with us in the development of specific chapters. Over several years, David Philbrick has provided stimulation for our thinking about early-onset depression and it is fitting that the client described in Chapter 7 is his, not ours. Louise Wicks is an unsung heroine of the Newcastle CBT Centre; we have learned much from her steadfast hopefulness working with chronic depression. One of her clients is described in Chapter 9. Kevin Meares and Matt Stalker, also of the Newcastle CBT Centre, have contributed greatly to our reflections on the links between trauma and depression. Chapter 12 owes much to our stimulating conversations with them.

The CBT Diploma led by the Centre has, since 2008, been delivered in partnership with colleagues at the School of Psychology at Newcastle University, and prior to that for several years with Durham University. Our students have been guinea-pigs to many of our ideas and deserve a lot of credit for feeding back so constructively. There are too many to mention everyone individually, but thank you all. Several other clinicians and academics have contributed in different ways, in particular Dorothy Dunn, Mark Latham, Clare Lomax, Theresa Marrinan, Thomas Meyer, Lucy Robinson, Ailsa Russell and Richard Thwaites.

Thanks also to Anthony Bash, Beth Bromley, Jen Cottam, Tim Diggle, Paul Golightly and Michael Hodson who gave generously of their time to offer feedback on draft chapters, in addition to a number of anonymous reviewers who contributed very helpfully at the proposal and early development stages. James Ewing and Elizabeth Freeman have also been steadfast supporters: thank you. Last, but not least, our families have championed our cause and found a great deal of patience to let us write, when writing was certainly not the only task at hand: thank you Jim, May and Gillian, and most especially Rachel, Thomas, Luke and Jacob.

1

Introduction

Practitioner Guidance

If you have opened this book to find out if it will be useful to you, it will be helpful at the outset to be clear about its aims and intended readers. This is a clinically oriented book exploring how to provide Cognitive Behavioural Therapy (CBT) to clients suffering from Major Depressive Disorders (MDD). It is not a self-help book for people feeling depressed; there are several books of this kind already available (e.g. Gilbert, 2009). The main intended readership is CBT therapists working in clinical services, including students of CBT. It isn't written with any particular profession in mind; in fact one of the refreshing aspects of CBT is its multi-disciplinary nature. In recent years there has been an opening of routes into becoming a CBT practitioner; this book welcomes you and encourages your interest whatever path you are on. CBT interventions are also used widely by other practitioners and professionals, who would not consider themselves to be CBT therapists, but nevertheless find CBT a useful approach. This book will be helpful to you because it will provide a clear grasp of the theoretical frameworks and evidence base underpinning cognitive-behavioural interventions. For the same reasons, academics, researchers, psychologists, psychiatrists, psychiatric nurses, social workers, counsellors, occupational therapists and all students of mental health will find the book of interest.

Therapy manuals describe the essential components of a treatment but they sometimes fall short of explaining *how* that therapy should be delivered, particularly with more challenging presentations. In this book we aim to do both, and this is what we mean by practitioner guidance. Whilst one of the attractions of CBT, at least in its basic forms, is the relative ease with which practitioners and clients can grasp its fundamentals, it is a considerable challenge to provide CBT competently and responsively, particularly with complex or difficult-to-treat cases (Garland, 2015). Rich with case studies and examples, this book marries treatment components with how to go about providing them. There is also an emphasis on trouble-shooting because not all CBT interventions work smoothly every time; methods that generally work well can be a poor fit for particular clients. So this book explores how to provide CBT that is *responsive to the needs of particular clients*, particularly in challenging cases. Most of the clinical examples are based on clients within healthcare settings, since this is where most CBT is provided, but the guidance can be applied in a range of other sectors such as education, forensic, social work, probation, occupational health and independent practice.

We want to be clear at the outset that the emphasis is on treating *major* depression, in particular those clients who have not responded to established CBT therapies. Major depression is a very common mental health problem and the leading cause of ill-health and disability worldwide, a surprising fact when one considers the range of other physical and mental health conditions that have a disabling effect on human wellbeing. According to World Health Organization estimates, more than 300 million people are now living with depression, an increase of more than 18% between 2005 and 2015 (WHO, 2017). Lack of support for people with mental disorders, coupled with a fear of stigma, prevent many from accessing the treatments they need to live healthy, productive lives. This is a very concerning situation. In contrast with mild depression, major depression is associated with significant impairment to social and occupational functioning and huge personal, relational and economic costs when it is left untreated. It is heartening that evidence-based therapies, such as CBT, can make such a positive difference (Driessen & Hollon, 2010), but they are not yet effective for all clients and more research and development is needed.

For readers unfamiliar with the difference between major depression and milder mood disturbances, we have listed the criteria for Major Depression published in the tenth edition of the International Classification of Diseases (ICD-10; World Health Organization, 1992), in Table 1.1. To reach criteria for Major Depression the client must have two of the first three core symptoms (depressed mood, loss of interest in everyday activities, reduction in energy) plus at least two of the remaining seven symptoms.

These symptoms must be present for at least 2 weeks, but in clinical practice many clients will have experienced them for several months or even years. It is worth noting that severity is not only determined by symptoms: it is also their *impact* on occupational and social functioning. In relation to this, common distinctions between moderate and severe depression, and their typical impacts, are listed in Table 1.2. The presentation of clients varies considerably: some people's functioning reduces markedly with mild symptoms while others maintain surprisingly good functioning in spite of severe symptoms.

Table 1.1   Diagnostic symptoms of Major Depression listed in ICD-10

	Symptom
1	Depressed mood*
2	Loss of interest*
3	Reduction in energy*
4	Loss of confidence or self-esteem
5	Unreasonable feelings of self-reproach or inappropriate guilt
6	Recurrent thoughts of death or suicide
7	Diminished ability to think/concentrate or indecisiveness
8	Change in psychomotor activity with agitation or retardation
9	Sleep disturbance
10	Change in appetite with weight change

ICD-10: International Statistical Classification of Diseases and Related Health Problems, 10th Revision (see WHO, 1992).

CBT Model of Depressed Mood

CBT is usually provided through 16–24 treatment sessions over a 3- to 6-month period using an individualized formulation, or case conceptualization (DeRubeis et al., 2005). Later in the book we will review CBT's evidence base and explore several opportunities for its further development. However, we should be clear at the outset this book does not directly address brief or low-intensity cognitive-behavioural interventions for milder depression, such as guided self-help or computer-assisted CBT. Readers are encouraged to access other specialist texts devoted to this important area (Hughes, Herron & Younge, 2014; Papworth, Marrinan & Martin, 2013).

Table 1.2 Common functional impairments in moderate and severe depression

Functional domain	Moderate impairment	Severe impairment
Family relationships	Quiet, negative, passive	Withdrawn, disengaged, reluctant to talk
Education and work	Sometimes absent, less consistent effort (or more effort to maintain performance)	Often absent, reduced performance, lack of concern about consequences
Peer relationships	Decreased socializing, more isolated pursuits	Very isolated, socializing discontinued
Stress level and anxiety	Difficulties minimized or worried about privately	Feelings withheld, fears minimized by withdrawing
Suicidal ideation	Vague, occasional thoughts	Plan or method actively considered
Other self-harm	Occasional thoughts but no plans or attempts to harm	Self-neglect, possible cutting or other self-injury

To provide an orientation to some of the main issues, a CBT model of depressed mood is presented in Figure 1.1. This applies a generic 'hot-cross bun' model to the specific phenomena of depression. In this model a number of links are made that constitute a depressed mood: negative thinking, reduced activity, negative emotions and unpleasant body states. People who have not experienced severe depression sometimes struggle to understand why it cannot be shaken off or overcome more easily. In fact, clients with major depression experience a *much* greater intensity of negative emotions and distressing thoughts compared with 'normal' dysphoric moods.

For two linked reasons it is helpful to start with this basic model. Firstly, in many respects depression can be understood as a spectrum from normal dysphoria through to severe depression, and some of the phenomena observed in dysphoric moods, such as negative thinking and reduced activity, are also observed in severe depression. We will return to the relationship between normal and abnormal moods in Part II of the book. Secondly, Figure 1.1 neatly illustrates one of the fundamentals of CBT: emotional problems do not *persist* on their own. They are *maintained* by the cognitions and behaviours linked to them (Beck, 2011; Beck, Rush, Shaw & Emery, 1979; Martell, Addis & Jacobson, 2001). Attempting to feel differently through choice or effort, without engaging with other parts of the model, usually leads to no change, or just adds frustration into the mix. In contrast, it is usually more effective to change a behaviour or test out a belief to find out if it is accurate or helpful. This is at the heart of CBT.

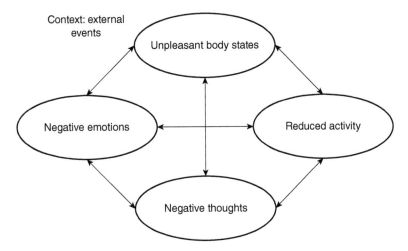

Figure 1.1   CBT model of depressed mood

Notice also that moods are not just emotions. Emotions can be quite short-lasting experiences triggered by specific events, whereas a mood tends to be a longer-lasting affective state. Although it is strongly affective in nature, there is usually more than one emotion involved, such as sadness, guilt or shame (Beck, 1976). Cognitive and behavioural aspects are fundamental in shaping how moods affect an individual. Moods colour how we perceive and think about the world; they orient our actions towards and away from different possibilities. We can be in the mood for doing X, but not Y, and so on.

This speaks to two other principles within CBT: firstly, we can believe something is true and feel sure about it, but we are actually mistaken; secondly, we can do what is helpful or necessary at one point in time, but later it develops into an unhelpful habit. There is good evidence that major depression is associated with unhelpful thinking and self-defeating behaviours. Inaccurate beliefs can *feel* true and unhelpful behaviours can *feel* helpful, because of their short-term effects. The general principle of testing out beliefs and experimenting with new behaviours is woven into the fabric of CBT. Of course, these principles are straightforward to understand intellectually, but they are less easy to apply in practice, particularly with challenging cases. This is one of the reasons for writing this book. As the book progresses we will see that CBT is not usually so simple as explaining to clients the benefits of thinking less negatively and becoming more active. Cognitive and behavioural changes need to be subtly and carefully targeted, particularly when working with clients with moderate or severe impairments.

Challenges for Therapists

This book engages with concrete experiences, not just theories or ideas, and we will focus on therapists' experiences, as well as clients'. We'd like to start that now by exploring your experience of working with depressed clients. This is a task we've used to good effect many times in training workshops because it helps to explore the sorts of challenges therapists face working with depression. If you're not a therapist, bring to mind a time you've been supporting a friend or family member who has been feeling very down.

Memory Task

Bring to mind a particular depressed client you have worked with in the past. Try to remember your first meeting, then subsequent sessions. Across the course of treatment, what *feelings* did you experience during your work together? Try to remember as many feelings as possible, not just information about the case. Take a few minutes to do this and list the feelings in a notebook before you read on.

When we first did this task we were surprised by the responses and we repeated it with different groups in various settings, finding the same pattern time and again. It is this: most therapists recall significantly more negative than positive feelings from their work with depressed clients. If this fits with your recollections, that is very normal. Table 1.3 lists common responses from our workshops: positive feelings are reported but they are consistently less common.

Could this be some kind of recollection bias? Perhaps therapists tend to remember experiences with more challenging clients? This may be true, but we don't believe it is the whole story. Encountering depressed moods in another person can be difficult, triggering a range of responses whether in a partner, friend, colleague or therapist. Being given permission to acknowledge and express difficult feelings can help therapists feel relieved that they aren't the only one who finds this work challenging. It can be de-shaming to 'fess up' to feelings of pessimism, frustration or even dread. But then there is a potential problem: if it is normal for therapists to experience negative feelings, how can they respond mindfully to those emotions so they form part of a creative understanding of their clients' experience, rather than react to them unreflectively?

In fact, this is a fundamentally hopeful situation because it demonstrates that therapists are *engaging* with the emotional world of their clients. Such engagement is essential

Table 1.3 **Feelings commonly experienced by therapists working with major depression**

Negative emotions	Positive emotions
Anxious	Comfortable
Disappointed	Empathic
Discomfort	Hopeful
Down	Rewarded
Drained	Satisfied
Dread	Sympathetic
Frustrated	
Heavy	
Helpless	
Hopeless	
Irritated	
Low	
Overawed	
Overwhelmed	
Panicky	

for the client to be supported, understood and taken seriously. Negative emotions are not bad: as long as they are noticed, reflected on and directed in a helpful way. It is when they go un-noticed or un-reflected that unhelpful behaviours result. To enable meaningful cognitive and behavioural change it is essential to have emotions and moods at the centre of CBT, not the periphery. This means that therapists need to be sufficiently aware of the impact of therapy on their own moods, and use supervision and reflective practice to make sense of them in the therapeutic process.

Follow-up Task

Choose one of the negative emotions from Table 1.3, preferably one you have experienced during your work with a depressed client. Consider the therapist behaviours that could result if this feeling was not noticed or was reacted to in an un-reflective way. Then consider possible therapist behaviours if the feeling is noticed and reflected on, for example in clinical supervision.

This task reveals a key challenge for therapists: while paying attention to their emotions, and the emotions of their clients, how to facilitate a process of *change*? Like all evidence-based psychotherapies, CBT requires therapists to balance support with change, and this is illustrated in Figure 1.2 (Webb, DeRubeis, Dimidjian, Hollon, Amsterdam & Shelton, 2012). When supportive elements are over-emphasized, therapists are over-concerned with building and maintaining a strong personal bond. They are empathic about their client's predicament, but if there is insufficient attention to change, that predicament is likely to be maintained rather than improved.

Conversely, if change-oriented techniques are over-emphasized, without building a sufficiently strong personal bond, the negative emotions reported by therapists in Table 1.3 are prone to recur. It can be frustrating and unsatisfying for therapists when depressed clients don't engage in the treatment as it has been outlined to them, for example, cancelling sessions, not doing homework, struggling to contribute to agenda setting, forgetting what was discussed in previous sessions, and so on. Therapists can experience this as thwarting, uncooperative, ungrateful or even sabotaging. In those same moments clients can experience their therapists as remote, business-like and safely distanced from the despair of depression. The aim is to balance and integrate bond and tasks, a theme we will return to throughout the book.

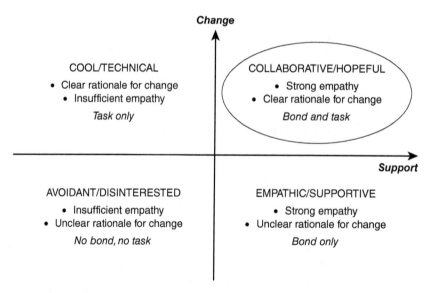

Figure 1.2   Balancing support and change in CBT for depression

Evidence-Based Practice

How can therapists learn to respond to these various challenges? The answer lies partly in a further theme: follow the evidence. All therapists want their treatment to be effective, and most recognize the need to ground it in an approach that isn't only personally satisfying, but also has empirical support. CBT for depression has a strong evidence base from randomized controlled trials (RCTs) and other types of evidence: therapy process studies, practice-based evidence, experimental studies of cognitive and behavioural processes, and so on. Clinical guidance tends to emphasize RCTs above other types of evidence and this is understandable to establish which treatments work for which disorders (NICE, 2009, 2017). Even when a breadth of evidence is considered, an awkward fact cannot be avoided: there is often a gap between the evidence base and its translation into clinical practice.

CBT for depression has a strong evidence base but there are several gaps, anomalies and ambiguities regarding its translation (Driessen & Hollon, 2010). For example, treatment manuals can be simultaneously supportive and frustrating. If the treatment components specified in manuals are empirically supported, it makes sense that this is what therapists should be doing. However, this overlooks two key points. Firstly, most manuals have a greater emphasis on *what* should be done than *how* to do it. How to deliver the therapy tends to be left to trainers and supervisors, and if training and supervision are not adequate, therapists can be left under-supported: the manual tells them what to do but falls short of explaining how (Roth & Pilling, 2007). Some manuals are also heavily task-focused. Rather than establishing a *balance* of bond and tasks they create the impression of therapy as a mainly technical exercise. In fact, all CBT skills are interpersonal skills. There is no way of setting an agenda or agreeing a homework task without a client present. Everything is done together. It is vital that therapists deliver the treatment components known to be effective, rather than drifting into an unstructured personal bond; but it is also important they are encouraged to be creative in delivering those components in a personalized and interpersonally-sensitive way (Waller & Turner, 2016).

Secondly, manuals are not always updated after RCTs have been completed and subsequent research becomes available. Not all treatment components are equally potent, so if manuals are not updated, therapists can be adherent to treatment procedures that are not strictly necessary and may be wasteful of treatment time. There have been 40 years of research since the inception of CBT for depression, but the lag-time for those findings entering routine clinical practice has been surprisingly long, especially when guidance, training and supervision have not been updated in a timely way. Alongside other influences, this book has grown out of a synthesis of that evidence, woven into the results of our own research and experience of providing therapy, supervision and training. The integrated approach that has resulted is introduced in detail in Part II.

We have learned a great deal from RCTs, but just as much from conducting single case analyses with our own clients. The reason is simple: clients with major depression *vary* a great deal. RCTs report average effects across large numbers of clients. The average effect of a treatment is important to know, but it creates the impression that most clients are average, as if they are drawn from an underlying normal distribution. The average client is a myth. All clients are unique, and the task of treatment is to apply the models and methods of CBT in a way that responds to individual need, not to apply what works for most people most of the time. For that reason our research and development strategy has been to take learning from RCTs and focus it on single case analysis. By recognizing the uniqueness of each individual we have learned a lot about what works for whom, and this is reflected in the case examples presented throughout the book.

The Heterogeneity of Major Depression

The *heterogeneity* of major depression is a huge challenge for CBT therapists. By this we mean multiple variations in the presentation of depressed clients. CBT provides a coherent framework to understand and treat depression, but this needs to be applied responsively to clients who often have very different needs. Heterogeneity can be encountered within the depression itself: some clients are in their first onset of major depression, others are in a pattern of repeated recurrences. Others have chronic and persistent depression that rarely, if ever, fully remits. The heterogeneity may be expressed in interactions with other mental health problems. Many have comorbid disorders such as Generalized Anxiety Disorder (GAD), Social Anxiety Disorder, Obsessive Compulsive Disorder (OCD) or Post-Traumatic Stress Disorder (PTSD). There is also the heterogeneity of clients' life circumstances: some are struggling with poverty, inadequate housing, unemployment or abusive relationships; others with physical health problems, such as illness or chronic pain. The varieties can be daunting and at times overwhelming, for client and therapist.

To respond to this breadth, our experience has taught us the importance of being *flexible* and *hopeful*. This will also be a recurring theme throughout the book. If you want to treat major depression, develop your capacity for hopefulness and expand your imagination to find flexible ways of delivering the therapy. Hope is not simply optimism or looking on the bright side. It is embodying and enacting the belief that no matter how bad a client's situation, there will be a way of improving it. With the above examples, none of the problems are *sufficient causes* of depression.

An individual's depression is not an inevitable consequence of comorbid disorders, social disadvantage, trauma or abuse. People can experience these problems and *not* fall into depression. When depression does occur its causal path usually involves multiple factors. Even for clients with traumatic histories, personality problems, social problems or chronic depression, the problem – at least in part – is the impact of those experiences on *how that individual thinks and behaves*. To follow through that logic, anyone can become depressed and everyone can recover or, at least, they can learn how to respond to depressed moods in ways that reduce their suffering. This book is an exploration of how to be hopeful and flexible working within the parameters of CBT, particularly when clients' depression is complex or difficult to treat. To do this effectively, heterogeneity has to be accepted and explored, not over-looked or over-simplified.

When therapist hopefulness and flexibility increases, the usual consequence is greater empathy, reward and satisfaction doing this therapeutic work. This has been our experience over an extended period, and a significant motivator to share our enthusiasm in this book. Of course, enthusiasm and hopefulness need to be harnessed with interventions that have the *potency* to respond to the types of challenges we've outlined. So how can CBT respond to these challenges? How can therapists adapt treatment to the needs of different clients?

The Heterogeneity of CBT

Beck et al.'s (1979) *Cognitive therapy* was the pioneering CBT treatment for depression and it is still the most widely researched and best-established work. We introduce it in detail in Chapter 2. Compared with before the turn of the millennium, CBT therapists now have multiple other options with the development of various other standalone treatments: Behavioural Activation, Rumination-Focused CBT, Mindfulness-Based CT and other third-wave approaches such as Compassion Focused Therapy and Acceptance and Commitment Therapy. These are welcome developments because, as we have outlined, depression is a multi-factorial problem. But, perversely, in clinical practice it is not always easy to know which model to adopt. Should I focus exclusively on a favoured approach and become familiar with it, at the risk of ignoring other models? Should I diversify and learn about new approaches, at the risk of losing fidelity and increasing confusion? Are third-wave therapies as effective as established approaches? These are the sorts of questions we've been asked many times at training workshops, and this book is partly the product of our endeavours to answer them.

Multiple approaches create therapeutic possibilities, and the field now has great breadth and depth, but in our view it lacks *coherence*. Competition between models is inevitable, and useful if it helps to find out which approach works best for particular clients. The downside is that shared treatment processes tend to be overlooked and differences magnified. An unintended consequence is confusion in the minds of therapists, and our approach has been to seek *integration*. We believe CBT therapies relate to each other on a spectrum, though we are not implying this was the intention of their developers. Different models attend to different phenomena, and since depression is such a heterogeneous disorder, there are a lot of phenomena to consider. We have illustrated these relationships in Figure 1.3.

- *Cognitive Therapy/Cognitive Behavioural Therapy (CT/CBT)*. CT/CBT's main concern is to develop functional beliefs and cultivate realistic thinking. A key way of doing this is scheduling enjoyable activities and conducting behavioural experiments; engaging in activities to test out predictions and put beliefs to the test. Cognitive change is the primary aim (Beck et al., 1979; Beck, 2011; DeRubeis et al., 2005).
- *Behavioural Activation (BA)*. BA considers behaviours in detail through functional analysis of their antecedents and consequences, the aim being to increase positive reinforcement and encourage engagement with rewarding aspects of the environment. This is guided by idiosyncratic personal values; behavioural change is the primary aim (Kanter, Busch & Rusch, 2009; Martell et al., 2001; Martell, Dimidjian & Herman-Dunn, 2010; Richards et al., 2016).

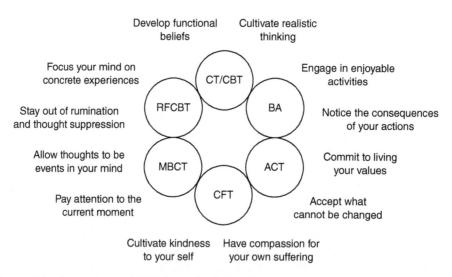

Figure 1.3   A spectrum of CBT therapies for major depression

- *Acceptance and Commitment Therapy (ACT)*. ACT encourages commitment to personal values, increasing contact with valuable experiences, maximizing what can be changed and accepting what cannot: this can otherwise become a source of conflict, pain and suffering. Behavioural change is essential to establish a different relationship to one's experience (Hayes, 2004; Zettle, 2007).
- *Compassion Focused Therapy (CFT)*. CFT cultivates compassion for one's own suffering and seeks to develop internal capacities for kindness. Many depressed people are compassionate to others but critical and judgemental of themselves; the challenge is learning how to be compassionate to oneself. In relation to depression, cultivating a compassionate self-to-self relationship is primary (Gilbert, Baldwin, Iron, Baccus & Palmer, 2006; Gilbert & Procter, 2006).[1]
- *Mindfulness-Based Cognitive Therapy (MBCT)*. MBCT encourages a non-judgemental acceptance of experience and helps clients learn how to pay attention to the current moment, including bodily experience; in this way thoughts and other mental events are experienced as events in the mind, rather than distressing truths. This helps to disrupt unhelpful processes such as cognitive rumination and emotional suppression (Ma & Teasdale, 2004; Teasdale, Segal, Williams, Ridgeway, Soulsby & Lau, 2000). Cultivating mindful awareness is the primary aim.
- *Rumination-Focused Cognitive Behavioural Therapy (RFCBT)*. RFCBT targets unhelpful repetitive thinking and helps clients to learn more effective ways of information processing, such as concrete/experiential processes in preference to abstract/conceptual thinking. This enables greater 'flow' between mind and experience, which helps to maintain realistic and helpful thinking, returning full circle to the original aims of CT/CBT (Watkins et al., 2007, 2011).

These therapies contain a lot of wisdom, some of it shared, some of it unique – but at this point it is not clear what is specific and what is common to all. Our strategy has been to prioritize the *psychological processes that maintain depression*, rather than work within the parameters of one model. The challenge has been the large number of maintenance processes, and as we have tackled each one, we have experimented with various treatment components from the above therapies. In following this method, we have discovered that CBT can have a broad range of effects: reality-orienting, activating, problem-solving, engaging, accepting, self-compassionate, mindful, mentally freeing, and so on. Clients need these, and benefit from them, to different degrees. They do not necessarily need separate types and courses of CBT to experien16ce these benefits; a single course of integrated CBT can be sufficient, at least for some clients.

---

[1]The proponents of CFT do not view it as a Cognitive Behavioural Therapy but its theory and techniques can be used to augment CBT. This is the approach we take in this book.

Integrated Approach

Psychotherapy integration is usually *between* therapy schools such as cognitive-behavioural, systemic, interpersonal or cognitive-analytic. This book seeks integration *within* the field of CBT. Our approach does not capture all aspects of the therapies illustrated in Figure 1.3. They each have their own integrity, and this book is not intended to undermine that. Rather, we have sought to maximize points of contact between them, to develop a CBT treatment that is sufficiently potent to treat complex and difficult-to-treat cases. Depending on the needs of the client, therapy can have a reality-orienting, activating, problem-solving, engaging, accepting, self-compassionate, mindful or mentally freeing effect. The resulting treatment is strongly process-oriented and described in detail from Part II onwards. In developing this approach, we have sought to make a virtue out of a necessity. For the past 20 years our clinical base has been the Newcastle CBT Centre, a specialist CBT service providing therapy at Step 4/5 in the English stepped care system (NICE, 2009, 2017). All depressed clients referred to our service have recurrent, complex or chronic difficulties. They have all received previous courses of CBT, and/or other psychotherapies, and these have either been ineffective or not had a lasting effect. The question that has repeatedly confronted us, is: what treatment should we offer when established CBT has not been effective, or not had a sustained effect?

In fact, this question is not unique to specialist services. In Part I of the book we introduce the best-established CBT therapies for depression, Beck's CBT and Jacobson and Martell's BA, and we review their evidence bases. At the present time these therapies produce a *sustained recovery* in approximately two-fifths of clients (Driessen & Hollon, 2010). This is the best available evidence from RCTs, where the treatment effects tend to be larger than routine practice. A proportion of clients drop out or do not respond to CBT, and some who respond are vulnerable to relapse in the post-treatment period. These rates are comparable with other evidence-based treatments: drop-out, non-response and relapse are challenges for all treatments, not just CBT. CBT is at least as effective as other therapies, and may be more effective under certain conditions. Nevertheless, three-fifths of clients remain depressed or have a significant vulnerability to depression after a course of established CBT.

We have illustrated this situation in Figure 1.4, showing the transition from Step 3 to Step 4 in the English stepped care system. For every five clients presenting with major depression at Step 3, two will need more specialist or intensive therapy at Step 4/5 and one of the others is likely to be re-referred, having suffered a relapse or recurrence at some point in the future. This book describes our response to what can be offered when established CBT has not worked, or not had a lasting effect. It explores how

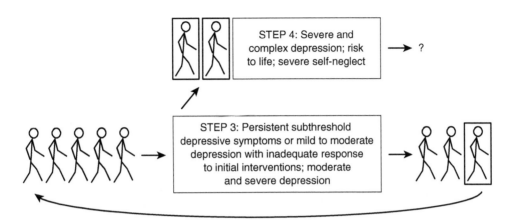

Figure 1.4   **Outcomes from established CBT projected onto stepped care pathways**

treatment can be adapted, adjusted or intensified for clients stepping up to Step 4/5 or recurrently presenting at Step 3. It also explores the factors that enable established courses of treatment, such as CBT or BA, to be delivered successfully.

We want to be unambiguous at this stage that *clients should receive an established course of CBT or BA as the first-line intervention*, exactly as recommended by current clinical guidance (NICE, 2009, 2017). We actively encourage therapists to deliver high-quality established CBT or BA in the first instance. When CBT or BA are effective they do an excellent job in bringing clients out of depression and helping them stay well in the future. For this reason, we devote Part I of the book to established CBT protocols including relapse prevention, where CBT has a stronger evidence base than most other therapies. The integrated approach that follows, from Part II onwards, has been developed for clients who do not currently achieve a sustained recovery: for those recurrently presenting at Steps 3 or 4/5.

The integrated approach is not a new brand of therapy; it is a way of organizing treatment components from existing CBT therapies. As will become apparent, a lot has been learned about how to prioritize and target CBT interventions for different types of clients. An analogy would be attempting to complete a jigsaw puzzle without the picture-board: the last 20 years has generated a lot of new pieces from various models, evidence and clinical techniques. A bigger picture is starting to emerge. This book integrates the pieces in a particular way, with the aim of creating an accessible up-to-date treatment that makes sense clinically, has theoretical coherence and is also evidence-based. The strategy underpinning the integration is three-pronged, and it is illustrated in Figure 1.5.

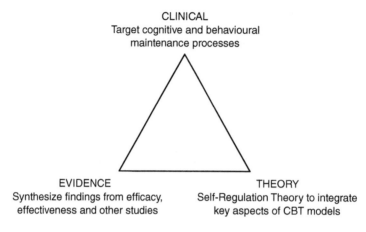

CLINICAL
Target cognitive and behavioural
maintenance processes

EVIDENCE
Synthesize findings from efficacy,
effectiveness and other studies

THEORY
Self-Regulation Theory to integrate
key aspects of CBT models

Figure 1.5   Rationale for an integrated CBT model

- *Clinical Integration.* Rather than work within a single CBT model, we have sought to incorporate the full range of *cognitive and behavioural processes that maintain depressed moods.* We have then experimented with treatment components from established therapies to respond to those various maintenance cycles. The main contributing therapies are CT/CBT, BA, ACT, CFT, MBCT and RFCBT. Additionally, we have drawn on Continuation Cognitive Therapy to support relapse prevention (C-CT: Jarrett et al., 1998, 2001; Jarrett & Thase, 2010).
- *Theoretical Integration.* Therapy should always be guided by an explicit cognitive-behavioural model. We have developed a model that uses Self-Regulation Theory (SRT; Carver & Scheier, 1999) together with several of the *principles* underpinning Interacting Cognitive Subsystems (ICS; Teasdale & Barnard, 1993). SRT is concerned with self-identity, affect, motivation and goal-directed behaviour. ICS views depression as an interaction of multiple cognitive subsystems. SRT has added to our understanding of suppressed motivation, reduced goal-directed behaviour and self-devaluation. The principles underpinning ICS have added to our understanding of over-generalization, memory processes and rumination. Additionally, the model has drawn from the Differential Activation Hypothesis (Teasdale, 1988), Retrieval Competition Hypothesis (Brewin, 2006) and Dynamic Systems Theory (Hayes, Yasinski, Barnes & Bockting, 2015).
- *Empirical Integration.* Various sources of evidence have been synthesized and they are broadly convergent: in other words, they point towards a generalizable picture of CBT's mechanisms and effects. Different types of evidence include clinical trials (open, randomized), single case research, case series, practice-based evidence, meta-analyses, epidemiological and cohort studies, experimental and observational studies. Within the book, the proposals we put forward have three 'levels' of evidence and, as

far as possible, without disrupting the flow, we try to make it clear which level applies at each point:

o   Level 1: Claims that are already empirically supported in the field
o   Level 2: Proposals that are consistent with the evidence base, but are our interpretation of it
o   Level 3: New hypotheses that need further empirical tests

Of course, readers will be wondering: at this point in time, writing in 2018, what evidence is there for this integrated approach? There are three answers.

- *Treatment components.* The various treatment components are all derived from the existing CBT evidence base; Parts II, III and IV of the book set these out in detail.
- *Therapy research.* Some years ago we conducted a case series with an earlier version of this approach (Barton, Armstrong, Freeston & Twaddle, 2008). The post-treatment and follow-up data for those cases are presented in Figure 1.6. They were Step 4 cases with complex difficulties, and the outcomes were comparable to established CBT. What encouraged us was the follow-up data: one year after the end of therapy clients were continuing to improve, rather than relapsing back into depression.
- *Practice-based evidence.* Over the past 10 years, we have developed this approach with more than one hundred depressed clients, all with recurrent, chronic or complex depression that has either not responded to established CBT, or the CBT has not had a lasting effect. The book describes eleven of those clients in detail, as case illustrations. We have selected cases using the following criteria: (a) clients who illustrate a particular sub-type, complexity or clinical issue; (b) clients who had a full course of treatment; (c) clients who were willing to be included in the book. It is not a random sample, for example, treatment drop-outs are not included, and there is no comparator group. However, we have selected challenging cases, not the most successful cases, and the pre–post changes on their standardized measures demonstrate how effective this approach can be, particularly with difficult-to-treat depression.

In Chapter 13 we provide a synthesis of the cases and the various themes within the practitioner guidance across the chapters. We re-visit the issue of empirical tests and discuss different strategies for treatment development and ways of extending the evidence base with this client group.

From Beginners to Experts

This book has been written with different readers in mind. If you have no basic knowledge of CBT then it will be probably be too advanced. We recommend you read a more general introduction to CBT first, such as Kennerley, Kirk & Westbrook (2016).

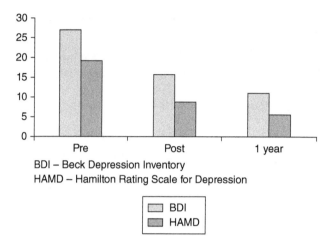

BDI – Beck Depression Inventory
HAMD – Hamilton Rating Scale for Depression

Figure 1.6   Post-treatment and 1-year follow-up outcomes from Barton et al. (2008)

In what follows a lot of general knowledge of CBT is assumed, such as: treatment structures, goal setting, agenda setting, activity scheduling, collaboration, Socratic guidance, thought challenging, behavioural experiments, and so on. If you're not sure what these are, it is best to start elsewhere. Otherwise, the book has been written for everyone, from therapists beginning to work with depression, to experts in the field and all points in between.

As Figure 1.5 suggests there is a triangle of knowledge in CBT that appeals to phenomenology, evidence and theory and each will be given equal weight. Sometimes our focus needs to emphasize our client's experience, which can be full of surprises. At other times we need to emphasize the evidence base; the different types of evidence mentioned above, and your own evidence collected as treatment progresses. At other times we need to emphasize the theoretical principles of CBT, and invoke models that capture the processes maintaining a particular client's difficulties. Over a course of therapy we need to triangulate experience, evidence and theory as we approach each problem, question or issue. This is the method we will follow, as far as possible, throughout the book.

We should acknowledge, however, that there has been inevitable selectivity on our part. CBT for depression is such a vast field that to do it justice with a comprehensive synthesis of evidence and theory would create a very different book. It would be a scholarly work of primary interest to academics, not practitioners. So there have been several compromises in developing this line of work and writing the book. To keep it useful, accessible and up-to-date we've kept the focus on what is most relevant to clinical practice, and consequently certain theories and evidence bases are touched upon rather than given the space they fully deserve.

Developing therapists are recommended to work through each chapter in turn. Part I focuses on established CBT protocols, and there are various reasons for including these. To understand integration, one needs to understand the components that are being integrated. As we have already stated, the integrated approach is for clients who have already received a standard course of CBT and it has either not been effective, or not had a lasting effect. We want to be explicit about the treatment components clients have already received. If a standard course of treatment has not been sufficient, we need to be curious why not and consider what else can be provided. The integrated model is an *evolution* of established protocols, not a competitor brand; it builds on these interventions and augments them. By introducing them in Part I, we are able to address questions of the relationship between different CBT models in an explicit way.

In Chapter 2 we introduce Beck's CBT, illustrated with a clinical case. The client, like all case illustrations in the book, has consented for her anonymized treatment to be included. We review and synthesize the current evidence base, including rates of drop-out, treatment response, relapse and treatment mechanisms. In Chapter 3 we introduce behavioural therapies, most prominently Jacobson and Martell's Behavioural Activation (BA). In a similar format to Chapter 2, we review its evidence base and provide a case illustration. In Chapter 4 we focus on relapse prevention, including Continuation Cognitive Therapy (C-CT) and Mindfulness-Based Cognitive Therapy (MBCT). A synthesis of techniques, models and evidence is the basis for the integrated approach that follows in Part II.

Part II introduces the integrated approach. In Chapter 5 we describe the *self-regulation model* used to understand how depression is triggered and maintained, particularly for cases that have been unresponsive to established treatments. We provide a case example and discuss various cognitive and behavioural maintenance processes. In Chapter 6 we describe the treatment components and processes that help to reverse depressed moods and overcome major episodes. We explain the sequence of treatment and the different evidence-based components, some of which are essential for all clients, and others that are optional depending on need.

Part III applies the integrated approach to challenging sub-types of depression associated with non-response, relapse or recurrence. These create various challenges for therapists; some emotional and personal, others technical and practical. Adjustments need to be made to treatment parameters such as the balance of support and change, the therapeutic dose, the pace of change and treatment focus. As before, there are case examples in each chapter. Chapter 7 focuses on early-onset depression that occurs in adolescence and early adulthood. Young people who suffer major depression are at heightened risk of lifetime recurrences, and early intervention is a particular focus. Chapter 8 considers highly recurrent depression, a common presentation in clinical services. Compared with early onsets, similar cognitive and behavioural processes apply but a different emphasis and focus is needed. Chapter 9 explores chronic and persistent depression where clients have experienced symptoms and functional impairment over an extended period of at least 2 years, although in many cases the duration is several years, or lifelong. We explore adjustments needed to treat clients with chronic presentations, some of whom can be helped to a full recovery, while others need a more acceptance-based approach, learning how to respond differently to depressed moods.

Part IV considers how to treat complex depression, often associated with comorbidities and other complexity factors. Chapter 10 develops an understanding of complexity based on the *interaction* of depression with a range of biopsychosocial factors. This differentiates complexity from severity, recurrence and chronicity, phenomena with which it is frequently (and unhelpfully) confused. The majority of clients with major depression have at least one comorbid disorder – often an anxiety disorder – and although this is a well-known fact, guidance for therapists under these conditions is remarkably sparse. In Chapter 11, guidance is offered for practitioners working with comorbid anxiety and depression, and clinical cases are used to illustrate the approach. Chapter 12 applies these principles to trauma and Post-Traumatic Stress Disorder (PTSD) including the impact of early trauma, abuse and neglect. Theories of psychopathology vary in the weight they give to early experiences. A happy childhood is not insurance against depression, and for some clients early experience is not the appropriate focus. Nevertheless, early adverse experiences such as trauma, abuse and neglect increase the *risk* of adult depression and for that reason we give it due prominence in this part of the book. The final chapter, Chapter 13, provides an overview and synthesis of the main themes of the book, in light of the integrated approach. We revisit what we have learned about the heterogeneity of depression and CBT; how the integrated approach differs from established therapies, and next steps in the development of this work.

As far as possible it is best to use this book in conjunction with supervised clinical practice. Because the emphasis is on therapeutic skills and treatment processes, most new learning will be found in applying the ideas in practice, rather than just abstract consideration. At no point do we shirk from how difficult this work can be, but we hope to communicate the tremendous satisfaction we've gained from treating hundreds of clients over the past 20 years. For complex, unresponsive or difficult-to-treat cases, successful therapy seems to be 'against the odds' – but over time our learning from clients, supervision, training and research has radically improved those odds. Depression is treatable: even complex and difficult-to-treat cases can be helped, and this is the learning we want to share in this book.

Summary

This chapter has introduced the overall aim of the book: to provide guidance to CBT practitioners working with major depression, particularly complex or difficult-to-treat cases.

This book:

- Requires a basic prior working knowledge of what CBT is and how it is used in clinical practice.
- Is best used in conjunction with supervised clinical practice.
- Will be useful for trainees, specialists and expert therapists – each will learn different things from it.
- Explores the challenges CBT therapists face treating major depression, including effects on their own mood.
- Helps therapists balance support and change within the therapy they provide.
- Explores the heterogeneity of depression, in other words the wide variety of clinical presentations that meet criteria for major depression.
- Maintains a balanced emphasis on different types of knowledge within the field: experiential, theoretical and empirical.
- Draws on different types of evidence including RCTs, single case research, practice-based evidence, cohort and experimental studies.
- Encourages therapist hopefulness and flexibility – not to drift from evidence-based protocols, but to deliver CBT responsively and imaginatively.
- Focuses on which treatment components need to be prioritized for different clinical presentations.
- Introduces an integrated CBT approach that harnesses techniques and treatment components from different evidence-based therapies.
- Explores treatment adaptations for difficult-to-treat cases that have not had a sustained recovery following established CBT; these include complex cases with comorbidities, developmental factors, biological processes, social processes and healthcare complications.

PART I
ESTABLISHED CBT THERAPIES

The aim of Part I is to provide an overview and introduction to established CBT, in other words, the best-developed cognitive and behavioural therapy protocols that have been tested in clinical trials and are supported by clinical guidance. Chapter 2 introduces Cognitive Behavioural Therapy, originally called Cognitive Therapy (Becket al., 1979), covering the acute phase of treatment, the period from assessment through to the end of regular therapy, usually 16–24 sessions over 3–6 months. Chapter 3 uses a similar format to introduce behavioural therapies, particularly Behavioural Activation (BA). Chapter 4 covers booster sessions and other interventions aimed at relapse prevention such as Continuation Cognitive Therapy (C-CT) and Mindfulness-Based Cognitive Therapy (MBCT). Case examples are used to illustrate key points and the current evidence base and clinical guidance for each approach is synthesized and summarized.

Cognitive Behavioural Therapy

Cognitive Model

The best-established CBT for depression is the model and treatment first proposed by Aaron Beck in the 1970s (Becket al., 1979). Beck and colleagues include behavioural components in their treatment but mainly emphasize the cognitive aspects of depression, in two key respects. Firstly, cognition is given a *causal* status by conferring a vulnerability to depression in some individuals. This cognitive vulnerability, or susceptibility, is purported to have its roots in early childhood experiences and their impact on the unique cognitive organization and beliefs an individual develops. A collection of beliefs, assumptions, attitudes or rules around a specific theme is called a *schema* (Beck, 2011; James, Reichelt, Freeston & Barton, 2007). Schemata represent the particular way an individual constructs and views themselves, other people and the world. People with adverse early experiences can develop unhelpful core beliefs that form into *maladaptive schema*. These can have a depressing effect on mood when activated later in life. Beck's model is illustrated in Figure 2.1 with a clinical case, Angela.

Case Illustration | Angela: cognitive vulnerability

Like all case illustrations in this book, Angela is a real client who has consented for details of her therapy to be included. We have, however, changed a number of details to protect her anonymity. Angela was a 40-year-old married woman with three

(Continued)

(Continued)

children who worked part-time as a teaching assistant. She was referred for therapy with a 4-year history of depression and excessive worry following relationship problems with her husband. Assessment revealed a key part of her early experience was being part of a large family, often feeling overlooked and neglected by her parents. This led to her feeling she was worthless (*core belief*) and believing she needed other people's approval to feel good about herself (*unhelpful assumption*). These beliefs and feelings persisted into adulthood. However, this was the first time she had experienced a major depressive episode. Angela *compensated* her schema by being submissive and acquiescent in key relationships. This strategy met with others' approval, particularly her husband, which in turn helped Angela to feel wanted and worthwhile. As long as she received others' approval, Angela was protected from depression.

In particular life circumstances, maladaptive schemata can be triggered and a preponderance of negatively biased thinking results: this affects the individual's view of themselves, their world and their future. These negative automatic thoughts can occur at the edge of an individual's awareness and trigger a range of unpleasant affective, behavioural, motivational and somatic effects such as sadness, guilt, shame, reduced energy, behavioural withdrawal, reduced capacity for pleasure, and so on. Once an individual is in a depressed state their propensity for negative thinking continues and negative thoughts become more believable (Barber & DeRubeis, 1989).

Case Illustration | Angela: triggering events and negative automatic thoughts

After 4 years of marriage, Angela's husband became dissatisfied with their relationship and regularly criticized her appearance. This was deeply upsetting for Angela and provoked thoughts and images of herself as ugly and unattractive. Sometime later she discovered her husband had been having affairs and this activated her core belief of being worthless. Angela believed she needed her husband's approval to feel good about herself, therefore its withdrawal had a very distressing effect on her. She felt too weak to challenge him and instead hid what he had done and tried to regain his approval. Thoughts that she was ugly and worthless triggered feelings of shame, hurt and anxiety and these maintained her submissive behaviours. Angela's passivity presented no challenge to her husband's behaviour, and as he continued to dominate the relationship and act disrespectfully, there were repeated situations triggering Angela's thoughts of being ugly and worthless. Hence a maintenance cycle was formed with links between negative thoughts, negative emotions and passive behaviours, nested within an aversive interpersonal situation: see Figure 2.1.

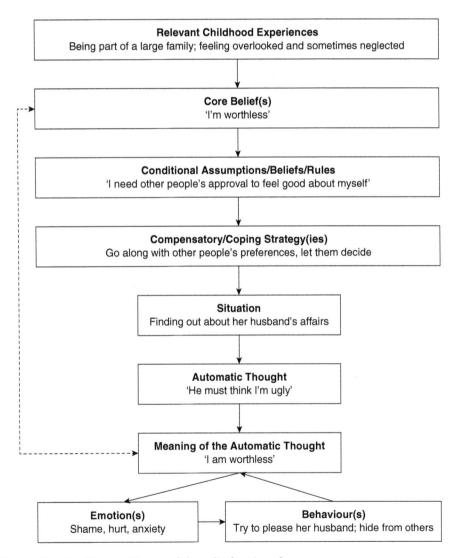

Figure 2.1   Beck's cognitive model applied to Angela

Treatment Phases

Figure 2.2 illustrates the usual treatment phases within Beck's therapy. The data-points represent scores on the Beck Depression Inventory (Beck, Steer & Garbin, 1988) completed by Angela at each therapy session. These show a gradual decrease from moderate depression to remission, achieved across 4 months of acute phase treatment.

The treatment phases are overlapping rather than discrete and it's normal for treatment plans to be individualized. In the main body of treatment, the first batch of sessions usually have a strong behavioural emphasis, then the focus shifts towards negative automatic thinking, then onto underlying beliefs, assumptions and rules for living. The acute phase sessions are followed by continuation booster sessions to protect the client from relapse and, ideally, a follow-up session around a year after the end of treatment. Session frequency is tapered from twice-weekly initially reducing to weekly, fortnightly and then monthly boosters.

Assessment and treatment rationale

The main treatment phases are preceded by one or two assessment sessions to explore the client's history and life circumstances, including precipitators and maintaining factors within the current episode. During the assessment sessions, the therapist presents a rationale for cognitive therapy by illustrating the depressing effect of overly negative thinking. This helps the client recognize that their problems are partly due to the way they are viewing and constructing their situation, not just the situation itself. It's also usual to form a list or map of current problems that forms the basis for agreeing treatment goals.

Part of the function of assessment is the exchange of information; equally important is forming a trusting therapeutic alliance. As we outlined in Chapter 1, it is essential that the therapist expresses genuine curiosity and empathy with the client's predicament as well as supporting their wish to overcome their problems. Mutual trust needs to be translated into collaboration on therapeutic tasks. The therapist encourages the client to engage in treatment, taking a share in responsibility for change. This can take a lot of therapeutic skill since clients are, by the very nature of depression, often pessimistic or even hopeless about therapy being beneficial. Clients need to engage in therapy to *find out* if it will be helpful. If the therapist holds too much responsibility for change it is unlikely the client will gain much benefit.

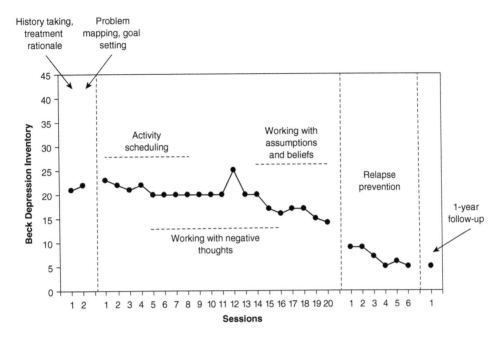

Figure 2.2   Treatment phases within Beck's therapy

Case Illustration | Angela: assessment (sessions 1–2)

Angela described long periods of low mood when she felt helpless as if her life was out of control. Her Beck Depression Inventory score was 21, indicating moderate severity. Since separating from her husband 2 years previously, she had been going through the motions in life and had lost a lot of confidence. Angela also had a habit of cognitive avoidance in which she would suppress upsetting memories and problems rather than face them and try to solve them. The initial treatment goals were: to overcome depression and return to normal mood (Beck Depression Inventory less than 10); to regain self-confidence and normal control of life; to face problems rather than avoid them. As treatment proceeded, these goals were shaped to become more concrete and specific.

In the early sessions, the therapist communicated empathy for Angela's predicament; it was important that the depth of her hurt was acknowledged and understood.

(Continued)

(Continued)

This was balanced with questions exploring what Angela could do to help herself. Her husband's behaviour had been shocking and distressing to her, but therapy should not aim to change another person; the client has to reflect on what they wish to change within *their own* thinking and behaviour. These changes might then have a positive impact of their life situation, including other people. Because Angela had quite a passive interpersonal style it was important to share responsibility for change, so she was encouraged to be as active as possible and contribute to decision making. Submissive clients can experience others as powerful and behave accordingly, so it was important her therapist was not pulled into a dominant role within the therapeutic relationship.

Activity scheduling

The usual first phase of treatment is scheduling and engaging in activity, focusing on problematic symptoms and behaviours that interfere with daily life such as passivity, avoidance, lack of gratification and unexpressed affect. From Beck's perspective the problem with these behaviours is that they maintain negative automatic thoughts and unhelpful beliefs. As Beck et al. (1979: 119) comment, 'for the behaviour therapist, the modification of behaviour is an end in itself; for the cognitive therapist it is a means to an end – namely, cognitive change'. The primary problem as Beck sees it is the client labelling themselves in a negative fashion, such as worthless, ugly and weak. Avoidant and passive behaviours are problematic because they keep those mental labels in place. At the outset of treatment, when depression is usually at its most severe, the most effective way to encourage cognitive change is by changing the behaviours linked to those thoughts. As Beck et al. (1979: 119) note: 'change in behaviour allows the identification of negative appraisals … and provides an opportunity for the patient to evaluate his ideas empirically'.

To begin this process clients complete a baseline measure of activity to establish current behavioural patterns. This is done using a Weekly Activity Schedule (WAS) that can be adapted to individual need. The usual format is an hourly record of activity during waking hours. As far as possible clients complete the schedule throughout the day and make ratings of the amount of pleasure, achievement or purpose associated with each action. The WAS serves three key functions:

1. It gives the therapist a clear idea of what and how much the client is doing in their daily life – this may be different to the impression created by the client.

2. It increases the client's reflection on their activities and how they are linked to their thinking and mood.
3. It provides a baseline from which behavioural changes can be measured.

The WAS also has the advantage of starting therapy with a manageable task: observing and recording experiences, rather than challenging and changing them. Sometimes clear patterns emerge, for example, diurnal variation in activity and mood. Reviewing a WAS also generates a window into the client's *appraisals* of their activities helping to make links between behaviour, thinking and emotions more apparent – see Figure 2.1. Therapy then moves from observing current behaviour to scheduling activities that the client has discontinued during the episode of depression. Scheduled behaviours have to be manageable, especially as the client may not feel like doing them when the time comes. They should gradually build up from simple to more challenging tasks. This is called graded task assignment.

Case Illustration | Angela: activity scheduling (sessions 3–8)

Although she was moderately depressed, Angela had quite a busy daily life. However, the WAS revealed generally low ratings of pleasure, achievement and purpose doing these activities. Therapy focused on overcoming various types of avoidance and increasing assertiveness with other people, such as contacting friends, approaching a colleague at work about a disagreement and opening her divorce papers. Angela gradually built up the confidence to face phone-calls with her solicitor and husband. By session six, she was able to attempt assertive behaviour with her husband as part of a behavioural experiment. As predicted she felt extremely anxious during the phone-call but her husband was not as angry and dismissive as she had predicted. This provoked a small but noticeable reduction in her belief in being a weak person.

Working with negative thoughts

Behaviour change, particularly through behavioural experiments, can bring new information to light and help thinking to become more realistic and helpful. As the client's mood starts to improve, their capacity to work productively on thoughts tends to increase, though there is a lot of individual variation. The purpose of working more explicitly on negative thoughts is firstly to notice when they are present, since they can occur automatically at the edge of awareness, and then to balance them to become more accurate and helpful. Thoughts and beliefs need to be *tested out* for accuracy and helpfulness – this is the essential feature of this stage in therapy. This can be done with a variety of techniques such as thought records, pie charts, behavioural experiments and positive data logs. Beck et al.'s (1979) framework to conceptualize negative thinking is the Negative Cognitive Triad and this is illustrated in Figure 2.3.

This aspect of Beck's model claims that negatively biased thinking is concentrated in thoughts about self, world/others and future (Beck, 1972). We have represented this as a triangle in Figure 2.3 with examples of negative global thinking that can be difficult to discuss, test and disconfirm. Specific thoughts are included in the middle of the triangle to reflect the need to funnel down or 'drill for detail'. In our training workshops this is one of the most difficult skills for therapists to develop. Depressed clients tend to *pull* the dialogue up into a broad range of disorganized, vague and generalized thoughts about self, world and future. The therapist's task is to counteract this by *drilling down* for detail to enable cognitive change to take place.

Self
e.g. unlovable, useless, worthless,
stupid, weak, ineffective, failure

Specificity

*'My friends will think
I'm worthless if
they know what I've
been through'*

*'My husband will hate me
if I stand up to him'*

World
e.g. wars, disease, poverty,
injustice; others as critical,
separate, un-interested

Future
e.g. hopeless, uncertain,
confused, futile, bleak

Figure 2.3   The negative cognitive triad

A central part of the change process is exploiting the link between specific thoughts and particular emotions. As thinking becomes more accurate and helpful, negative emotions should also reduce in frequency and intensity. Table 2.1 summarizes the cognitive themes that accompany the most prominent emotions experienced during depressive episodes. This is an extension of Beck's (1976) theory of *content specificity*; that different feeling states are associated with specific cognitive contents. In therapy sessions it is important to aim for an emotional intensity that is manageable for the client – the so-called Goldilocks principle of emotions being 'not too hot, not too cool'. When emotions run hot it is important to ask explicitly what the feelings are, how intense they are and whether the client is able to manage them. Cognitive change relies on thoughts that are sufficiently hot, since these are the thoughts that will be biased and overly negative, but not so hot that the client is unable to reflect and learn from them.

Table 2.1 Emotions and specific cognitive themes

Emotion	Cognitive theme
Sadness	Loss, grief, mourning
Frustration	Blocked progress towards a goal
Anger	Unfairness, injustice, violation of rights
Guilt	Self-blame, perceived cause of harm
Embarrassment	Socially visible mistake
Shame	Loss of social respect, status, rank
Disgust	Aversion to something noxious, horrible
Fear	Perceived threat or danger
Disappointment	Failure to achieve a goal or standard

Case Illustration | Angela: testing out negative thoughts (sessions 9–16)

Angela had very generalized thoughts about being worthless, ugly and unattractive, and the shame and hurt associated with them was so intense it would have been counter-productive to work on them directly early in treatment. Instead, her

(Continued)

(Continued)

therapist drilled for detail and found specific thoughts that were still upsetting, but more manageable to work with. Firstly, Angela often voiced negative appraisals of others' opinion of her, and these provoked feelings of shame and embarrassment (e.g. 'people will think I'm worthless if they know what I've been through'). With respect to this thought, Angela undertook a mini-survey of close family and friends to find out how they perceived her. This was an extremely anxiety-provoking task, but resulted in a lot of positive feedback. She also shared details of her husband's behaviour with a close friend and was shocked to find her friend was furious with her husband, not her. This was the beginning of Angela learning that it was better to face problems than avoid them. A breakthrough came in session 15. Angela's shame was beginning to reduce and she began to disclose the full extent of the abuse her husband had perpetrated on her, most of it emotional and some of it sexual. This was a very upsetting process for her, but it brought certain facts into the open: it became clear she had not acted in a shameful way. As her distress reduced, her belief in being worthless and ugly also began to reduce.

A second group of thoughts concerned the predicted negative consequences of being assertive with her husband, which provoked intense fear and anxiety (e.g. 'my husband will hate me if I stand up to him'). Angela firmly believed that she was unable to stand up to her husband, becoming increasingly worried as their divorce proceedings came to a head that she would lose her home if she was assertive about her needs and preferences. She spent two therapy sessions considering the costs and benefits of assertion versus submissiveness. In this period Angela lost her temper with her husband after he had been unreliable over childcare. To Angela's amazement, her husband apologized for his behaviour and was not critical of her. This was the beginning of Angela being more assertive about her needs. The divorce agreement was settled within the next 2 weeks. Angela kept her home, disconfirming her worst fear.

Working with assumptions and beliefs

This can be the most challenging phase for clients because it addresses fundamental levels of cognition: the beliefs, assumptions and rules for living that pre-date the depressive episode and usually have their roots in early childhood experiences (James & Barton, 2004). Beck's theory holds that these types of cognition constitute the vulnerability for depression, and that addressing these beliefs can help the client understand what led them into depression, and make changes to stay well in the future. It is essential when working at this level that the client's mood has improved sufficiently for them to *reflect* on their underlying beliefs and not simply *ruminate* about them (Nolen-Hoeksema, 1991). This is the main reason why work on underlying assumptions and core beliefs tends to be concentrated in later sessions, though there may be some clients or situations when it is possible earlier in the treatment. The client's reflective capacity has to be strong enough to make links between past and present experience, and recognize that strongly held beliefs are not necessarily true, or helpful, just because they are familiar or strongly felt.

Case Illustration | Angela: exploring core beliefs and assumptions (sessions 17–20)

Angela was able to reflect on her beliefs about being ugly, worthless and weak: as her mood lifted they became much less believable than at the start of treatment. She was able to identify that feeling worthless had its roots in early childhood experiences, whereas beliefs about being ugly and weak developed during her marital problems. She began to recognize that approval-seeking from others meant she acted as if her value depended on that approval: hence the devastating impact of her husband's behaviour. This was an uncomfortable realization that emerged gradually over several sessions. However, it helped Angela to recognize the need to develop greater self-acceptance and let go of her husband's support and approval. This was a long-term piece of personal development that coincided with the divorce process and continued for many months after regular treatment had ended. By the end of twenty sessions Angela had achieved her treatment goals: her Beck Depression Inventory score was 7; she had begun to regain self-confidence and normal control of life; she had also learned to face problems, not avoid them.

Relapse prevention

Because major depression is a recurring problem, it is essential to help clients prepare for challenges after their regular sessions have finished. There is good evidence this can reduce the risk of relapse. As shown in Figure 2.2, Angela received six booster sessions over 6 months, following her regular treatment, and this helped her to consolidate her gains. She achieved a full recovery and was well one year after treatment. Relapse prevention is such an important topic we have devoted Chapter 4 to it, and we describe Angela's booster sessions in detail there.

Evidence for CBT

Clinical outcomes

Beck's CBT has been tested in several randomized controlled trials. The most recent and rigorous meta-analysis, including these studies, has been conducted by Cuijpers, Karyotaki, Weitz, Andersson, Hollon & Straten (2014). Table 2.2 provides summary information about average symptom reduction in the CBT treatment 'arms' within the reviewed studies. As can be seen in Table 2.2, CBT produces a 12- to 14-point mean reduction in Beck Depression Inventory scores and a 10-point mean reduction in the Hamilton Rating Scale for Depression. Confidence intervals measure the level of certainty that the mean is an accurate estimate, based on the number of studies that have been conducted. Intervals tend to be broad when there are only a few studies and narrower when there are more studies. The confidence intervals around these means are narrow because of the large number of studies; therefore we can have a high level of confidence in the findings. Table 2.3 reports response and remission rates from the same meta-analysis. In contrast to symptom reduction, this provides categorical data on the proportion of clients achieving different clinical outcomes.

Table 2.2 Average symptom reduction in CBT trials for moderate/severe depression

Measure	Number of studies	Baseline score (mean)	Post-therapy reduction (mean)	95% Confidence interval
BDI	45	25.73	14.43	13.11–15.76
BDI-II	14	28.03	12.75	10.49–15.02
HAM-D	35	19.93	10.25	9.37–11.12

BDI: Beck Depression Inventory (Beck et al., 1988; Beck, Ward, Mendelson, Mock & Erbaugh, 1961). Scale: 0–9: minimal; 10–18: mild; 19–29: moderate; 30–63: severe.

BDI-II: Beck Depression Inventory-II (Beck, Steer & Brown, 1996). Scale: 0–13: minimal; 14–19: mild; 20–28: moderate; 29–63: severe.

HAM-D: Hamilton Depression Rating Scale (Hamilton, 1960, 1967). 17-item scale: 0–7: normal; 8–13: mild; 14–18: moderate; 19–22: severe; ≥ 23: very severe.

Source: Adapted from Cuijpers et al., 2014

Again the results support the efficacy of CBT for moderate/severe depression, that is, its effects under controlled trial conditions. Fewer studies contributed data than in Table 2.2, due to the information reported in the publications, so confidence intervals were somewhat wider, but approximately 50% of clients responded to CBT (i.e. achieve 50% symptom reduction) and approximately 40% achieved full remission (i.e. symptoms returned to normal levels). Approximately 60% of clients no longer met diagnostic criteria for Major Depression after treatment, but this finding should be treated with some caution. Diagnosis is an effective way to confirm or disconfirm the presence of a disorder but it is not a sensitive measure of change: for example, in this meta-analysis approximately 40% of untreated clients no longer met diagnostic criteria after the same 3–4 month period.

Another key outcome is the proportion of clients who drop out of treatment and do not receive a full dose of therapy. A recent meta-analysis of thirty-five studies reported a proportion of 0.17 clients dropping out of CBT in this way; in other words, of all clients entering treatment 17% drop out or fail to receive the full number of sessions (95% confidence interval: 0.13–0.21; Cooper & Conklin, 2015). Overall, the above findings translate into a moderate effect size for CBT when compared with a range of active control conditions (d = 0.67; Driessen & Hollon, 2010). The number needed to treat (NNT) is 2.75: this means that, allowing for all other variables and influences, for every three clients entering CBT one will be successfully treated.

Table 2.3 **Response and remission rates in CBT trials for moderate/severe depression**

Measure	Number of studies	Proportion	95% Confidence interval
Diagnosis *Not* meeting criteria for Major Depression post-treatment	17	0.66	0.58–0.73
Response Achieving at least 50% reduction in symptoms	9	0.53	0.39–0.66
Remission Post-treatment score of HAM-D <6	8	0.42	0.29–0.55

HAM-D: Hamilton Depression Rating Scale (Hamilton, 1960, 1967). 17-item scale: 0–7: normal; 8–13: mild; 14–18: moderate; 19–22: severe; ≥ 23: very severe.

Source: Adapted from Cuijpers et al., 2014

Change processes

Therapists need to know whether or not a treatment works. They also need to know *how* it works: the fact a treatment is effective does not prove its underlying theory. Put simply, change mechanisms (or *mediators*) may be different from those put forward by the treatment's proponents, even if the therapy is effective. This generates a key question concerning change processes in CBT: when CBT is effective, does it work for the reasons proposed by Beck et al. (1979)? In other words, is clinical improvement the result of *cognitive change*: more accurate thinking, more helpful assumptions and more adaptive self-beliefs?

Evidence about treatment processes focuses on events within the therapy, from referral through to discharge. Process research also has to consider external events during this period because non-therapy factors, such as life events and other interventions, can also have a significant impact. We know from RCTs that CBT strongly influences clinical outcomes but like any psychological treatment, it is only one factor. A recent meta-analysis suggests that psychological treatments only explain approximately 20% of the variance in clinical outcomes (Wampold, 2001; Wampold, Minami, Baskin et al., 2002). So when clients have a good outcome it isn't just due to the treatment – several other factors have an impact, either through their interaction with therapy or via independent effects. By the same argument, when clients have a bad outcome, it is not usually just due to the treatment.

These can be uncomfortable truths for therapists trained to believe in the efficacy of a treatment and responsible for the quality of its delivery. It is good that therapists believe in the treatment and share responsibility for delivering it well: both of these are essential to enable good outcomes. However, it's not good if therapists believe the client's outcome is *entirely* down to them. This simply isn't true. Instead we need to consider a range of client, therapist, treatment, historical and contextual factors that interact dynamically over time to lead to the eventual outcome: good, bad or indifferent. Most process research in this field has focused on cognitive change, client and therapist variables and the client–therapist relationship.

Cognitive change

There is a lot of evidence to support cognitive change across courses of CBT. Clients who respond to therapy have significant reductions in negative cognition as predicted by Beck et al. (1979). This also fits with a wealth of empirical evidence examining Beck's claims that is broadly supportive of the negative cognitive triad (Clark, Beck & Alford, 1999). However, there are two caveats: evidence for change in schemata, assumptions and core beliefs is more equivocal and we will return to this when we consider relapse prevention and cognitive vulnerability in Chapter 4. Secondly, non-CBT treatments, most notably anti-depressant medication, also produce comparable reductions in negative thinking (Cristea, Huibers, David, Hollon, Andersson & Cuijpers, 2015). So changes in cognition before and after CBT do not prove that cognitive change mediated the clinical improvement. They simply confirm that when clients are depressed prior to treatment they tend to produce a lot of negative cognition, and when they are recovered afterwards they do not. It is possible that another mechanism is responsible for symptomatic relief, one that has an independent effect on negative thinking.

Researchers have investigated the temporal sequence of cognitive change and mood change within courses of therapy. The most replicated finding concerns sudden gains. Many clients experience a gradual improvement across the course of treatment ('steady gains') but a proportion experience a sudden large improvement in symptoms from one session to the next (Tang & DeRubeis, 1999). The majority of these gains are not reversed, so for most clients who experience them, a sudden gain is a good prognostic indicator. Client speech in the therapy session immediately preceding the gain has been judged (by blind raters) to have a high level of cognitive change. Interestingly, measures of therapeutic alliance in the session following the improvement show reliable increases – so there appears to be a discernible sequence of cognitive change, symptomatic relief and strengthened therapeutic alliance, as would be predicted by Beck et al.'s model (Tang, DeRubeis, Beberman & Thu, 2005). Sudden large mood changes create a good opportunity for research of this type, but in general it is a complicated and difficult area to research (Lorenzo-Luaces, German & DeRubeis, 2015). The complications include temporal confounds, where relationships between variables at time 2 could be explained by their prior relationship at time 1. There are also third variable explanations, where relationships between variables could be explained by another variable that has not been measured.

Another complication is ambiguity in what is meant by cognitive change: does it refer to the content of client's thoughts, which is what we have focused on so far? Does it mean cognitive processes such as reasoning, attention and decision making? Does it mean cognitive structures such as general knowledge, memories or schemata? Does it mean cognitive skills that clients learn during treatment to help them respond differently to mental events? Or does it mean cognitive techniques such as thought records, pie charts, behavioural experiments and positive data logs? These are all legitimate aspects of cognition. Relevant studies cover all of these aspects and this makes it a difficult field to synthesize and meta-analyse. Overall, the current evidence is broadly consistent with Beck et al.'s proposed mechanisms, but the CBT change theory is unproven due to plausible alternative explanations. However, one clear finding is that the impact of CBT is not limited to changes in the content of thought. In particular, clients with good outcomes appear to learn that thoughts are thoughts, not facts, and develop a different relationship to their mental events (Driessen & Hollon, 2010). We will expand on this further in Chapter 4 and beyond.

Client and therapist factors

Another strand of process research is client and therapist characteristics associated with better (or worse) clinical outcomes. Some client factors are *prognostic*, in other words, they predict response to multiple treatments, not just CBT. Other client factors are *prescriptive*, in other words, they suggest an advantage (or disadvantage) for CBT relative to other treatments. One study found that clients with a relatively brief duration of the current episode, later age of onset and absence of family history of affective disorder did better in CBT (Sotsky et al., 1991). Other studies have identified that clients with chronic and severe depression are less likely to respond well to CBT compared with other treatments, such as Interpersonal Therapy (IPT), Behavioural Activation (BA) or anti-depressant medication (ADM), but this has not been a consistent finding (Dimidjian et al., 2006; Dobson et al., 2008; Elkin et al., 1989). However, a high level of therapist experience and skill does appear to be needed to treat chronic and severe depression with CBT, and outcomes have sometimes been less good when this has been absent (Coffman Martell, Dimidjian, Gallop & Hollon., 2007). For an unknown reason, clients who are married tend to have better outcomes in CBT – this is both a prognostic factor (they do better than unmarried people in CBT) and a prescriptive factor (they do better in CBT than some other treatments; Jarrett Eaves, Granneman & Rush, 1991). There are inconsistent findings in relation to clients with personality disorders, some of whom have worse outcomes in CBT compared with anti-depressant medication (ADM), while others have better outcomes in CBT compared with other psychological therapies (Hardy Barkham, Shapiro, Stiles, Rees & Reynolds 1995; Hollon Jarrett, Nierenberg, Thase, Trivedi & Rush, 2005; Joyce et al., 2007; Shea et al., 1990).

Recent research has explored client factors by investigating treatment *moderators* within controlled trials. A moderator is a variable that significantly influences outcomes in one or more treatment arms. For example, if female clients responded better to CBT than males we would say that response to CBT is *moderated* by gender (it is not). These trials have compared CBT with anti-depressant medication (ADM) (DeRubeis et al., 2014) and Interpersonal Therapy (IPT) (Huibers et al., 2015). Statistically significant moderators were used to calculate whether individual cases were matched or mismatched to the treatment arm most likely to give them symptomatic relief. This was calculated by applying machine learning to individual patterns of scores on the moderating variables, generating a Personalized Advantage Index (PAI) for each client. Clients who were randomized to their optimal treatment arm, as predicted by the PAI scores, had better outcomes. This is a very exciting development because it could lead to *prescriptive decisions* about treatments that are evidence-based *and* personalized. However, at present there is some need for caution: moderators across trials tend to vary quite a lot and thus far PAI scores have generated 'retrospective' predictions. In other words, once the trial has been completed, these variables indicate whether or not clients were randomized to the optimal treatment. If treatment moderators are generalizable across depressed populations, and PAIs can generate *prospective* predictions, this would be truly revolutionary. It's important for therapists to be aware of these developments because of the potential long-term impact on their role. In the decades ahead, scores on standardized measures could be used to guide prescriptive clinical decisions, not just about who receives CBT and who receives other treatments, but which targets need to be prioritized within the treatment of choice.

Regarding therapist factors, two main aspects of treatment fidelity have been studied: *adherence* – the degree to which therapists conform to CBT procedures and deliver the treatment components prescribed in protocols; and *competence* – the responsiveness and expertise with which the therapy is delivered, bearing in mind the needs of the client in question (Webb et al., 2012). Therapists can be adherent but not competent, competent but not adherent, or both adherent and competent. Studies suggest that adherence and competence are both highly desirable but the relationship between the two is not straightforward. Non-adherence is clearly unhelpful but 'slavish' adherence to a protocol may indicate unhelpful inflexibility in certain circumstances (McGlinchey & Dobson, 2003). Few studies have systematically considered the relationship between therapist competence and clinical outcomes but the evidence from two major trials is that a high level of training is needed if CBT is to be delivered well, otherwise less experienced therapists are less effective treating chronic or severe cases (DeRubeis et al., 2005; Elkin et al., 1989).

In summary, at the present time there is no convincing evidence to exclude a client from CBT based on their personal characteristics. However, clients with severe and chronic depression are likely to do less well if their therapists are inexperienced, poorly trained, unsupported or inadequately supervised. Brief duration of the current episode, later age of onset and absence of family history of affective disorder are associated with better outcomes.

Client–therapist relationship

The most studied client–therapist variable is the *therapeutic alliance*, the strength and quality of the collaborative relationship between client and therapist. This is a well-known feature of the *common factors* hypothesis about psychotherapeutic change. This hypothesis suggests that *non-specific* factors common to many types of therapies explain the effectiveness of treatments, rather than cognitive mediation or other modality-specific mechanisms (Wampold, 2001). It is beyond the scope of this chapter to review all the relevant evidence: suffice to say it is beyond doubt that the therapeutic alliance is a very important element in the CBT change process. Most studies report a moderately strong correlation between alliance measures and clinical outcomes (Martin Garske & Davis, 2000).

If therapists imagine that CBT is a solely technical exercise they are deeply mistaken about cognitive theory, as well as the prevailing evidence. From a CBT perspective, a good therapeutic alliance is an essential precursor to engaging and persisting in the tasks of therapy. As we've observed with the sudden gain phenomenon, the alliance can be strengthened by cognitive change and mood enhancement *within* the treatment. This makes intuitive sense: clients are likely to increase trust and collaborate more fully with therapists who are helping them to improve. Strengthened alliance supports more demanding therapeutic tasks that can lead to more change, and so on. We saw this in Angela's case earlier in this chapter. One of the most demanding tasks for her was disclosing the extent of the abuse she had suffered from her husband. She later fed back that it was only possible to do this, after fifteen sessions, because of the alliance that had been built with her therapist up to that point.

This suggests a close interaction of interpersonal and technical elements within CBT, as predicted by CBT theory. It also reveals a paradox within the common factors hypothesis: the only way to achieve a *common* effect is to deliver a *specific* therapy. There is no such thing as common factors therapy. When the therapeutic alliance influences the change process in CBT it manifests as a *distinctive CBT alliance*, not a general or common alliance. The same is true for alliances in other therapies: they have a highly specific nature within those modalities. What is 'common' or 'non-specific' is that the alliance matters in all treatments, not just CBT, but it doesn't follow that it has the same nature or character within different treatments, even if it is always an important factor. Nor does it follow that the magnitude is the same across different therapies.

Practitioner Tips: Cognitive Behavioural Therapy

- When presenting the treatment rationale for CBT, help your clients notice the impact of overly negative thinking on their mood. This will begin a process of learning that thoughts can be inaccurate or unhelpful. Thoughts are thoughts, not facts.
- Encourage clients to share responsibility for change at the start of treatment even if they are doubtful or pessimistic CBT will help. Clients need to engage in therapy to *find out* if it will help.
- In most circumstances, focus on scheduling concrete activities in the first phase of CBT. Meeting with the client twice weekly for the first batch of sessions can help to

build therapeutic alliance and gain momentum. Make sure that behaviour change is calibrated with current behaviour, not normal non-depressed behaviour.

- Seek to form strong therapeutic alliances oriented around therapeutic tasks. Clients and therapists need to be sufficiently focused on change, not just support and understanding. Pay particular attention to cognitive change and seek to consolidate it within and between therapy sessions. If clients improve suddenly this is usually a good prognosis.

- When working with negative thoughts aim for a high level of detail to counteract rumination and global thinking. Make links to specific emotions and body states: the greater the cognitive and emotional specificity, the more likely cognitive change will occur.

- Follow the 'Goldilocks principle' for emotions within sessions: not too hot, not too cool. If a client's feelings are too intense or distressing for them to reflect and learn, it is best to switch to a more manageable task. If a client is avoiding or suppressing feelings, gradually focus more on emotions so they learn how to approach them and tolerate them.

- Undertake schema-level work, if it is needed, when the client's mood has started to improve. By this stage the client has to be able to *reflect* on their thoughts as mental events, not facts. Carefully assess which beliefs are long-standing and which have been triggered by the depressive episode.

- Access good-quality clinical supervision, particularly when working with severe and chronic cases (see Chapter 9 for further guidance on treating chronic and persistent depression). Supervision should support your adherence *and* competence, not just one or the other: in other words you should be following evidence-based protocols but in a way that is responsive to your client's needs.

- Benchmarking outcomes against clinical trials sets a high standard, because outcomes in RCTs are known to be better on average than clinical services. Nevertheless, as you become more experienced, and assuming you're in receipt of good-quality training and supervision, your clinical outcomes should approach 50% response: that is, approximately 50% of depressed clients should experience a 50% reduction in symptoms.

- Approximately 20% of clients drop out of clinical trials and this rate is known to be greater in clinical services. Drop-out rates for less experienced therapists are likely to be higher, but as therapists become more experienced the rate should reduce down to the 20% level. To achieve this therapists need to reflect on treatment failures, not avoid thinking about them, and try to understand what stopped therapy being effective on those occasions. However, beware of unhelpful self-blame. Multiple factors influence clinical outcomes; it is good for therapists to reflect on their part in outcomes (good and bad), but it is only a part.

- Expect challenges and setbacks after regular treatment has ended. It is best to normalize them and view them as opportunities to practise CBT skills to learn how to stay well – see Chapter 4 for more guidance.

3

Behavioural Activation

Beck's CBT is an *inside-out* treatment because it stresses the role of clients' thoughts, assumptions and beliefs in maintaining their problems. From a CBT perspective, individuals *construct* their environment via their interpretations of it, and treatment consists in developing more accurate thoughts and helpful beliefs. By way of contrast, Behavioural Activation (BA: Martell et al., 2001; Martell et al., 2010) and the less well-known Behavioural Activation Treatment for Depression (BATD; Lejuez, Hopko, LePage, Hopko & McNeil, 2001) are *outside-in* treatments because they emphasize the role of the environment in precipitating and maintaining depression. From a BA and BATD perspective, individuals are *acted upon* by their environment in ways that are more or less difficult to deal with. In response, individuals *act upon* their environment, and depression results when behavioural responses are insufficient to adapt to environmental demands. The focus of BA treatment, therefore, is to help people develop a behavioural repertoire that responds more effectively to demanding environments, and, where possible, access rewarding experiences within them. In this chapter we will explore the theory underpinning BA and BATD (the shorter abbreviation will be used hereafter), the accompanying evidence, key aspects of the treatment, and the strengths and weaknesses of this approach. A clinical case will be used to illustrate key points, and practitioner tips are included at the end of the chapter.

Behaviourism

Most readers will be familiar with the name, if not the writings, of Ivan Pavlov (1849–1936), and will have a basic grasp of his famous dogs. This is one of the origins of *Classical Conditioning (CC)*, which proposes how organisms learn by *association*. A ringing bell is repeatedly paired with the provision of food; the dogs learn, not through conscious choice, to salivate in response to the bell, even after food is withheld (Pavlov,

1902). If the food is withheld long enough, the dogs stop salivating. The dogs learn by *association* rather than conscious effort. Automatic associations can also be observed in human responses, for example, to traumatic events: the survivor of a bomb might flinch at the sound of fireworks, even though he knows the difference between the two. Classical Conditioning demonstrates how the environment, via such interactions, acts upon organisms' involuntary responses. In CC terms, the *antecedents* or triggers of involuntary behaviours are the key element.

B.F. Skinner (1904–90) further developed the study of environmental influences on human behaviour. We are not, he argued, simply *acted upon* by our environment through involuntary responses; we also *act upon* our environment through voluntary behaviours. We *operate* within and upon our environment, learning to adapt to it depending on how it responds to us. This theory built on Edward Thorndike's Law of Effect:

> Responses that produce a satisfying effect in a particular situation become more likely to occur again in that situation, and responses that produce a discomforting effect become less likely to occur again in that situation. (Thorndike, 1898)

Skinner gives the example of a person whose office lies upstairs in their workplace (Skinner, 1938). There is a lift, and by pressing the call button, the lift is summoned and the goal of reaching the upper floor is achieved. The next day, the behaviour of button-pressing is repeated with the same outcome, and so the pattern repeats. The behaviour (button-pressing) is met with a consistent response in the environment (lift arriving) and this encourages the behaviour's repetition: the behaviour is *reinforced*. If the lift persistently fails to arrive, the behaviour will not be reinforced; the person will give up on button-pressing and the behaviour will be *extinguished*. In short, some behaviours are met with environmental responses that serve useful functions, encouraging the repetition of those behaviours (*reinforcement*), while some are met with responses that fail to operate as needed and the behaviour dwindles (*extinction*). This is the basis of *Operant Conditioning* (OC) in which the consequences of behaviours are the key element.

Taking this analysis a step further, let's suppose the button-pressing leads to other consequences: the door opens on a minuscule lift crammed full of smokers (the person doesn't smoke); or there's a tap on his shoulder and his boss is glowering at him, saying 'Don't you realize that this is the EXECUTIVE lift?' These would be *aversive consequences* that would discourage the behaviour's repetition. Under these conditions the behaviour would be *punished*: the likelihood of it being repeated would reduce. In this context *punishment* is not meant in any moral or ethical sense. OC seeks to account for those behaviours that are most likely to be promoted, and those most likely to be discouraged, through a lack of response or aversive responses in the environment.

One further refinement: a behaviour can be reinforced by something desirable being made present, or something aversive being taken away. If I add herbs to a stew it tastes better, so I am more likely to add them next time. The behaviour is *positively reinforced* – the *added* taste and enjoyment has a reinforcing effect. If I develop a headache and take paracetamol, the headache goes away or at least diminishes, so next time I am more likely to take paracetamol. The behaviour is *negatively reinforced* – the *reduced* pain has a reinforcing effect. Likewise, punishment can be positive or negative. If a particular running machine in the gym provokes ankle pain, I will learn not to use it. The behaviour is *positively punished* – the *added* pain has a punishing effect. On the other hand, if a behaviour persistently reduces something desirable, that will reduce its frequency. For example, if I lend a friend some books and he keeps failing to return them, sooner or later I will stop lending him books. The lending behaviour is *negatively punished* – the continuing *absence* of the books reduces the lending behaviour. As with the term punishment, *positive* and *negative* do not imply value-judgements: they merely indicate whether a reinforcer or punisher is the consequence of something being made present or taken away.

Behavioural Treatment of Depression

First generation behavioural treatments originated with Lewinsohn (1974), Ferster (1973) and Seligman (1975). The best-known is Seligman's work on *learned helplessness* where depression-like changes were observed in dogs, studied under conditions we would now think of as ethically questionable. They were administered a mild electric shock, which prompted them to move from the location of the shock to a shock-free area. The shock-free area was then also electrified, so the dogs were then unable to escape shocks, whatever position they moved to. The dogs learned the association between their behaviour and its consequences: no matter what they did there was no way to escape the shock. Helplessness resulted from a set of *learned associations* between the situation, their behaviour and its consequences. The dogs gave up trying to escape the shock, even after the situation reverted to the original arrangement. In behaviourist terms, the dog's escape-oriented behaviour was *positively punished* to *extinction* and depression-like inactivity resulted. Notice that helplessness was not maintained by avoidance; it was the result of *giving up* on attempts to avoid. We can recognize parallels with human experiences when a person expects that, however they act, they will fail to escape something aversive in their environment. This can also have a cognitive impact on *self-efficacy*: that is, their belief in being able to control or influence subjectively important outcomes (Bandura, 1977).

This understanding of depression formed the basis of early behavioural interventions treating depression through OC principles. From this perspective, the fundamental problem is that an individual's experience becomes dominated by punishing interactions with the environment. If the consequences of behaviours are not sufficiently rewarding, an individual will learn to do less of that behaviour. If the behaviour had a significant role in maintaining positive mood, then doing it less creates fewer opportunities for reinforcement, which leads to further reduction, and so on. Positive reinforcement is gradually reduced and this cycle of punishing interaction, reducing frequency of behaviour and reduced reinforcement explains the persistence of depression. The core treatment principle is to increase opportunities for positive reinforcement by activating behaviour – to restore normal mood and behaviour patterns (Hollon, 2001).

Contemporary BA therapies have taken these behavioural principles and applied them within a *contextualist* understanding of depression. Depression is often precipitated when contextual events impact on an individual, such as major life stress, significant losses, transitions, unexpected changes, illness, disability and so on. These impacts are highly individual, or *idiographic*: the way such circumstances (*antecedents*) map onto behaviours and their consequences differs considerably across individuals. The fundamental hypothesis in BA is this: contextual changes lead to idiographic behavioural changes that result in a loss of *positive reinforcement* in some individuals. The impact depends on highly specific behaviour patterns. In some people this can lead to the reduction and extinction of behaviours that were previously reinforced, and were key to maintaining enjoyment and euthymic mood. The contextualist model of depression is illustrated in Figure 3.1 with a clinical case, Bob.

Case Illustration | Bob: contextual events

Bob was a 54-year-old man who presented with severe major depression. His difficulties commenced around 10 years previously with increasing pressure and bullying in his workplace, eventually leading to redundancy from his position as a factory manager. He subsequently obtained office work but found it unsatisfying and gave it up. In the intervening period he withdrew from a range of social activities that he formerly found enjoyable, including an interest in horse racing and hill walking. He had developed the habit of spending a lot of time indoors, and would spend long periods thinking about his past.

(Continued)

(Continued)

A contextualist formulation attends to the real-world situations in which clients find themselves, not how they construe their self, world or future. In OC terms, Bob's work activity became aversive. Rather than eliciting enjoyment it began to trigger stress, anxiety, frustration and anger – all negative emotions. With a worsening of this situation he eventually left that environment. His behaviours within that job were punished to extinction. He initially experienced *relief* leaving the work situation, but the alternative work he found lacked the *rewards* of his previous job. In the absence of positive reinforcement, the work-related behaviours that had formerly been key to maintaining Bob's euthymic mood remained extinguished.

Sadness, frustration and anger are understandable, and non-pathological, responses to a punishing environment. Withdrawal from subsequent unrewarding work was also understandable, but that in itself did not trigger the onset of Bob's depression. However, when Bob's withdrawal from work *generalized* to other behaviours and situations, his mood became much more depressed. Thus, in the absence of work his motivation to engage in other mood-enhancing behaviours (e.g. the horses, the hills, socializing) dwindled, leaving him with a reduced sense of purpose and feelings of deep sadness, frustration, anger and dissatisfaction. In summary, the changed situation (*context*) had an emotional impact (*negative*) and a punishing effect on Bob's work (*behaviour*). His inactivity became generalized, so reduced reinforcement became the pattern across the whole of Bob's life, not just in relation to work. The BA formulation stresses the role of these *secondary* behavioural changes that we see in Bob's case – not just the failure to access rewards in work, but a more general reduction in positive reinforcement.

Treatment Rationale

The model presented in Figure 3.1 is used to help socialize clients to the BA approach. From the first assessment session the therapist attends to the client's life context, behaviours and their affective consequences. There are three key aspects to the treatment rationale:

1. *Contextual and behaviour changes contributed to the client becoming depressed.* This can be established by reviewing the course of the depressive episode and enquiring directly about changes in action and context.
2. *Certain behaviour patterns are keeping the client depressed.* This is usually a combination of new behaviours, that are having unhelpful consequences, and the absence of former behaviours, that might have helpful consequences if they were activated.

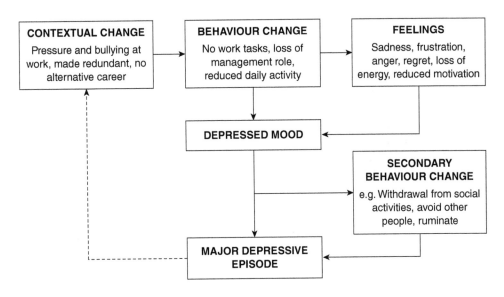

Figure 3.1 Contextualist model of depression illustrated through a clinical case, Bob (adapted from Martell et al., 2001)

3. *Behaviour change is the way to improve mood and recover from depression.* The client needs to reflect on their actions to find out which behaviours are helpful and which are hindering. This forms the basis of *behavioural activation*: doing more of the helpful and less of the unhelpful.

One of the biggest challenges for therapists is focusing on concrete events and behaviours, rather than the client's thoughts or beliefs. In this respect BA has a very different character to CBT because the therapeutic targets are actions, not thoughts. Consequently, therapists need to disattend to the client's cognitive construction of a situation and not explore whether their thoughts are accurate or helpful. Instead the line of questioning is much more concrete: explore time, place, events, actions, feelings and consequences. This can feel quite jarring to therapists initially because the therapeutic work bypasses *meanings* and attends more to concrete experiences. As we'll explore further in Part II of the book, this attentional shift is probably an important element in BA's effectiveness, or at least a significant factor in enabling behavioural change. BA is not a cognitive therapy, but bypassing meanings, particularly during severe depression, can provoke a helpful shift in cognitive processing out of a ruminative mode into a more concrete-experiential mode.

The focus on actions in context has to be carefully supported because behavioural change during depression is usually achieved gradually, not suddenly. The main reason is that depressed clients do not always *feel like* enacting the behaviours that could be helpful to them. Their emotions and body states tend to deplete normal energy which can make it effortful and difficult to enact usual behaviour. Additionally, at least in the initial phase of treatment, the degree of reward from helpful behaviours is likely to be much less *potent* than is usually the case. So although clients may have understood and accepted the treatment rationale, it is highly plausible they will sometimes drift into ruminating about the meaning of being depressed and base their actions on current motivation, rather than what has been agreed and scheduled.

Functional Analysis

Figure 3.2 outlines the key stages of therapy. Unlike CBT with its distinct but overlapping phases, BA tends to have an iterative pattern across the acute phase with an alternating sequence of functional analysis, preparation and activation. Once the treatment rationale has been accepted, functional analysis is the BA method of formulation. It asks the questions: 'What is the function of a given behaviour? What triggers it? What effects does it have?' The function of a behaviour is analysed using an A–B–C model:

A – the *antecedents* or triggers
B – the *behaviour* or actions
C – the *consequences* or effects

A functional analysis seeks to capture how different environments become associated with unique patterns of behaviour and result in particular mood-states for that individual. Consequently there is a big emphasis on exploring *variability* in behaviour, with detailed analysis of particular situations. It is expected there will be highly specific interactions between the individual, the situation, their actions and the resulting feelings and moods. The overall aim is to identify the effects of behaviours on moods, symptoms and related problems, then reduce depression symptoms through behaviour change. Depending on the functional analysis this can be reducing avoidance, graded exposure to challenging tasks, activity scheduling and/or initiating positively reinforced behaviours.

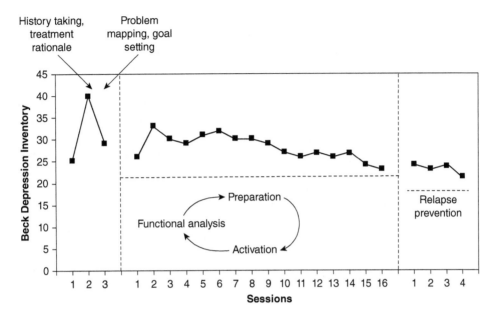

Figure 3.2   Treatment structure of BA, illustrated through Bob's response to treatment

Case Illustration | Bob: functional analysis of staying indoors

During assessment Bob was able to identify that he had developed the habit of spending a lot of time indoors. A number of functional analyses of this behaviour were conducted over the first 4–6 sessions. There was no assumption staying indoors was triggered the same way each time, or had the same consequences. Across various situations, two patterns emerged regarding the antecedents and consequences: firstly, Bob tended to stay indoors on days when his mood was initially worse and, secondly, after deciding to stay in he would experience a noticeable reduction in negative feelings such as tiredness, anxiety and dread. This is a common behavioural pattern in depression and in a BA model it is given the acronym TRAP – Trigger Response Avoidance Pattern.

TRAPs maintain depression in a subtle way. Not surprisingly, clients tend to experience more negative than positive affect when in a major depressive episode. Negative emotions and unpleasant body states are highly salient and can be very distressing. Situations and behaviours that reduce the intensity of negative affect therefore have a strong likelihood of being reinforced – not because they intensify positive affect, but because they reduce negative affect. This is illustrated in Figure 3.3, which depicts the typical affective consequences of Bob staying indoors on days when his mood was initially bad. The data-points in Figure 3.3 are hypothetical, not actual measures, but they represent the typical pattern of positive and negative affect across the day when Bob stayed indoors.

Notice that soon after avoiding going out, Bob would experience relief in negative affect (NA) that could last 2–3 hours. This is a good example of *negative reinforcement*, in other words, the reduction, subtraction or removal of a consequence that makes it *more* likely the behaviour will recur. The function of avoidance was to reduce Bob's negative affect such as tiredness, anxiety and dread, and avoiding going out would do that 'job' very effectively for a 2–3- hour period. Consequently, a habit of staying indoors was formed. The trap in this case was the medium- and long-term consequences of that habit. As the day progressed the initial relief in

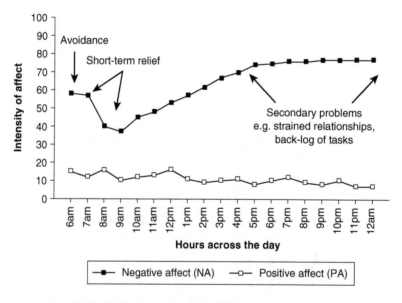

Figure 3.3   TRAP: Trigger Response Avoidance Pattern applied to Bob staying indoors (hypothetical data)

tiredness, anxiety and dread was overtaken by other negative emotions such as boredom, guilt and shame. It could also lead to a backlog of tasks Bob had agreed to do, and this would create tensions in his marriage. Avoiding going outdoors also limited Bob's exposure to *positive reinforcement*, for example, behaviours that could produce an increase in positive affect (PA). When a functional analysis was conducted over the whole day, Bob was able to recognize that avoidance offered short-term relief but longer-term worsening. Avoidance was a problem to be tackled, not a solution to be encouraged.

Preparation

Functional analysis is the basis for deciding what to do more (*activation*) and what to do less (*deactivation*). It is important to stress these are shared decisions. BA is not the therapist *instructing* the client to do more of X and less of Y, or advising them of the types of behaviours people generally find helpful and reinforcing. It is discovering *together* what is helpful and hindering for this particular client in this particular situation, then making plans for behaviour change. Recognizing a behaviour as unhelpful is just the first step. There then needs to be a process of planning and preparation – that is, making concrete plans for specific changes. Notice the emphasis is on *concrete* and *specific* behaviours: clients need to leave therapy sessions with clear agreements on what they are going to do and where and when they are going to do it. Plans, schedules and diary charts can be very helpful for this purpose. It is also helpful to consider the behaviour in detail; to imagine doing it or preferably rehearse it during the therapy session.

Therapist and client also need to consider whether the behaviour is feasible and manageable at that stage in treatment. Like activity scheduling in CBT, behaviour changes need to be *calibrated* with current behaviour, not the client's usual non-depressed behaviour. It is a common problem to agree a behaviour that is too demanding for the client to manage, or requires a level of energy and motivation that is absent at the agreed time. Overall there are a number of helpful questions for therapists and clients to ask during the planning and preparation process:

1. Is there shared agreement about the behaviour change?
2. Is the proposed change concrete and specific (e.g. time, place, detail of what to do)?
3. Is the client able to do the behaviour in the session, or at least imagine doing it?
4. How different is the behaviour from what the client is currently doing?
5. What barriers might get in the way of the client doing the behaviour (e.g. contextual factors, low energy, negative affect, reduced motivation)?

Case Illustration | Bob: scheduling going out on walks

Bob was able to connect the treatment rationale with the functional analysis of avoiding the outdoors. He recognized that staying indoors was stopping him enjoying the activities he used to do, particularly hill walking which had been a passion until he left work 10 years previously. He set the goal to climb a Munro (a Scottish peak over 3000ft/914m, popular with hill walkers and previously well within Bob's abilities). The therapist agreed this was a good goal but negotiated not to set a date to do it, because early in treatment it was difficult to know how much time Bob would need to build up his energy and confidence for this task. This is *graded task assignment*: starting with small manageable steps and building up to more challenging goals. Instead Bob and his therapist considered how far he was able to walk currently when he did go out (*calibration*). The agreed first stage was a 300 metres walk around the area where Bob lived. This was concretized by setting a time and day and considering barriers to action. The biggest clue to barriers was in the functional analysis: if the function of staying indoors was to reduce negative affect (NA), what might happen to Bob's affect when he went out for a walk? Bob needed to be prepared for negative affect increasing in the first instance, and this was a key part of the planning process.

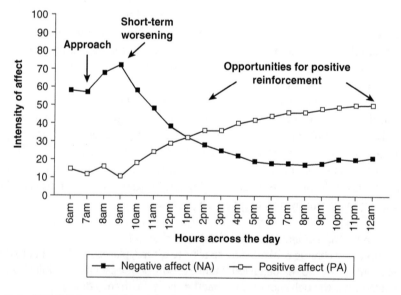

Figure 3.4   **TRAC: Trigger Response Alternative Coping, applied to Bob going out on walks (hypothetical data)**

Activation

Unlike CBT, activities are not set up as experiments to test out the client's expectations or predictions. The purpose of the activity is to *create opportunities for positive reinforcement*, so the therapeutic aim is to prepare and enable the client to do the agreed actions, not test out the accuracy of their beliefs about what will happen. It is therefore helpful to consider all potential barriers in advance so the client is as prepared as possible and able to do the agreed behaviour. This can be presented as an alternative way of responding to difficulties, also known as TRAC – Trigger Response Alternative Coping, illustrated in Figure 3.4. As in Figure 3.3, the data-points are hypothetical, not actual measures, but they represent the typical pattern of positive and negative affect across the day when Bob started to go out on walks.

Short-term worsening is a very common pattern when avoidance is being overcome. Approaching unfamiliar situations and reactivating former behaviours can increase negative affect in the first instance. It can also be very challenging to enact approach behaviours when mood is depressed and anxiety is high. It is therefore essential to prepare clients for this eventuality and find out how they plan to respond if they don't *feel like* doing the behaviour and/or doing it makes them feel worse initially. Figure 3.4 is a helpful graph to show to clients to help them understand the rationale for change: approaching rewarding tasks can be difficult initially, it also may not be immediately rewarding, but the purpose is to create longer-term opportunities for positive reinforcement. Short-term worsening can have a punishing effect unless it is expected, manageable and tolerated. In the behavioural model of depression, the fundamental problem is deficits in positive reinforcement and low levels of PA. The purpose of behavioural activation is to re-organize action around PA and positive reinforcement, rather than NA and negative reinforcement.

Case Illustration | Bob: going on walks and noticing the consequences

Bob understood he might need to act against inclination if he didn't feel like going on a walk. He was also prepared to feel worse initially and this is what happened on some occasions, but not all. He planned a gradual increase in walking distances and began recording how far he walked and the different feelings and body states he

(Continued)

(Continued)

experienced before, during and afterwards. Across the 3 months of the acute phase he gradually built up distance and confidence. He rated his fitness 1/10 on week 1 and 7/10 on week 12. Bob's behaviour changed because he *enjoyed* the walks. The first few walks were challenging and not particularly enjoyable, but by the fifth walk there were a number of rewarding consequences: fresh air, feeling connected with nature, having conversations with passing strangers, feeling fitter, a sense of accomplishment, and so on. This was the beginning of *positive reinforcement*: the act of walking increased positive affect (PA) and this increase made the recurrence of walking more likely.

The iterative sequence of functional analysis, preparation and activation repeats most therapy sessions when the client returns to discuss their homework. Homework is usually an agreed action from the previous session, and it is normal to review this in the first part of each session. A functional analysis framework can be used, so each week there is an opportunity for further learning about triggers, behaviours and consequences within the client's daily activities. This iterative pattern will tend to uncover other TRAPs. In Bob's case he initially worried and ruminated during the walks, tried to avoid strangers and avoid eye contact when someone spoke to him. This led to activating further TRACs within the walks, for example, planning to say hello to the first person he saw each day.

When positive reinforcement has sufficient impact, *behavioural generalization* occurs where behaviours from one situation begin to generalize to others. Without it being discussed in therapy, Bob started to contact old friends he hadn't spoken to for some time – the act of saying hello to strangers on walks generalized to saying hello to friends on the phone. There can also be *behavioural diversification* within situations. For example, when Bob was indoors at home, rather than spending most of his time watching TV and thinking about his past, he became engaged in researching Munro walks and looking for voluntary work. Neither of these was explicitly discussed or activated within treatment, but reinforcement of key behaviours in certain situations can trigger a process of generalization and diversification that increases opportunities for positive reinforcement across different aspects of the client's life. For example, by session 14 Bob was reporting 'a desire to get out there and enjoy myself' and by session 16 he was going out regularly to the shops, meeting up with acquaintances, giving blood and so on.

Positive reinforcement of helpful behaviours can lead to a gradual extinction of unhelpful behaviours, but sometimes unhelpful habits persist in spite of progress elsewhere. A good example was Bob's habit of rumination in which he would analyse his past, worry what might go wrong during a walk and conduct internal 'post mortems' of what he had said to strangers. There was a *pull* for Bob and his therapist to explore the content of his ruminations and it can be difficult to resist the temptation to explore the meaning or accuracy of these sorts of thoughts. In a BA model, rumination is best approached as an *internal behaviour*. So several functional analyses of ruminative behaviour were conducted rather than engaging with the content of Bob's thoughts. This revealed that Bob tended to ruminate when he was feeling down, and worry when he was feeling anxious, so his first learning was to spot when ruminative behaviour occurred: the associations between antecedents, behaviours and consequences have to be *noticed*. He also learned that rumination and worry generally made him feel worse and were largely unproductive in helping him understand his past and cope with new challenges. This learning was achieved by sticking with functional analysis of his ruminative behaviour, rather than exploring thought content.

Across the treatment, Bob kept a daily diary with summary information about where he had been and what he had done each day. He also made daily ratings of the intensity of two key emotions: sadness and happiness. Figure 3.5 illustrates the effects of the activation process on Bob's emotions across the acute phase, continuation phase and follow-up period – 15 months in total. Notice the shallow initial gradients of decreasing negative affect (NA) and increasing positive affect (PA) in the acute phase, and compare this with the symptomatic changes illustrated in Figure 3.2. In both figures the change process is steady and incremental.

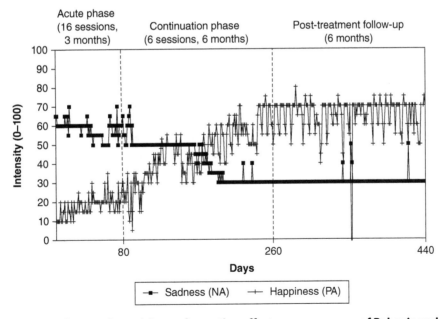

Figure 3.5   Changes in positive and negative affect across a course of Behavioural Activation (Bob's actual data)

Although Bob reported a lot of subjective benefit of being more active and feeling better, this had a relatively small effect on his depression symptoms. These were still in the moderate range by the end of the continuation phase. Recall, however, in Chapter 1 we emphasized that depression severity is not just symptomatology. It is also how well an individual *functions* with their symptoms. Within the continuation phase, positive affect (PA) increased above the level of negative affect (NA), and by the end of the continuation phase Bob had achieved his goal to climb a Munro, he was meeting with friends and acquaintances regularly, he had begun to explore opportunities for voluntary work and he was reporting feeling subjectively better. The follow-up period confirmed that, for the most part, Bob sustained these behavioural changes once the therapy sessions had finished.

Troubleshooting

BA has an attractive simplicity and face validity for both clients and therapists. However, it is unusual for a course of BA to proceed without any hitches or setbacks. In fact, a lot of learning can be gained from setbacks when they are approached in a helpful way. In our experience, three common types of problem are encountered, and it is useful for therapists to consider the best way to respond to these sorts of difficulties.

- *The agreed behaviour was not attempted or completed.* This can happen quite regularly, particularly in the early phase of treatment. Sometimes the client doesn't feel like doing the behaviour when the time comes, or they feel too unwell to manage it, or an unexpected obstacle gets in the way. The main guidance is to review what happened to make sense of why the behaviour was not enacted. One way to approach this is to conduct a functional analysis of what the patient did instead of the agreed behaviour. The most common problem is the agreed behaviour was overly demanding and it needs to be broken down into more manageable steps. It can also be helpful to revisit the rationale for change so that clients understand they may need to *act against inclination* if they don't feel like doing the behaviour when the time comes.
- *The agreed behaviour was enacted but it was not rewarding.* It is great that the client managed to do the behaviour, and therapists need to make sure they reinforce the fact the client did it. The main guidance is not to gloss over the consequences of the actions, even if they were unrewarding or disappointing – review them in detail. One possibility is the client's expectations need to be adjusted during depressed moods. For example, initial rewards are likely to be less than usual, so there needs to be a rationale to persist with behaviours when their consequences initially lack *potency*. Another possibility is that the client enacted the behaviour but was not fully *engaged* in performing the action, for example, going through the motions, ruminating or having their attention elsewhere. In this eventuality, it is worth repeating the behaviour to rehearse and enact it with fuller

engagement. Another possibility is that the client and therapist need to learn from the fact the action was unrewarding. This can mean choosing a different situation or adjusting the behaviour to activate next time. The process of reviewing what happened creates *associative learning* – the client comes to associate actions with their consequences and this enhances their capacity to adapt to their environment and find more rewarding experiences within it (Kanter et al., 2009).

- *The agreed behaviour was activated but it was subsequently appraised as insignificant.* Sometimes clients do the behaviour, gain some benefit but later compare what they have done with pre-depression behaviours and start to doubt its significance (e.g. 'all I did was cut the grass – that's nothing'). The homework review at the start of the next session can then be coloured by post-event rumination rather than reflecting on concrete events, actions and consequences. In this situation concentrate on the actual consequences of the behaviour, rather than the post-event appraisal. Find out if there was any reward from doing the behaviour by sticking to the BA model: focus on the actual, concrete consequences of doing the behaviour rather than disputing or debating the meaning the client has subsequently attached to it.

Evidence for BA: Clinical Outcomes

While behavioural interventions in the treatment of anxiety disorders gained widespread acceptance through the 1970s and beyond, the advent of CBT overshadowed an equivalent expansion in the field of depression. However, it did not escape the attention of behaviourally oriented therapists that Beck's CBT had a strong behavioural emphasis in the initial phase of treatment (*activity scheduling*). They reasoned that the behavioural and cognitive components in Beck et al.'s CBT (Beck et al., 1979) could have *differential effects*, raising the question of how much added value the cognitive components contribute in addition to behavioural change. In the early 1990s a Washington research team led by Neil Jacobson conducted a component study of Beck's CBT to test the relative contribution of the cognitive and behavioural components. Clients were randomly allocated to one of three treatment arms:

a. Behavioural Activation (BA) alone
b. BA plus a cognitive focus on Negative Automatic Thoughts (AT)
c. BA plus a cognitive focus on Negative Automatic Thoughts and Core Schema (CBT)

It was expected that (b) and (c) would show some advantage over (a), but the question was how much? The results are depicted in Figure 3.6. In fact, both the acute phase and 2-year follow-ups found no differences between the treatment arms: they were all equally effective in treating major depression. If there are comparable outcomes for behavioural treatments without cognitive components, why not omit cognition altogether and concentrate entirely on behavioural change? This finding gave impetus to the development of Behavioural Activation as a standalone treatment, and this has led to a number of subsequent clinical trials.

The Cuijpers et al. meta-analysis mentioned in Chapter 2 reported that there was an insufficient number of BA trials to accurately estimate the proportion of clients achieving response and remission (Cuijpers et al., 2014). However, post-treatment symptom changes were reported for both the BDI and HAM-D, and these data are summarized in Table 3.1.

The reductions are numerically comparable to the effects of CBT, albeit with a smaller number of trials contributing data. Cooper & Conklin (2015) have also reported a similar drop-out rate to CBT for BA (proportion of 0.22; 95% CI 0.13–0.33). In these respects BA appears to have comparable outcomes to CBT, which fits with the component study conducted by Jacobson et al. in 1996 (see Figure 3.1).

Although there is a relatively small number of BA trials treating moderate/severe depression, there is evidence BA could have an advantage over CBT in the treatment of severe cases. Figure 3.7 summarizes the main outcomes for severe depression across three treatment arms in a trial conducted by Dimidjian et al. (2006): BA, CBT and SSRI anti-depressant medication. This trial was included in the

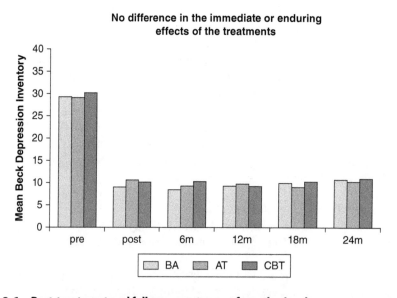

Figure 3.6 **Post-treatment and follow-up outcomes from the Jacobson component study (from Jacobson et al., 1996; Gortner, Gollan, Dobson & Jacobson, 1988)**

BDI: Beck Depression Inventory (Beck et al., 1988; Beck et al., 1961) Scale: 0–9: minimal; 10–18: mild; 19–29: moderate; 30–63: severe.

Table 3.1   Average symptom reduction in BA trials for moderate/severe depression

Measure	Number of studies	Baseline score (mean)	Post-therapy reduction (mean)	95% Confidence Interval
BDI	4	25.97	14.42	9.83–19.01
BDI-II	3	29.79	22.91	18.36–27.46
HAM-D	15	18.55	11.17	8.77–13.57

BDI: Beck Depression Inventory (Beck et al., 1988). Scale: 0–9: minimal; 10–18: mild; 19–29: moderate; 30–63: severe.

BDI-II: Beck Depression Inventory-II (Beck et al., 1996). Scale: 0–13: minimal; 14–19: mild; 20–28: moderate; 29–63: severe.

HAM-D: Hamilton Depression Rating Scale (Hamilton, 1960, 1967). 17-item scale: 0–7: normal; 8–13: mild; 14–18: moderate; 19–22: severe; ≥23: very severe.

Source: Adapted from Cuijpers et al., 2014

Cuijpers et al. (2014) meta-analysis and is presented separately here to illustrate a key point: all treatment arms were effective but BA and SSRI (selective serotonin reuptake inhibitors) were superior to CBT when treating severe cases.

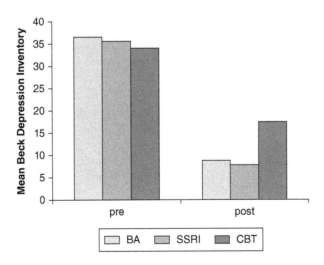

Figure 3.7   Dimidjian et al. (2006) trial of BA, CBT and SSRI medication for severe depression

BDI: Beck Depression Inventory (Beck et al., 1988; Beck et al., 1961) Scale: 0–9: minimal; 10–18: mild; 19–29: moderate; 30–63: severe.

This is a key finding because although meta-analyses of BA have demonstrated robust effects, studies have included clients with a range of mild, moderate and severe depression (Ekers, Webster, Van Straten, Cuijpers, Richards & Gilbody, 2014). It is difficult to draw direct comparisons when the CBT literature has almost exclusively focused on moderate/severe cases. The Dimidjian et al. (2006) trial proved the principle that BA can be more effective than CBT when treating severe depression, and this result has big implications for an integrated approach, not least because activity scheduling is the main treatment phase in CBT when clients' depression is at its most severe (Coffman et al., 2007; Dobson et al., 2008). We will return to discuss the potential mechanisms in Chapter 6.

There is also reason to believe that it is easier, and less costly, to train therapists in BA than CBT, a key finding from the recent COBRA trial (Richards et al., 2016). This pragmatic trial found that BA was non-inferior to CBT for major depression in naturalistic UK NHS services. Some of the CBT clients received a relatively small dose of treatment, which may have limited its effectiveness, but this is an important finding regarding the translation of therapies from RCTs into real-world practice. As we observed in Chapter 2, the effects of CBT in RCTs often depend on highly skilled experienced therapists. At the time of writing, secondary analysis of the COBRA study has not yet been published so we do not yet know whether there were differential effects of CBT and BA for more severe cases. The Jacobson et al. (1996) and Dimidjian et al. (2006) trials would suggest either no difference or an advantage for BA.

Since the 1996 component study the main thrust of BA research has been to challenge the dominance of CBT through randomized controlled trials and this is an understandable strategy given the prominence and influence of RCTs in healthcare commissioning and clinical guidance. However, with a few exceptions there has been relatively little attention paid to *process research* within BA. This is surprising given that the behavioural tradition is identified with experimental case analysis and steeped in the measurement of individual behaviour change. At the present time we simply do not know whether BA works for the reasons put forward by its proponents, that is, the restoration of positive reinforcement through functional analysis and individualized behavioural activation. The efficacy and affordability of BA is becoming very clear and should not be ignored, particularly in the treatment of severe depression. Its development will be further strengthened by increasing tests of purported change mechanisms in the years ahead.

Practitioner Tips: Behavioural Activation

- When presenting the BA treatment rationale, help your clients notice the impact of contextual and behaviour changes on their mood. This will begin a process of *associative learning* about specific situations, actions and their consequences.

- Disattend to the meanings and beliefs the client ascribes to their situation and instead focus on their concrete experiences: explore time, place, events, actions, feelings and consequences.
- Draw attention to *variability* in the client's behaviour with functional analyses of antecedents and consequences in particular situations. The aim is for the client to discover which of their behaviours are helpful and which are hindering.
- Make sure that behaviour change is calibrated with current behaviour, not normal non-depressed behaviour, so that changes are manageable.
- Make *concrete* plans for behavioural change: clients need to leave therapy sessions with clear agreements about what they are going to do and where and when they are going to do it. Ideally they will rehearse the behaviour and consider any barriers to enacting it.
- Help your client notice the difference between actions that temporarily reduce distress through avoidance (TRAPs), and those that increase pleasure, enjoyment and satisfaction (TRACs). The aim of behavioural activation is to organize action around positive affect (PA) and positive reinforcement, in preference to negative affect (NA) and negative reinforcement.
- If rumination becomes a barrier to behaviour change, approach it as a behaviour in its own right and conduct functional analyses of specific occasions when the client has been ruminating. Stay out of addressing the content of the rumination; instead help the client notice what triggers it and what consequences it has.
- Review all homework whether or not the client enacted the agreed behaviours. Use functional analysis to make sense of what the client has done. Decide together whether a behaviour should be repeated, adjusted or modified – allowing for the fact that positive reinforcers are likely to have reduced potency at the beginning of treatment.

Relapse Prevention

This chapter will consider the effects of established CBT in minimizing or preventing depressive relapse after a client has responded to treatment. Firstly, evidence will be reviewed as to whether or not CBT has an enduring effect after regular therapy has been completed. Then specific relapse prevention interventions will be introduced: Continuation Cognitive Therapy (C-CT) and Mindfulness-Based Cognitive Therapy (MBCT). These are contrasting but complementary interventions, delivered after the acute phase of treatment, to try to reduce the risk of relapse in clients most vulnerable to it. Evidence for their effectiveness is reviewed and case illustrations are presented.

Most of the evidence summarized in this chapter comes from CBT trials, not BA. This is because there have been fewer BA studies devoted to continuation and relapse prevention. However, limited evidence does not mean a lesser effect. On the contrary, BA trials with follow-ups have shown similar effects to CBT (for example, see Figure 3.1) but this is a more developed area within CBT and that is reflected in this chapter. However, the principles underlying relapse prevention are equally applicable to behaviour change. The chapter ends with a brief synthesis of the key evidence and guidance from Part I that lays the foundation for the integrated approach in Part II.

Does CBT Have an Enduring Effect?

To be clear about definitions, Figure 4.1 illustrates different trajectories for a client as they progress into depression, then during and after their treatment. *Precipitation* is the onset of a disorder and *maintenance* is the period in which it is perpetuated rather than self-correcting and returning to normal. A treatment *response* is observed when there is a clinically significant reduction in clients' symptoms, and *remission* occurs when those symptoms have returned to the normal range. After a sustained period of remission, usually 6–12 months, clients are regarded as having made a full *recovery*. *Relapse* occurs after remission and prior to recovery, in the period when clients' mood has normalized but has not yet been sustained over a significant period. *Recurrence* is classified as a separate depressive episode that occurs subsequently, after the client has recovered from the current episode (Kupfer, 1991).

Relapse is a significant problem for all depression treatments. Across the population of people affected by depression, each successive major episode increases the risk of further episodes and there is a subset of clients at heightened risk of *relapse* (returning into the same depressive episode) and *recurrence* (the emergence of a new episode at a later point). We will explore how this affects delivery of CBT for highly recurrent depression in Chapter 8.

There have been two recent meta-analyses investigating the *enduring effect* of CBT, in other words, the capacity of CBT to protect against relapse after acute phase treatment has finished (Cuijpers, Hollon, van Straten, Bockting, Berking & Andersson, 2013; Vittengl, Clark, Dunn & Jarrett, 2007). Studies have tended to vary in how they define and measure relapse but there is a consistent pattern of findings: 29% of clients suffer a relapse in the year after achieving remission following CBT, and 54% suffer a relapse/recurrence in the following 2 years. These rates are not expressed as a proportion of clients entering treatment; they are expressed as a proportion of clients achieving remission. This means that around one-third of the 50% of clients who respond to CBT suffer a relapse in the following 12 months, and around one-half in the following 24 months.

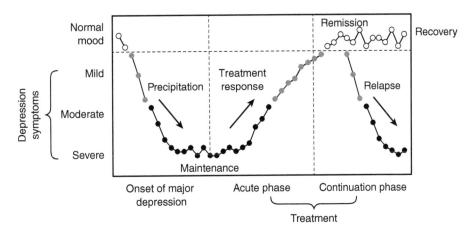

Figure 4.1   Treatment phases and client outcomes

By any standard these relapse rates are disconcertingly high, but there is good evidence that CBT has a *more* enduring effect than some other therapies. The most common comparator has been anti-depressant medication (ADM). When CBT and ADM are discontinued after the acute phase, CBT protects against relapse significantly better than medication (39% vs 61% relapse after 68 weeks; Vittengl et al., 2007). Not only that, there is no significant difference in the protective effect of *discontinued* CBT versus *continuing with* ADM. In other words, clients who respond to a discrete course of CBT have comparable protection against relapse, compared with clients who respond to medication and continue with that treatment (Cuijpers et al., 2013). In relation to all therapies, including CBT, relapse and recurrence are very significant problems that need to be faced and tackled, not avoided. In relation to CBT, there is encouraging evidence that it mediates some relapse prevention compared with other treatments. This finding has prompted the development of specific interventions aimed to further improve CBT's enduring effect.

Continuation Cognitive Therapy (C-CT)

C-CT was developed by Robin Jarrett in the 1990s to address the problem of relapse and recurrence (Jarrett et al., 1998; 2001). The basic idea is simple: rather than terminate treatment at the end of the acute phase, a number of booster sessions are made available to help clients maintain their therapeutic gains. These are scheduled in the 6–12 months between remission and recovery, the period in which clients are at risk of relapse. Original studies delivered up to eight booster sessions spaced out over an eight-month period, though subsequent evidence suggests not all clients need this amount. As we will discover shortly, current guidance is to provide C-CT to clients at the highest risk of relapse. Fortunately, these are the clients who benefit most from it.

Consolidate and generalize learning

The first point to emphasize is that it is *not* the purpose of booster sessions to increase the dose and time-course of the acute phase. This is an important point to communicate to commissioners and service managers: booster sessions are not the consequence of earlier inefficiencies; they are investments in clients' future wellbeing. Spending time now can save time and resources later. Continuation is a separate phase of treatment: sessions are less frequent and the therapeutic focus changes considerably. The first step is to review and *consolidate learning* from the acute phase. Rather than continue working on the client's problems, the therapist and client stop and reflect on the process of treatment. They review which sessions or homework tasks the client found most useful. They synthesize and distil clients' learning into key points that they found to be most helpful. This process makes the learning more *explicit*, whether it has a cognitive, behavioural, affective or contextual focus.

The process of reviewing and synthesizing learning is intended to make it more *available* for clients when they most need it. This is important because it is sometimes difficult for depressed clients to remember details of what happened during their treatment. Autobiographical memories are less specific during depression, and the client's remission presents an opportunity to remember more details and deepen the impact of the learning from the acute phase (Williams, 1996). To illustrate the continuation process we'll revisit the booster sessions delivered to Angela (Chapter 2) and Bob (Chapter 3).

Consolidation: Key Learning Points from the Acute Phase

Angela (CBT)

1. I'm not worthless, ugly or weak
2. It is better to face problems than avoid them
3. It is better to be assertive with others rather than just go along with what they want
4. It doesn't help to keep looking for other people's approval; I need to feel OK about myself as I am
5. Depression is controllable – as long as I stay aware of my thoughts and challenge them when I feel down

Bob (BA)

1. Staying indoors makes me feel bored and doesn't really help
2. Activities like walking give me a feeling of achievement, as long as I build them up gradually
3. Thinking too much makes my depression worse; it's best to discuss things with other people rather than try to sort it all out in my head

When key learning has been identified, the therapist encourages the client to *generalize* it in their daily life. The idea is to apply it not only to the problems tackled in treatment, but also to other situations where it could be relevant and useful. Examples include Angela becoming more assertive with colleagues at work, or Bob extending the range of activities he does outside and inside the house. The rationale is this: *consolidation* and *generalization* will increase the impact of learning from the acute phase and enable it to have a more enduring effect.

Relapse signatures and cognitive reactivation

Alongside this deepening of knowledge and skills there is a parallel activity preparing for, and learning how to respond to, triggers and challenges. The more a client can respond helpfully to naturalistic challenges in their daily life, the less likely they will be to relapse back into depression. The client's formulation from the acute phase can be helpful to consider types of triggering events that might present a challenge to mood and wellbeing. In Angela's case it could be a disagreement with a colleague or conflict with her ex-husband over childcare. In Bob's case it might be a reminder about the past, or inclement weather getting in the way of his walking plans.

The client is also encouraged to spot *early warning signs* of relapse. These might be particular symptoms, somatic states, emotions, thoughts or behaviours. Family and friends sometimes also spot setbacks before the client does, and this can be incorporated into plans for staying well. However, for two reasons the primary strategy is not to *avoid* triggers at all costs: firstly, challenges are a normal part of life and they are generally unpredictable; secondly, trying to avoid challenges can maintain an *avoidant orientation* that increases the risk of depression in the longer term. Within this framework, challenges, setbacks and relapse are defined as follows:

- *Challenges* – these are stressful or demanding experiences that threaten wellbeing and euthymic mood; they tend to be unpredictable and are best *not* avoided; rather they need to be faced and dealt with when they occur.
- *Setbacks* – these are temporary mild depressed moods precipitated by challenges; they are early warning signs of relapse and the client needs to respond as helpfully as possible to them to prevent further worsening.
- *Relapse* – this is a downward spiral of mood following a set back that deepens and returns the client into a major depressive episode.

It is understandable that clients are concerned about relapse: evidence suggests they should be, because the statistical risks of it occurring are high. However, if concerns are translated into *worry, avoidance or self-limitation* this is likely to be counter-productive.

Almost certainly this is one of the direct benefits of C-CT: it addresses the tendency of some clients to worry about relapse, but not take active steps to counteract it. C-CT is also helpful for clients who are *under-concerned* about relapse – it brings the issue to their attention. If clients have responded well to CBT and their depression is in remission, there can be a temptation for client and therapist to disattend to relapse risks. Raising the issue can feel like spoiling the party, but continued wellbeing is not achieved by either passive worry or blind optimism (Forand & DeRubeis, 2014). Clients need the skills to deal with challenges when they occur. It is better to *approach* relapse prevention, trying to bring about the desired outcome *(staying well)* rather than to avoid the issue, or simply hope for the best (Trew, 2011). The distinction between approach and avoidance is not just semantic; it has a fundamental impact on the client's orientation and we will explore this further from Part II of the book onwards.

The client is therefore encouraged to *accept* that challenges will happen from time to time, because that is a normal part of life. This does not necessarily mean actively seeking them out, but it does mean accepting that they will occasionally happen. The important skill is to notice the effects of challenges when they occur. When they provoke setbacks, such as negative thinking, avoidant behaviour or dysphoric moods, these are warning signs that require attention. When setbacks occur the key issue is whether there is then a depressiogenic reaction or a 'CBT' response. Does the client react to setbacks with overly negative thinking about their self, world and future? Do they become helpless and behaviourally withdrawn? If the answer to either is 'yes' there is a risk of a downward spiral and relapsing back into depression. If, on the other hand, the client responds by applying the skills learned during the acute phase of treatment, and consolidated during C-CT, then those skills can help to reverse the set back and assist in staying well.

The available evidence suggests certain clients are at greater risk of depressiogenic reactions than others. It also suggests that clients vary in their capacity to apply CBT skills when they most need them. For some clients their learning is automatic; the impact of acute phase treatment produces more balanced thinking and increased behavioural engagement, and there is an automatic *compensatory response* when mood begins to worsen. Dysphoric moods are *self-corrected*, much as we would expect in normal functioning. Other clients need to use deliberate methods and techniques during setbacks to prevent worsening. Whether the processes are automatic or deliberate, or a combination of the two, the critical question is: do clients access the CBT knowledge and skills they need at the point their mood begins to worsen?

For this reason it is important that staying well is an active and experimental process, not just an exercise in *declarative knowledge*. Clients often know what they *should* do in challenging situations, but fall short of being able to do it. They may have memories of what helped during therapy, but if those memories are not accessed during the setback, they are less likely to have a protective effect. This is the tremendous advantage of

C-CT: it creates a period of time (usually around 6 months) in which the therapist can support and *scaffold* the process of staying well, in other words, rather than the client noticing challenges, warning signs and attempting to respond on their own, the continued presence of the therapist makes this a much more supported process.

One of the best-established models to understand these processes is John Teasdale's *differential activation hypothesis* (Teasdale, 1988; Teasdale & Barnard, 1993). Teasdale proposed that what takes some clients back into depression is a *cognitive reactivation* of the thoughts, beliefs and cognitive processes that were present during the depressive episode. As depression becomes more recurrent, cognitive reactivation can be triggered by quite minor challenges, even mild negative emotions such as normal sadness. Rather than negative thoughts provoking negative emotions – the traditional Beckian view – the causal path is reversed and negative emotions trigger negative thoughts. The process is *differential* because of the contrast between clients in remission and people who have never been depressed. In normal mood there is no difference in their levels of negative or unhelpful thinking. During sad mood, for example through an experimental mood induction such as listening to sad music or watching a depressing movie, the remitted depressed clients (on average) show increased negative and unhelpful thinking compared with never-depressed people (Miranda & Persons, 1988). The key issue is clients' thinking and behaviour under stress or challenging conditions – how *robust* is their balanced thinking and behavioural engagement in the face of mild stress or negative affect? The proposed mechanism of relapse is therefore: (a) minor stress or mild negative emotions present a challenge; (b) unhelpful cognitive processes are reactivated, particularly for people with highly recurrent depression; (c) a downward spiral of mood develops, unless compensatory skills are applied at this point in the process. Whether or not clients are able to reverse the downward spiral depends on how they respond to the challenge.

In fact, there is quite a lot of supporting evidence showing that the extent of an individual's *cognitive reactivity* is a good predictor of relapse (Segal, Kennedy, Gemar, Hood, Pedersen & Buis, 2006). Studies have shown that, compared with anti-depressant medication, CBT produces lower average levels of reactivity, and this fits with CBT having an enduring effect. Nevertheless, even if average levels are lower, some people will have a strong propensity for reactivation and these are the people at greatest risk of relapse in the post-treatment period. Teasdale and colleagues emphasized the cognitive aspects of reactivation, but the same principles apply to behaviour. For example, negative emotions in a remitted client may reduce their behavioural engagement, even if their behaviour during euthymic mood is indistinguishable from never-depressed people. Whether a cognitive or behavioural emphasis is taken, there is clear value in finding out the impact of challenges on clients' cognition and behaviour, and taking the steps necessary for the client to learn how best to respond.

Stress tests

The idea behind a stress test is to find out the impact of challenges in clients' daily lives. If the impact is large, the client needs to be well prepared to counteract setbacks so they don't provoke a downward spiral into a full relapse. There are therefore two parts to a stress test or mood challenge: firstly, how big an impact does the challenge have on the client's mood? Secondly, how able is the client to reverse (or *compensate*) those effects using their CBT skills? Notice this is a long way from avoiding challenges in the blind hope of not getting depressed. On the contrary, it is actively facing challenges to find out what effects they have, and learn how to reverse them. The advantage of naturalistic challenges is that they have high face validity, and are directly relevant to the client's daily life.

Case Illustration | Naturalistic challenges in the post-treatment period: Angela (CBT)

Angela's remission from depression helped her to recognize that she wanted to change her job. She had been based at the same school for several years, and over that time the school leadership had become more demanding and less supportive. Two sources of stress emerged from this: firstly, she became very anxious prior to a job interview, and this reactivated concerns about being disapproved, unwanted or rejected. Angela faced the job interview, rather than avoid it, and her fears were disconfirmed. Secondly, having received and accepted the job offer, she was confronted by anger and resentment from the leadership in her former school. This situation provoked unexpected upset, but Angela was able to use a booster session to reflect on the situation. Rather than spiralling into overly negative thinking she was able to appraise the school leader's reaction as confirmation she would be better moving to the new school. This reappraisal minimized the setback and helped her to restore euthymic mood. Angela's remission was further strengthened by moving to her new post, which she preferred over her former job.

The advantage of naturalistic challenges is that these experiences are fully embedded in the client's daily life and form a natural part of their recovery. The disadvantage is that they are often unpredictable and less amenable to behavioural experiments. One way to overcome this is for the client to undertake a deliberate mood challenge such as remembering difficult memories, watching a sad film or listening to sad music. This can be done within a therapy session and the client's expectations can be elicited in advance to test out their predictions. This can be particularly helpful if clients are under-estimating or over-estimating the risk of relapse. Either expectation can be dis-confirmed: under-estimators may be surprised by the extent of reactivation, and this can alert them to the need to pay more attention to staying well. Over-estimators may be surprised by their robustness in the face of a mood challenge, helping them to trust more fully in their capacity to stay well.

Case Illustration | Angela (CBT) – mood induction stress test

Twelve months after the end of the acute phase, Angela participated in a mood induction stress test with the aim of finding out the extent of her cognitive reac-tivation and capacity to counteract it with CBT skills. This was set up as a behav-ioural experiment with Angela keeping an emotion and thought diary for 2 weeks prior to the mood induction session, during the session itself, then for 2 weeks afterwards. The purpose of the emotion ratings was to calibrate the mood induc-tion with natural emotional fluctuations in her daily life. The emotion ratings are presented in Figure 4.2.

The induction of sad mood was achieved by playing the music often used in mood induction experiments (Prokofiev's 'Russia under the Mongolian Yoke', played at half speed). As can be observed in Figure 4.2, the sad mood induction had a temporary effect on Angela's emotions for about 30 minutes, and the intensity was comparable with the feelings she experienced during a stressful day later that month.

The induction was within a 2-hour therapy session on day 14 of the process and by the end of the 2 hours Angela's mood had returned to normal, supported by some up-beat pop music to help reverse the temporary induction. The focus of interest was the extent to which the induced mood would reactivate depressing thoughts, beliefs and cognitive processes that had been active 12 months previously. Angela had been stable in remission during that period and was now in full recovery. It is important to choose the timing for a stress test wisely. The value is to find out the robustness of remission or recovery, so clients need a sustained period of wellbeing to benefit from this type of experiment.

As part of the test, Angela and her therapist recalled the unhelpful thoughts she had believed with great conviction prior to her treatment. There were six key thoughts and she rated her conviction in these beliefs 2 weeks before, during and

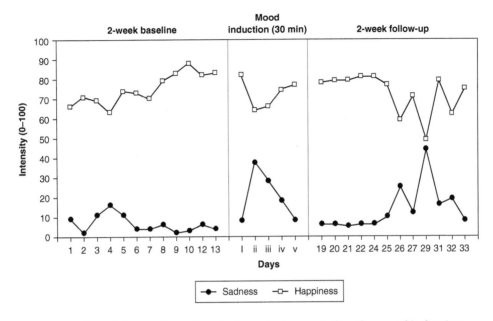

Figure 4.2   Angela's emotion ratings before, during and after the mood induction stress test

2 weeks after the mood induction. The unhelpful thoughts were: *It helps me to put the lid on problems and avoid them; If my ex-husband doesn't believe I'm valuable, then I'm not; I only want my ex-husband's approval; I'm worthless; I'm ugly and unattractive; I'm unable to stand up to my ex-husband and be assertive with him.* By the same method Angela rated her conviction in six complementary helpful beliefs she had acquired by the end of treatment: *It makes things worse if I put the lid on problems and avoid them; Whatever my ex-husband thinks doesn't affect my value; My ex-husband's approval doesn't matter to me; I'm valuable; I'm attractive; I can stand up to my ex-husband and be assertive when I need to.* Angela found it difficult to predict whether the sad mood would affect her beliefs or not – she simply didn't know. Because of the uncertainty she was anxious it would affect her and set her back. However, she accepted the rationale that either way it was better for her to find out. If unhelpful beliefs were reactivated, that would suggest there was more work to do. If they were not reactivated, that would suggest she could have more confidence in her recovery. The results are presented in Figure 4.3.

As would be expected for a client in recovery, in her daily life Angela had a much higher conviction in the helpful than the unhelpful beliefs, as evidenced in the 2 week baseline phase. Prior to the mood induction she reported it had been helpful to monitor these beliefs – it helped her to realize how much she had changed and progressed. The key issue was whether the sad mood induction would reactivate her conviction in the unhelpful beliefs. As can be observed in Figure 4.3, this is not what happened. Angela's conviction in the helpful beliefs was robust to sad mood, with only very slight shifts in belief. In the debrief afterwards Angela reported that negative thoughts had started intruding into her mind, but they were counteracted automatically by more balanced thoughts, without her having to make a conscious effort.

This discovery was a confidence boost for Angela. She began to trust her recovery more fully and rather than avoiding potential triggers, began to develop the confidence that she could withstand challenges and setbacks. An unexpected bonus was the further strengthening of Angela's conviction in her helpful beliefs – see the increasing trend-line in Figure 4.3. Angela was then discharged from the service. This gradual and planned withdrawal helped her to learn she was able to stay well independently without regular support. Her final feedback was this: *'I'm no longer protecting my ex-husband's false image. I'm filled with the power to say what I want to say and do what I want to do without having to live in inequality.'* Her conviction in being ugly, worthless and weak was approaching zero.

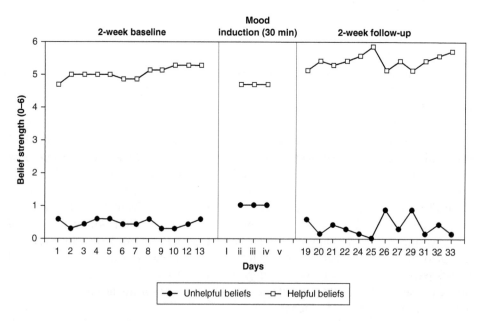

Figure 4.3 Angela's belief ratings before, during and after the mood induction stress test

Evidence for C-CT: clinical outcomes

Jarrett and colleagues have conducted three large-scale trials to investigate the effects of C-CT (Jarrett et al., 1998, 2001; Jarrett & Thase, 2010). As we mentioned earlier, the 12 month relapse rate for discontinued CBT is 29% (Vittengl et al., 2007). When an eight-session dose of C-CT was provided to treatment responders in these studies, the relapse rate was reduced to 10%, confirming the benefit of C-CT. Additionally, the largest benefit was received by those with the highest risk of relapse. The Jarrett studies identified three high-risk groups:

- *Highly recurrent depression*: clients who have suffered multiple previous episodes
- *Early onset of depression*: clients whose first major episode occurred before the age of 18
- *Unstable remission*: clients who have achieved remission but with occasional symptom reversals (or *residual* symptoms)

Relapse rates for these clients tended to be higher, but C-CT helped to reduce them. For example, clients with early-onset depression had a 67% risk of relapse (over 12 months) but C-CT reduced this to 16%. Clients with unstable remission had a 62% risk of relapse (over 12 months) but C-CT reduced this to 37%. This finding was replicated in a large-scale comparison between C-CT and continuation medication: relapse rates for C-CT and continuation fluoxetine were both reduced to18% in the 8-month continuation period (Jarrett & Thase, 2010). However, they rose to 45% (for C-CT) and 41% (for fluoxetine) over a 3-year follow-up. Is the glass half full or half empty? Even with eight sessions of C-CT, towards a half of clients with unstable remission returned to depression within 3 years – but this is significantly better than approximately 60% relapsing within 1 year, in the absence of C-CT.

Consequently, the appropriate clinical strategy is to *prioritize C-CT for high-risk clients*: that is, those affected by highly recurrent depression with early onset and/or unstable remission. On average, lower-risk clients do not need as many booster sessions in the post-treatment period. The evidence suggests to approach staying well on a case-by-case basis: use the client's depression history, clinical formulation and response to acute phase treatment to guide decision making about the amount and type of boosting needed after acute phase treatment.

Mindfulness-Based Cognitive Therapy (MBCT)

In Chapter 2 we considered the evidence concerning change processes in CBT. As we mentioned then, the evidence regarding the vulnerability hypothesis in Beck et al.'s model (Beck et al., 1979) has been mixed (Clark et al., 1999).

There is convincing evidence that *during depressive episodes* clients are affected by unhelpful core beliefs, maladaptive schemata and dysfunctional assumptions. There is also evidence, like negative automatic thoughts, that these beliefs reduce substantially after successful treatment – as occurred in the case of Angela. However, it has been difficult to find out whether core beliefs (and maladaptive schemata) *precede* depressive episodes, precisely because these structures may only be activated in the context of major life stress. For example, prior to her marriage did Angela really *believe* she was worthless? Or did she have a *susceptibility* to that belief – and it depended on circumstances whether the belief was formed? This is part of the mystery concerning the mechanisms by which certain people are vulnerable to depression and seem to remain vulnerable, even after successful treatment.

Although belief in maladaptive schemata and dysfunctional assumptions tends to reduce after successful treatment, there is no evidence, as yet, that their reduction is the *primary* mechanism of change. There will be particular cases where core belief change has a considerable impact – and it is very important to attend to it when it does – but it does not appear to be the main agent of change for most clients. The available evidence suggests acute phase CBT helps to *deactivate* unhelpful beliefs, schema and assumptions without necessarily modifying the *content* of those beliefs (Teasdale, Segal & Williams, 1995). Acute phase CT can build *alternative* helpful beliefs and when these are activated, unhelpful assumptions and beliefs tend to be deactivated. This perspective is consistent with Brewin's (2006) proposals about the mechanisms of action in CBT. He suggests that CBT alters the competition between different cognitive elements seeking retrieval into working memory. Some elements are strengthened by a course of CBT, and are therefore more likely to 'win' retrieval competition, whereas other elements are weakened and are less likely to be retrieved.

From a cognitive perspective there are therefore two types of change to consolidate in the relapse prevention phase of CBT: (1) changes in the *content* of negative thoughts; (2) *deactivation* of unhelpful beliefs/schemata and *activation* of helpful schema. There is also a third mechanism that we alluded to in Chapter 2 when considering different change-types. There is good evidence that CBT can help clients to develop *compensatory skills*. Even if thought-content is unchanged (and perhaps unhelpful beliefs are still active), clients who develop *different ways of responding* to thoughts appear to do well in CBT. In fact, this was one of the key findings emerging from early CBT trials: some clients learned that thoughts were thoughts, not facts. They were able to process their thoughts as events in the mind, rather than unquestioned truths. They learned to process depressing thoughts differently and develop a different relationship to them. In that sense CBT can have a *metacognitive* or *mindful* effect: clients can develop cognitive skills to relate differently to their thoughts and decentre from them, even if the thoughts themselves are largely unchanged (Hargus, Crane, Barnhofer & Williams, 2010). They pay attention to them in an accepting, non-judgemental way and this has a compensatory effect on mood, because unhelpful thoughts no longer produce such a painful sting (Teasdale et al., 2001).

Paying attention to concrete experiences

In light of these findings, Mindfulness-Based Cognitive Therapy (MBCT) was developed as a standalone intervention for relapse prevention, designed to help clients learn how to pay attention to their experiences in a different way, including mental events. Segal, Williams & Teasdale (2012) hypothesized that if clients could develop meta-cognitive skills, increase their capacity for mindfulness and attend differently to their concrete experiences, this would protect them from relapse, whatever gains they had received from acute phase CBT (and perhaps even if they hadn't received CBT). They saw mindfulness as a potential solution to cognitive reactivation: if clients experiencing reactivation could respond in a mindful way this would dampen the *ruminative processes* that tend to spiral out of control when depressing thoughts enter the mind (Raes, Dewulf, Van Heeringen & Williams, 2009; Watkins et al., 2011). Rumination is the repetitive stream of negative thoughts that characterizes much of depressed thinking. Mindfulness does not prevent the occurrence of negative and unhelpful thoughts – in fact, it is not *trying* to avoid, prevent, suppress or control unwanted mental events. It is cultivating the capacity to *notice* what is in the mind, rather than change it: the act of mindful noticing itself suspends unhelpful ruminative processes that can otherwise provoke a depressive spiral (Shahar, Britton, Sbarra, Figueredo & Bootzin, 2010).

MBCT also directs attention to the *body*. When depression becomes highly recurrent, clients can become prisoners in their own minds; feeling trapped by distressing thoughts, images and memories. These mental events grab attention and rumination further increases self-focus. This produces a vicious cycle: the more distressing the thoughts, the greater attention paid to them, the more they are processed in a ruminative way, creating more distressing thoughts, and so on. By placing attention more consistently on the body, the breath and other concrete experiences, the mind has less attentional 'fuel' to become embroiled in ruminative cycles. Clients become more attuned to their somatic and concrete experiences, which has a compensatory effect: they live less in their minds and more in their bodies.

MBCT is usually delivered in an eight-session group format to clients in remission from major depression. Clients are taken through various steps: (i) the rationale for mindfulness, (ii) dealing with barriers, (iii) mindfulness of the breath, (iv) staying present, (v) allowing/letting be, (vi) thoughts are not facts, (vii) self-care, (viii) dealing with future moods. An essential component of the intervention is meditative practice in between group sessions. This is important to develop attentional skills and increase mindfulness capacity.

Evidence for MBCT: clinical outcomes

The effectiveness of MBCT has been tested in several clinical trials. The first two trials found convergent evidence that MBCT was effective in preventing relapse in clients with remitted depression, if and only if those clients had three or more previous major episodes (Ma & Teasdale, 2004; Teasdale et al., 2000). Exploratory analysis suggested these clients also had earlier age of onset and significantly greater adverse experiences in childhood and adolescence. Counter-intuitively, MBCT slightly *increased* the risk of relapse in clients with less than three previous episodes. There is a differential effect of MBCT: it should be considered for cases of highly recurrent depression currently in remission, but not for people who have only suffered one or two prior episodes.

This pattern of results has been reflected in subsequent studies. Segal et al. (2010) reported no advantage for MBCT in clients with stable remission but a considerable advantage in those with unstable remission (28% vs 71% relapse). Similarly, Williams et al. (2014) found little advantage overall for MBCT compared with an active control condition: cognitive psychological education (CPE). This study dismantled the various components of MBCT and in the CPE condition provided psycho-education about depressive relapse and cognitive reactivation, but no meditation practice. Only the MBCT group received mindfulness meditation and was encouraged to practise it. This produced significant protection against relapse in clients with histories of childhood trauma, but not for the whole group.

A recent meta-analysis of six clinical trials found that MBCT reduced relapse by 43% in clients with at least three prior episodes (Piet & Hougaard, 2011). However, the overall pattern of results is clear and converges with the findings for C-CT: it is clients with significant *childhood trauma, abuse or neglect; early age of onset; highly recurrent depression* and/or *unstable remission* who are at greatest risk of relapse (Bondolfi et al., 2010; Godfrin & van Heeringen, 2010; Kuyken et al., 2008). Like C-CT, MBCT has the largest benefit for high-risk clients and is inert, or even unhelpful, for clients with lower risks and less complex presentations.

Practitioner Tips: Relapse Prevention

- All responders to CBT and BA need to receive relapse prevention.
- Booster sessions, continuation therapy or dedicated relapse prevention, such as MBCT, should be prescribed in higher doses for responders at highest risk of relapse. Key features of high-risk clients are:

  o significant childhood adversity – trauma, abuse or neglect
  o early onset of depression – first major episode before the age of 18
  o highly recurrent depression – three or more previous episodes
  o unstable remission – response to treatment but with intermittent symptom reversals or residual symptoms.

- When boosting conventional CBT with continuation sessions:

  o consolidate learning from the acute phase and support your client to generalize it in their daily life
  o encourage your client to reflect on potential triggers, but try to help them accept that challenges will happen from time to time rather than trying to avoid them at all costs
  o encourage your client to notice early warning signs when they have setbacks and could be falling back into depression
  o support your client to respond adaptively to challenges and setbacks using their CBT skills, whether the focus is cognitive or behavioural
  o particularly for high-risk clients, consider some form of stress test (naturalistic or planned) to find out the robustness of their remission to mood challenges
  o use stress tests to practise how best to respond to setbacks, and find out the robustness of the client's recovery.

- When delivering Mindfulness-Based CT remember:

  o MBCT has not been developed as an acute phase treatment for moderate/severe depression; it is mainly used as relapse prevention for people who are currently asymptomatic
  o ensure that clients have experienced a minimum of three previous episodes, and their depression is currently in remission
  o psycho-education may be sufficient to help low-risk clients, but high-risk clients, particularly those with childhood trauma, will need extensive meditation practice to help them stay well.

Summary of Evidence and Guidance from Part I

1. Sufficiently strong therapeutic alliances are essential for effective CBT and BA. Personal trust and confidence need to be translated into *therapeutic tasks* so that client and therapist can collaborate transparently about the optimal path to recovery. When cognitive or behavioural changes lead to symptomatic relief, therapeutic alliances are likely to be further strengthened, and this then creates an advantage for approaching more demanding therapeutic tasks.

2. When treating clients with *severe depression,* therapists need to focus on *activity scheduling* or *behavioural activation.* There is insufficient research to know whether the change mechanism is increased positive reinforcement (the BA hypothesis) or changes in clients' thoughts, predictions and beliefs (the CBT hypothesis). There may be an additive or interactive effect of the two, but CBT process research has not focused sufficiently on behaviour, and BA process research is under-developed.

3. In CBT treatment:

   i. After an initial period of activity scheduling, the client needs to test out the accuracy of their thoughts, predictions and beliefs. There is therapeutic benefit in more *realistic thinking* that will help to correct negative biases.

   ii. It is essential to target *specific examples* of clients' thoughts in *sufficient detail* to enable cognitive change. This means explicit links between particular thoughts and specific emotions that are manageably 'hot' to enable reflection and discovery.

   iii. Changes in *thought content*, towards less negative and more helpful beliefs, are highly desirable – but this is only one change mechanism. CBT can also deactivate unhelpful beliefs and build up more helpful alternatives.

   iv. CBT can also build compensatory skills such as mindful decentring: where clients learn that *thoughts are thoughts, not facts.* This enables a more reflective and less judgemental relationship with mental events, including depressing thoughts and memories.

4. In BA treatment:

   i. Clients have to find out whether their day-to-day behaviours are helpful or hindering in different situations. This means repeated functional analysis of behaviours, with detailed attention to antecedents and consequences. In particular, clients need to consider the medium- and long-term consequences of their behaviours, not just short-term effects.

   ii. It is essential to review *specific examples* of clients' behaviours in *sufficient detail* to enable associative learning.

iii. There is therapeutic benefit in increasing *opportunities for positive reinforcement*. These need to be explored on an idiographic, case-by-case basis.

iv. Clients need to base their activity on schedules and agreements, not whether they feel like doing a behaviour when the time comes, i.e. they will sometimes need to *act against inclination* to gain benefit.

v. Scheduled behaviours must always be manageable, even if they are less potent and rewarding initially than is usually the case.

vi. It essential to review agreed actions from the previous session whether or not they were enacted as planned.

5. Approximately 50% of clients respond to a course of CBT or BA. To help them maintain these gains it is essential to offer relapse prevention, through continuation booster sessions or Mindfulness-Based CT. Clients at highest risk of relapse need a proportionally bigger dose of C-CT or MBCT. They are clients with *significant childhood adversity, early-onset depression, highly recurrent depression* and/or *unstable remission*.

PART II
INTEGRATED APPROACH

Part I has introduced the best-established CBT therapies for major depression and we are unambiguous in our support of these treatments as first-line interventions. When Beck's CBT and BA are effective they do an excellent job bringing clients out of depression and helping them stay well in the future. However, in our view, difficult-to-treat cases who haven't responded to established CBT should not be given further standard CBT protocols. If those protocols have not been effective, it is better for clients to step up to another type of intervention.

Integrated CBT is an alternative next step. It harnesses the learning and evidence from Part I and seeks to apply it to the treatment of challenging cases. Compared with established CBT, integrated CBT is more individualized and less protocol-driven. It puts greater emphasis on cognitive and behavioural *processes*, that is, *how* people think and act rather than the *content* of what they think and do. It is based on a *maintenance model* of depression in the style of CBT for anxiety disorders. It generates bespoke treatment plans that are based on clear principles, an explicit model and evidence-based treatment components.

The integrated approach is informed by elements from a number of CBT and cognitive science models. It is rooted in a *self-regulation model* that emphasizes the role of self-identity, memories, goals and motivation. Therapist and client develop an individualized formulation of the self-regulatory processes that maintain depression, and a number of treatment components are available based on client need: some components are essential for all clients (*core*) and others are optional based on the emerging formulation (*optional*).

Integrated CBT has been developed to guide therapy with treatment-resistant and challenging cases that often have the following features:

- childhood trauma, abuse or neglect
- early-onset depression (first major episode before the age of 18)
- highly recurrent episodes
- chronic and persistent depression

- comorbid axis I disorders such as Generalized Anxiety Disorder (GAD), Obsessive Compulsive Disorder (OCD), Social Anxiety Disorder or Post-Traumatic Stress Disorder (PTSD)
- long-term interpersonal or personality problems
- social, economic, healthcare or cultural disadvantage
- heightened risk of self-neglect, self-harm and suicide
- unstable or non-response to previous courses of CBT

As the book progresses we will cover all of the above features but not all are covered in Part II. Part II introduces the self-regulation model and core treatment components, and the rest of book explores how the model is applied with different sub-types of depression under various conditions. Chapter 5 introduces the self-regulation model of depression: it is based on normal self-regulatory processes and the chapter illustrates how these are configured within euthymic and depressed mood. Chapter 6 describes the core treatment components and therapeutic processes that are needed to overcome depression and help clients stay well in the future. A clinical case, Chloe, is used to illustrate these processes in Chapters 5 and 6.

5

Self-Regulation Model of Depression

Self-Regulation Framework

As we have seen in Part I, established CBT protocols target negative thoughts and maladaptive beliefs, encouraging them to become more realistic and adaptive; they also target avoidant and unhelpful behaviours to increase rewarding activity and extinguish unhelpful habits. Integrated CBT shares the same aims but through a different approach. It formulates unhelpful thoughts and behaviours as the *products of self-dysregulation* and it targets the underlying self-regulatory processes and structures that generate unhelpful thoughts and behaviours (Dykman, 1998).

In the integrated approach we use a broad definition of self-regulation: it is the goal-directed cognitive, affective and behavioural processes through which an individual:

- constructs and maintains a valued self-identity
- learns how to notice and satisfy their needs and desires
- processes a range of mental states, emotions and body states.

Self-representations and mental states are regulated through values, goals and various feedback mechanisms, and when self-regulation is effective an individual is able to satisfy their basic, security, attainment and relationship needs through flexible interactions with the environment (Carver & Scheier, 1999). Self-regulation supports learning, adaptation and development across the lifespan, and when it is effective it helps to maintain euthymic mood.

In Figure 5.1 we propose a key set of relationships regarding the *content*, *process* and *structure* of self-regulation. The *content level* refers to an individual's concrete experiences; their thoughts, emotions and body states within the context of particular life situations. For example, imagine a mother with a newborn baby. She has a range of thoughts, some expressing delight and wonder, others self-doubt, others focusing on the beauty of her new child. The emotions are joy, awe and trepidation. The body states, including involuntary responses, are a mixture of discomfort, exhaustion and relief. From a self-regulation perspective, these experiences constitute *current mood* and they are the products of underlying psychological processes, interacting with inputs from the environment.

The *process level* refers to the motivational, behavioural and cognitive operations that *transform* experiences and information; they take one type of input, such as a thought, feeling, impulse, memory or goal, and turn it into something else, such as a plan, action, inference or decision. Moods influence motivation by shaping what people *feel like* doing. For example, this mother experiences a natural impulse to nurture her baby. Her motivation is oriented towards satisfying the baby's needs and this produces behavioural engagement and interaction, for example, feeding, cuddling and so on. Actions and interactions produce consequences, and reflective processes are needed to notice those consequences, conceptualize them and learn from them. Action and reflection are highly interactive within effective self-regulation. The outputs of reflection are further thoughts and mental events, which in turn influence emotions and body states; hence the process level feeds back into concrete experiences. Content and process are therefore in constant interaction. Reflection also generates new memories.

The *structural level* is long-term storage: memories, self-representations and goals that record the history, narratives, identity, values and aspirations of the individual. These underlying structures form a *dynamic system* with multiple memories,

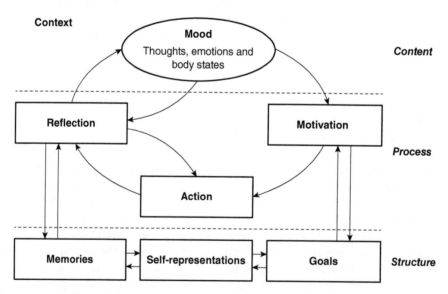

Figure 5.1   Self-regulation framework

self-representations and goals each with *differential accessibility*. This means that at any point, certain elements are more available and accessible than others. The birth of a child is a significant life event, so new autobiographical memories are likely to be laid down. These will feed into the mother's self-representations, and this in turn will influence her long-term and short-term goals. At any point in time, the configuration of these underlying structures provides inputs to the process level. Autobiographical memories feed into reflective processes, and goals feed into motivation. The three levels combine to form a highly interactive self-regulatory system, with multiple feedback loops, that has evolved to learn, adapt to the environment and satisfy needs and desires. We propose that self-regulation functions differently in different mood-states, and this is the basis of understanding euthymic and depressed moods.

Euthymic Mood: Self-Regulatory Processes

Euthymic mood

Euthymic (normal) mood is not characterized by exclusively positive thinking, positive emotions and pleasant body states. These are present in euphoric or joyful moods, whereas normal euthymic mood manifests a broader range of thoughts, emotions and body states: some positive, some neutral and some negative. However, there needs to be *sufficient positive affect* (PA) to maintain euthymic mood, and *sufficient tolerance of negative affect* (NA) when it is present.

Motivation

Euthymic moods with sufficient PA help to generate *approach motivation*; that is, *impulses towards desired states*, with positive anticipation and reward expectation. Approach motivation also generates a receptive openness to new experiences and a non-defensive orientation to interactions with others. In euthymic mood, approach motivation is primary and avoidance motivation is limited, as depicted in Figure 5.2 (Trew, 2011). Avoidance motivation is experienced as *impulses to avoid perceived threats*. The avoidant individual is closed to new experiences and has a more defensive orientation. He or she is alert to danger and poised to fight, flight or freeze in response to attack or risk of harm. Approach and avoidance interact and can both be useful, but the functional range of avoidance is much narrower: it can be helpful to avoid realistic threats, for example, to motivate escape from *entrapment* or unrewarding situations. But, as we will explore later, it has unhelpful consequences when applied broadly as a behavioural strategy.

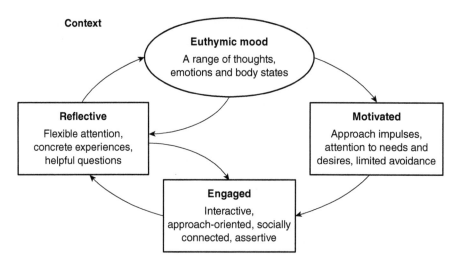

Figure 5.2   Self-regulatory processes in euthymic mood

Action

As the phrase suggests, approach motivation drives approach behaviour. When approach motivation is primary individuals *engage* in their actions because those actions are oriented towards desired outcomes, such as forming a strong attachment with a new baby. Actions are often *interactive*; not just an individual performing behaviours, but engaging with the environment and *relating* to others. Engaged actions help to satisfy needs and desires at different levels, especially when they are aligned with underlying goals and values. The birth of a new baby could help to satisfy relational desires and, hopefully, be a source of fulfilment and personal development. But, of course, what this means depends on circumstances for an individual and how they relate to their needs and desires.

Reflection

Reflective processes enable an individual to *pay attention* to experiences in a flexible way, plan, notice significant events and learn from them, for example learning about a new baby, recognizing the consequences of relating to him or her in certain ways, and so on. A key aspect is noticing the *consequences* of actions, in particular whether they align with needs, desires and goals. To do this, cognitive processing has to be sufficiently *concrete*, that is, focused on present experiences rather than abstract ideas. Reflective capacity is essential to understand self, others and world and when it operates well it leads to explicit learning and increases adaptation. Constructive reflection also relies on *helpful questions*: people need to think creatively to find answers and the result is enhanced conceptualization, for example, 'What does my baby like? How can I balance my needs with theirs? What sort of mother do I want to be?'

Depressed Mood: Self-Regulatory Processes

Applying this framework to major depression, from time to time the self-regulatory system has to accommodate periods of *self-devaluation*. This is what accompanies depressed moods and if the system fails to respond adaptively, persistent depression can result. In major depression, depressed moods fail to *self-correct*; something causes them to persist and this is the focus of the self-regulation model and integrated treatment.

Depressed mood

The basic premise of the model is this: from time to time euthymic mood is disrupted as a consequence of external or internal events. When precipitation is external, life events place stress on an individual's normal functioning (*outside-in*). These events can be past or current; single or multiple; they can be linked and have a cumulative effect; they can be big or small, sudden or gradual. Typically these are disappointments, misfortune, hardship, loss, conflict, oppression, illness or traumas. When precipitation is internal there is a change in self-regulation, for example as a result of sad memories being activated or a change in self-identity (*inside-out*). These events have a *self-devaluing* effect and this provokes depressed mood through negative thoughts, negative emotions and unpleasant body states.

This initial depressed mood is *normal*. It is a normal part of human experience to have temporary depressed moods in response to disappointments or sad memories, for example. However, there is a significant difference between a *depressed mood* and a *mood disorder*. A depressed mood is a relatively short-lived affective state that is likely to occur in certain circumstances. *A mood disorder results from depressed moods failing to self-correct*. We hypothesize that when a mood disorder develops, the failure to self-correct is due to the effect of depressed mood on motivation, action and reflective processes, with secondary effects on memory, self-representation and goal systems that we will address later in the chapter. A downward spiral forms because *depressed mood suppresses the processes that are needed to reverse its effects*. Depression works against

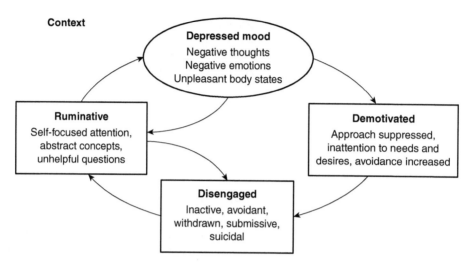

Figure 5.3 Self-regulatory processes in depressed mood

itself: the more depressed a person becomes the harder it is for them to reverse their mood, as illustrated in Figure 5.3.

We will consider each of these processes in turn and illustrate through a clinical case, Chloe. Chloe's case formulation is illustrated in Figure 5.4.

Case Illustration | Chloe: context and mood

Chloe was a 35-year-old married woman working as an engineer. Four years previously she suffered a miscarriage; this was a painful event both physically and emotionally, due to restricted use of painkillers, because of various medical conditions. Chloe was delighted to become pregnant one year later but suffered severe nausea, sickness and pelvic pain requiring hospitalization. This provoked anxiety about a further miscarriage and caused significant disruption to her work role. She was in a serious car accident during her pregnancy, but survived unscathed.

Prior to her son's birth, Chloe started to have the thought she was a bad mother (*self devaluation*), because the medication she needed carried a small risk of adversely affecting her child during his birth. She began to feel guilty that she was disadvantaging him and ashamed she did not feel stronger and more confident during her pregnancy. She felt she was failing in the task of being a good mother. These depressing thoughts and emotions accompanied periods of acute pain and physical discomfort that exacerbated her moods.

Chloe's experience of giving birth was painful and traumatic: the process was complicated by restricted pain relief and limited mobility. During extreme distress, Chloe was not fully consulted about certain medical procedures, felt shocked and terrified and believed she was going to die. Prior to being given a general anaesthetic, Chloe believed she would not survive the operation. She woke 2 hours later following the birth of her son, confused and shocked that they had both survived. Chloe then suffered a number of medical complications that required further surgery. She was diagnosed with post-natal depression 6 months later.

Depressed moods are very understandable in this situation. However, a *mood disorder is not an inevitable consequence of depressed moods*. Moods do not maintain themselves. We believe it is self-regulatory processes that determine whether depressed moods persist or self-correct, and we will consider each in turn.

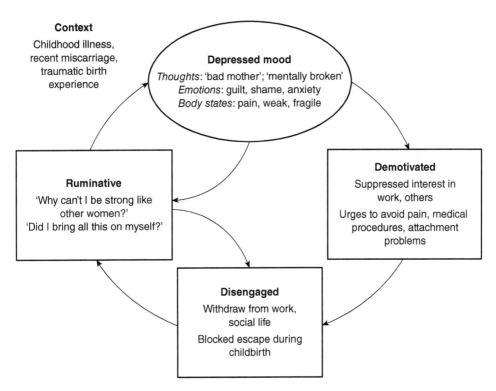

Figure 5.4   Case formulation for Chloe

Suppressed motivation

A number of factors contribute to depressed people becoming demotivated. For example, negative thoughts reduce expectations of activities being worthwhile and rewarding, and this can have a demotivating effect (Dickson, Moberly & Kinderman, 2011). Negative emotions can be demotivating when they interact with avoidance, for example, to prevent embarrassment, avoid shame, limit burden to others, etc. (Sherdell, Waugh & Gotlib, 2012). Unpleasant body states, such as reduced energy and psychomotor slowing, can have a demotivating effect because greater physical effort is required to initiate action (Treadway, Bossaller, Shelton & Zald, 2012; Yang et al., 2014).

We propose that there are three main ways in which demotivated states can become problematic and lead to behavioural disengagement:

1. *Approach impulses become suppressed.* There are fewer and weaker impulses towards desired states, with less positive anticipation and reduced reward expectancies. This can occur with specific needs and desires (e.g. loss of appetite), or it can have a more generalized effect across the hierarchy of needs – see Chapter 6. There is also less openness to new experiences and a more defensive orientation to interactions with others.
2. *Reduced attention to needs and desires.* As approach impulses become weaker, less attention is paid to them. Depressed people tend to pay more attention to their thoughts and memories, rather than identifying their needs by attending to emotions and body states – see the section below on rumination.
3. *Avoidant impulses increase.* Depressed people's impulses to avoid, escape or hide tend to increase. These impulses are understandable in the context of depressed moods, but if enacted they usually lead to later difficulties, even if the urge to avoid or escape is satisfied in the short term. Individuals vary in how much their demotivation is due to increased avoidance or suppressed approach: for most people it is an interaction of the two (Trew, 2011).

Case Illustration | Chloe: suppressed motivation

Prior to the depressive episode, Chloe had strong desires to have a family and was highly motivated at work (*approach*). However, her pregnancy and health problems limited access to work and affected her usual work performance. In the pre-natal, birth and post-natal phases Chloe's avoidance motivation increased: her threat system was heightened in response to earlier memories of medical procedures, intermittent uncontrolled pain, the road traffic accident, worry about future pain and concern about attachment problems with her son. Approach motivation was mildly suppressed in the pre-natal period and reduced markedly in the post-natal period, compounded by guilt, shame, pain and protracted physical discomfort.

Behavioural disengagement

Unless an individual acts against their inclination, the usual effect of suppressed motivation is some type of *behavioural disengagement*, in other words, withdrawal from normal behaviour. This can manifest in a number of ways, with a proposed taxonomy in Table 5.1. The self-regulation model emphasizes engagement or disengagement that *results* from actions. It is less concerned with what the behaviour is, and more concerned with whether or not it produces engagement, for example, in tasks or interactions with others.

The most obvious sub-type is *inactivity*, when depressed individuals lose motivation, have low expectations of reward, and become bored and under-stimulated as a consequence. Because motivation is suppressed, depressed people tend not to *feel like* acting, so not surprisingly their activity tends to reduce. As we explored in Chapter 3, inactivity can reduce positive reinforcement and PA, maintaining depressed moods and further suppressing motivation. In common with Behavioural Activation (BA), we agree that the consequences of behaviours are very important, because of the effects they have in maintaining or altering moods. In the self-regulation model, the affective consequences of behaviours are viewed as *feedback loops* back into the system. We do not refer to them as having *reinforcing* or *punishing* effects; rather they are one of several sources of feedback that influence the action tendencies of an individual. Alongside other inputs, they can have a powerful influence on future behaviour. In Chapter 6, we will consider the similarities and differences between BA and the self-regulation approach.

As summarized in Table 5.1, there are a number of other ways in which disengagement can manifest. Importantly, these do not necessarily entail *less activity*; they are concerned with *how* behaviour is enacted, in ways that reduce engagement. For example,

Table 5.1   Sub-types of depressed disengagement

Behaviour	Context	Cognitive self-appraisal	Emotions/affect
Inactive	Limited opportunities	Low expectations of reward	Bored, under-stimulated, flat
Avoidant	Hazards, threat, danger	Unable to cope, vulnerable	Anxiety, fear, dread, helplessness
Withdrawn	Isolation, rejection, loss, failure	Disconnected, alienated, unwanted	Sad, dejected, empty, disappointed
Submissive	Oppression, coercive control, entrapment	Inferior, defeated, weak	Shame, guilt, arrested anger
Suicidal	Reduced agency, mental defeat	Self-loathing	Resignation, hopelessness

avoidance will usually reduce engagement, but it can occur in someone who is active and busy (Ottenbreit, Dobson & Quigley, 2014). This is sometimes observed in agitated forms of mixed depression and anxiety, when being busy is a way of avoiding emotions and body states. Another variant is *social withdrawal*, where an individual becomes less connected and interactive with others. They are not necessarily less active; they are isolated and disconnected in their activities (Girard, Cohn, Mahoor, Mavadati, Hammal & Rosenwald, 2014). A related sub-type is submissiveness, which refers to role relationships. Submissive behaviour is not necessarily isolated; rather, it emerges out of reciprocation to powerful and dominant others. Another sub-type is when depressed people disengage from relationship with themselves: they have reduced *agency*. This results in less attention to needs and desires, fewer choices and plans, less self-respect, increased self-dissatisfaction and, in some cases, self-loathing. In severe cases *resignation* and *mental defeat* can occur, i.e. giving up on oneself or life. The ultimate form of disengagement is suicide: fatal disconnection from life itself (Handley et al., 2016).

In Table 5.1 we have included typical cognitive appraisals and affective states that accompany these sub-types. These are *indicative* of common patterns, not rigid categories. For most clients, behavioural withdrawal has mixed features, and the challenge in treatment is identifying which sub-types apply and how they interact with each other. As depression becomes more severe, disengagement tends to become more *generalized* and a greater number of these features are likely to be present. We have also included typical contextual factors, for example, avoidance associated with threat, withdrawal with rejection, submission with oppression, and so on. Individuals can find themselves in very particular situations, with idiosyncratic appraisals, so an individualized formulation is essential to understand these links. There are also two senses of 'context' to consider; one is the literal sense of real external events, such as threats, losses and oppression. In these cases, disengagement is 'outside-in'. The other sense is the 'cognitive context', in which benign situations are interpreted and experienced as threatening, ostracizing or oppressive. In these cases, disengagement is 'inside-out'.

Finally, it is important to note that disengagement is not maladaptive under all conditions (Koppe & Rothermund, 2017). It is within the normal range of human behaviour and not just a consequence of depression. We have already seen that avoidance can be useful within particular situations: for example, to escape imminent and realistic threats. Disengagement can also be helpful when a valued goal becomes unattainable. It is better to give up and re-prioritize if there is no prospect of a preferred outcome; to persist with something unattainable is a failure to adjust and accept a situation for what it is (Dickson, Moberly, O'Dea & Field, 2016). This also fits with evolutionary models of *involuntary defeat* – this is the hypothesis that there is an adaptive advantage for withdrawal in response to competitive loss. When an individual suffers a defeat or loss, it is better for long-term adaptation to withdraw submissively than continue fighting a dominant force (Gilbert, 2000). So under certain conditions, avoidance, withdrawal and submission have a functional range that can serve useful purposes. During depression, however, disengagement is over-expressed, over-generalized and tends to function in a maladaptive way.

Case Illustration | Chloe: disengaged behaviour

In the pre-natal period, Chloe had less opportunity for behavioural engagement at work. Her behavioural avoidance increased to try to prevent pain and limit the risks of a further miscarriage. During labour and delivery Chloe experienced *blocked escape* due to physical restraints and severe pain, to the point of feeling resigned to death (*mental defeat*). In the post-natal period she withdrew from normal social activities and had a gradual phased return to work that was difficult to balance with childcare and other health needs. She engaged in attending to her son's needs, but would sometimes avoid him when his crying triggered painful memories. Chloe continued to avoid the risk of pain when possible.

Ruminative cognitive processing

During depressed moods, reflective processes tend to become more *ruminative*. Depressive rumination is the tendency for unhelpful repetitive thinking and brooding on thoughts and memories (Nolen-Hoeksema, 1991). We propose that disengagement increases the risk of rumination, because the mind functions best when it is socially connected: withdrawal and avoidance reduce *connectivity*. This is one of the setting conditions that result in thinking becoming repetitive and unproductive. Because the depressed mind is functioning as a closed system, rather than an open system connected to other minds, attention becomes *inflexible* and *self-focused* (Lyubormirsky & Nolen-Hoeksema, 1995). Self-focus is not the problem; it is being *stuck* in self-focus, with limited flexibility and modulation of attention between internal and external cues. Negative mental events, emotions and body states grab attention and demand explanation, so processing resources are directed internally, rather than balanced or alternating with an external focus.

In this mood-state, it is difficult to decentre from mental events and simply notice what is there. Instead, depression pulls the mind into analysing its own predicament. This is the essential problem in depressive rumination: there is an internal demand to *conceptualize the depressed self from within.* Depressed people are trying to understand what is wrong and why they feel so down, and their concerns become more abstract and less grounded in concrete experiences. On the face of it this is an understandable goal. Major depression is an abnormal mood-state and it is natural for depressed individuals to want to make sense of ambiguous, novel or anomalous experiences. Rumination is an attempt to self-regulate: understanding what is wrong could be the first step in overcoming it.

However, the setting conditions for abstract thinking conspire to make it less effective. Attempts to conceptualize fall foul of inflexible self-focus and reduced reflective capacity (Watkins & Teasdale, 2001). Rather than increasing understanding, these conditions trigger repetitive mental loops that increase distress and re-initiate further attempts at conceptualization. This often manifests in the form of *unhelpful questions*, for example:

- Causal attribution (e.g. 'Why do I feel so down?')
- Conceptualizing deficiencies (e.g. 'What is wrong with me?')
- Implicational meanings (e.g. 'What does this say about me?')
- Anticipating consequences (e.g. 'Will I ever get out of this?')
- Comparative reasoning (e.g. 'How come other people cope better than me?')
- Counterfactual reasoning (e.g. 'Why don't I feel the way I should?')

There are three main consequences of these types of questions: firstly, the depressed mind only partially engages in trying to answer them. They are expressions of distress and frustration, not just attempts at conceptualization. Secondly, no answer is forthcoming, but rather than pause and reflect on this, the depressed mind moves on to other unhelpful questions. Thirdly, negative answers are generated and these tend to have self-referential content (e.g. 'It's my own stupid fault I let this happen'). This then feeds back into depressed mood and generates more inputs for further questions, so an iterative cycle of rumination is perpetuated, with negative thoughts and unhelpful questions interacting and feeding off each other: an interaction of content (thoughts) and process (questions).

The fundamental problem is that ruminative questions are detached from, or mismatched to, higher-order goals. Sometimes there is an explicit goal to figure out what is wrong, as a first step in deciding what to do. In this case there is a clear self-regulation strategy, but the ruminative process fails to deliver the desired output: a clear and helpful understanding is not usually forthcoming. The cognitive processes initiated by ruminative questions fail to increase understanding and instead iterative closed loops are instantiated. Rather than clarifying the problem, rumination produces a *self-critical dialogue* with the depressed mind asking itself unhelpful questions and producing unhelpful answers: this then perpetuates the depressed mood that triggered the conceptual demand in the first instance (Rimes & Watkins, 2005). The need to have a good-enough relationship with oneself is also threatened by repeated self-devaluation, a phenomenon we will re-visit in future chapters.

In other cases, rumination appears not to be goal-directed. Clients' attention is recurrently directed to certain memories, thoughts or body states and there is repeated brooding and dwelling on what has happened, or how things are; but not obviously to make a discovery, enhance understanding or make a decision. In this situation the self-regulation system has detected an anomaly, abnormality or goal-discrepancy (e.g. 'I don't usually feel this bad or dislike myself this much') and attention is directed where it needs to be, but there is not yet a goal or process to respond to the discrepancy and do something about it. Consequently, brooding and passive rumination result. This is analogous to an individual staring at an accident-site: unable to direct attention elsewhere, but not yet able to understand it or decide what to do.

One of the pernicious effects of rumination is that it further reduces reflective capacity, so depressed people tend not to notice how unhelpful their rumination is; they become embroiled in trying to understand the depressed self from within. In fact, they are unlikely to notice they are ruminating at the time, because attention is pulled into the *content* of their questions and answers. Over time, some depressed people recognize their tendency to over-think and begin to notice how unhelpful it is. However, this can trigger the opposite problem of cognitive avoidance and thought suppression: in other words, trying to empty the mind of all its contents and distract attention elsewhere (Beevers, Wenzlaff, Hayes & Scott, 1999). In many cases this produces an alternating pattern of rumination and cognitive avoidance, and this can be a considerable problem when the depressed person needs to emotionally process experiences or make decisions.

Case Illustration | Chloe: ruminative cognitive processing

In the pre-natal period Chloe became worried about miscarriage, pain and her future attachment to her son. Worry is a form of repetitive thinking focused on hypothetical threats and it shares a number of features with depressive rumination. Worry increases the risk of depressive rumination, and for Chloe this began to focus around the guilt she was experiencing in relation to her unborn son (e.g. 'Why can't I be strong like other women?', 'What if I don't bond with him?'). In the post-natal period, Chloe tried to make sense of her traumatic experiences including doubts about events at the birth (e.g. 'I'm mentally broken – so how come I'm still here?'; 'Is my son really mine?') There was also comparative rumination, regretting past events and comparing them with what should have happened (e.g. 'Did I bring all this on myself?').

Self-Regulatory Structures

Self-regulating processes can operate *outside-in*: this is when the environment is a stimulus for mental events, emotions and body states. They can also operate *inside-out*: this is when internal cognitive structures, that store knowledge and information, generate inputs for processing, such as memories, self-representations and goals.

Intrusive memories

Euthymic mood is associated with *specific autobiographical memories* across a range of experiences, not just positive (Conway & Pleydell-Pearce, 2000). When an individual is able to recollect their personal history in a high level of detail, this confers an advantage for pattern recognition, problem solving, goal setting and planning. It creates opportunities for learning and reflection. Within major depression, the autobiographical memory system functions differently. Firstly, memories that are congruent with depressed mood are more accessible; in other words, people are more likely to remember events from times when they were previously depressed. Not surprisingly such memories tend to be negative in content, for example, recalling disappointments, conflicts, losses and so on (Brewin, Reynolds & Tata, 1999). Secondly, a significant proportion of depressed people experience *intrusive memories*, that is, memories of negative events that enter awareness uninvited, not the product of deliberate recall (Starr & Moulds, 2006). Intrusive memories are often an input for rumination; they become subject to conceptualization and attempts to explain or mentally alter the past (Watkins & Teasdale, 2001). In addition, deliberate recollections of personal memories are less specific and more *over-general*. This can be frustrating for depressed clients when they are unable to remember details about past experiences, sometimes called a *memory blockade* (Griffith et al., 2016). In spite of their best efforts, depressed people struggle to access specific autobiographical

Case Illustration | Chloe: intrusive and over-general memories

In the pre-natal period Chloe experienced intrusive memories of her childhood illnesses, her miscarriage and the road traffic accident. In the post-natal period, she had intrusive memories of the birth experience, subsequent medical complications and interactions with her son. She was very frustrated by memory blockade, finding it difficult to recollect details from recent day-to-day experiences.

memories and this can become very disabling in highly recurrent and chronic depression. We will explore this further in Chapters 8 and 9.

Unhelpful self-representations

Autobiographical memories are essential to form self-representations, or mental models of self (Conway, 2005). It is a normal developmental task to create a self-identity based on life experiences, emerging personality traits and personal values. Self-identity is plural: self-representations are numerous and laid down in various developmental stages.

In Part III we will explore different aspects of self-identity: how they are influenced by early and later developmental phases, and particular vulnerabilities that can confer risks for depression. As illustrated in Figure 5.5, some self-representations are internalized through early learning and attachment experiences, such as mental models of being lovable, competent and safe. Others are self-generated and constructed from adolescence onwards, for example, investments in relationships, friendships, body, appearance, nationality, ethnicity, politics, religion, work, career, marital status, parenthood, interests, and so on. The key point is self-representations vary in how helpful and adaptive they are. When they are helpful they:

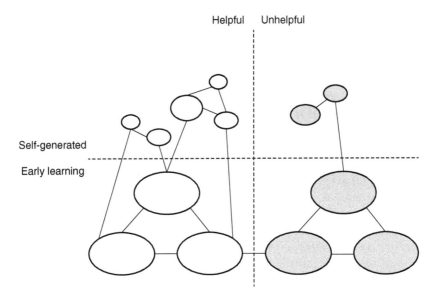

Figure 5.5   Networks of helpful and unhelpful self-representations

1. contribute positively to self-esteem
2. maintain self-efficacy and
3. enable an individual to interact in ways that satisfy their basic, security, attainment and relational needs.

When they are unhelpful or maladaptive they undermine self-esteem, reduce self-efficacy and obstruct interactions in ways that result in unmet needs.

We propose that self-representations are stored in networks of inter-connected nodes, and at any point in time some parts of the network are activated and other parts are deactivated (Hayes et al., 2015). The particular configuration of active nodes determines what *feels true* for that individual at that point. Active nodes make information *available to form beliefs* and influence felt-senses. In Figure 5.5, larger nodes represent more developed representations, and we will expand on this further in Part III. The main proposal is that during euthymic mood, helpful self-representations are activated and unhelpful self-representations are deactivated, whereas in depressed mood, there is a *phase shift* from helpful to unhelpful self-representations. Unsurprisingly, the activation of unhelpful nodes tends to provoke negative felt-senses, such as 'worthless', 'useless', 'unlovable', 'stupid', 'insecure', etc.

How, then, does this account differ from Beck's vulnerability hypothesis and other schema-based theories? Firstly, there is no assumption that a depressing felt-sense or belief, such as 'worthless' or 'useless', has previously existed in the individual's mind. It may be the first time those ideas have occurred or felt true. This can result from *deactivation* of helpful nodes, or *disruption* to them. In the case of deactivation, the helpful node is still available in the dynamic system and the therapeutic task is to find out what would help to reactivate it. In the case of disruption, erosion or even obliteration of a self-representation, the task is more challenging: how to repair or restore a formerly helpful self-representation that has been altered through aversive experiences or other events? This is not just an academic question: it is a pressing psychotherapeutic question, as we will explore in later chapters.

Secondly, unhelpful self-representations can form at any point in the lifespan, contrasting with Beck et al.'s proposal that they invariably result from aversive childhood experiences (Beck et al., 1979). As we have seen in earlier chapters, childhood trauma, abuse and neglect confer a risk for depression, and it is clear that those experiences can result in unhelpful self-representations forming and being internalized. We will explore various cases where this was true in later chapters. However, we have also observed that a happy childhood is not insurance against depression, precisely because unhelpful self-identities can develop at any point in the lifespan, even when early attachment experiences have been secure and positive.

From our perspective, this is the only credible explanation for late-onset depression, when people experience their first-onset of depression aged in their seventies or eighties. We think it is unlikely these people have had lifelong negative core beliefs, but have managed to avoid major depression for over six decades. It is more plausible that the developmental transition into later-life presents new challenges, such as losses and illness, and these can deactivate or disrupt helpful self-representations that have served the individual well up to that point. In this scenario, there is an opportunity for unhelpful nodes to form, even if they have not been present until now. It is well known there are sensitive phases of developmental transition when new self-representations form: old age is one; adolescence is another, which we will explore further in Chapter 7 (Praharso, Tear & Cruwys, 2017).

Thirdly, permanently active nodes will tend to manifest as stable beliefs, but it is equally likely that self-beliefs will fluctuate over time as a result of the overall activity of the network. Rather than viewing this as changes in *belief strength*, the network approach emphasizes the *strength of relationship between nodes*: certain self-representations strengthen or inhibit the activation of others, and it is the active configuration that determines what feels true and is believed. For example, people can hold mutually incompatible beliefs at the same time, depending on the activity of multiple nodes. To our mind, this is a richer way of modelling states of doubt, confusion or conflict that are common during depressive episodes.

In summary, during depressed moods, helpful self-representations are deactivated or disrupted, and unhelpful representations are reactivated or begin to form. Beyond a certain tipping point, the activation of unhelpful nodes has a *generalized effect* on the whole network and this is when a depressed mood can spiral into a more severely depressed state (Teasdale, 1999). In Part III we will extend the model in Figure 5.5 to consider specific vulnerabilities with individual cases.

Case Illustration | Chloe: unhelpful self-representations

There were three significant phase shifts in Chloe's self-identity during the precipitation and course of her depression. Firstly, intrusive memories of childhood illness, the miscarriage and the birth experience activated the unhelpful self-representation: *'physically frail'*. This had developed during childhood and was usually deactivated, unless cued by the threat of ill-health. Secondly, Chloe's self-representation as an *'intelligent mind'* was highly adaptive and self-defining, but the birth experience disrupted it to a profound degree. Her wishes at the time of the birth were disregarded by medical staff (*'as if I was just a piece of meat'*), and this had a devastating effect on Chloe's felt-sense of being an intelligent, self-respecting, agentive person. Thirdly, as would be expected, her self-representation as a *'responsible adult'* became more prominent in the transition to becoming a parent. However, in Chloe's case it began to take an unhelpful form: *'bad mother'*.

Passive goals

In euthymic mood, helpful self-representations activate *approach goals*, in other words, *desired future states* that feed into approach impulses. These contrast with *avoidance goals* that seek to prevent unwanted states. When approach goals are active they motivate current actions and orient them towards what the individual wants to happen. When helpful self-representations, such as *'intelligent mind'* and *'responsible adult'*, are disrupted or deactivated, this has an effect on associated life-goals. Life-goals are not usually obliterated during depression, even though there is significantly less goal-directed behaviour. Depressed people appraise that they have less influence over their life-goals and consequently they are less optimistic about achieving them (Dickson et al., 2011). We propose that this leads to *passive goals* – passively desired states with few associated actions. Rather than being concrete, tangible possibilities, approach-based goals become abstract desired states that are theoretically desired but appraised as unlikely to happen. As they become more abstract, they are prone to become objects of rumination (e.g. 'I'd love to have a partner, but who would want me?').

As we have already observed, this can have a suppressing effect on approach motivation, which then feeds into behavioural disengagement. The net effect is increasing *goal discrepancies*: over time, depressed people make minimal progress towards their approach goals because they are not fully engaged with them – they don't translate into action. Any distress provoked by being distant from a goal is usually worsened by depression, because the suppressing effect on motivation reduces goal-directed activity and can trigger rumination about the lack of progress. This then feeds into the memory system: there are no new memories signalling progress, which maintains self-devaluation and further exacerbates the goal discrepancy that triggered the cycle.

There are other common patterns: firstly, depressed people's attention sometimes narrows around a highly valued goal and there are phases of active engagement in pursuing it, alternating with phases of disengagement and inactivity. In some cases the highly valued goal is unattainable, but this does not stop intermittent goal pursuit (Barton et al., 2008). Secondly, people sometimes put their pre-depression goals on hold until they have recovered from depression and this increases *goal conditionality* (e.g. 'I'll go on holiday when I'm feeling better'). Ironically, this can limit engagement with the activities that would help mood to improve (Coughlan, Tata & MacLeod, 2016; Hadley & MacLeod, 2010). In contrast, approach goals during euthymic mood tend to be relatively independent, and certainly less conditional than is observed in depressed states. Thirdly, in many people depression provokes *avoidance goals*, for example, to avoid feeling worse, prevent other people seeing me like this, and so on. These are intended to self-protect – and they may have short-term protective functions – but in the longer term they contribute to the on-going suppression of approach motivation.

Case Illustration | Chloe: passive and avoidant goals

In the pre-natal period, Chloe's goals became more avoidant focusing on trying to prevent unwanted outcomes, such as uncontrolled pain and attachment problems with her son. This pattern persisted in the post-natal period with significant anxiety about her son being channelled into highly structured activities, pursuing the goal to limit relationship problems with him. Longer-term career and personal goals (*approach*) about having further children were put on hold.

Emergent Phenomena

The full self-regulation model of depression is illustrated in Figure 5.6. The interaction of demotivation, disengagement, rumination, intrusive memories, unhelpful self-representations and passive goals perpetuates the maintenance of depression. What maintains it is the *repeated interaction* of these processes and structures: this is what makes it difficult for the system to self-correct and return to normal mood. As we mentioned in Chapter 1, this closely reflects the *principles* of Teasdale & Barnard's (1993) Interacting Cognitive Subsystems (ICS) model, though there are several differences between this model and ICS in terms of the proposed subsystems. The self-regulation model has a greater emphasis on context, goals, motivation and action; however, it shares the emphasis on multiple subsystems that become stuck in depressed configurations.

A number of higher-order phenomena emerge as a consequence of these interactions. The following are not explained by any single factor, rather it is the repeated interaction of several factors:

- *Entrapment.* Depressed people often feel trapped and unable to escape aversive situations. This can have a contextual focus, for example, feeling stuck in life-situations without solutions or alternatives; it can also have an internal focus, feeling unable to escape unwanted mental states such as memories, thoughts and negative emotions. Within the self-regulation model, this is explained by multiple feedback loops creating a *depressive interlock* where the behaviour of each subsystem maintains the stuck state of the others (Teasdale & Barnard, 1993). This is analogous to a traffic gridlock: all vehicles are stuck because each needs another to move first. The system is in a state of *capture* and needs external inputs to un-stick the situation (Hayes et al., 2015). In clinical terms, this is the point at which individuals have considerable difficulty coming out of depression without external inputs.

- *Helplessness and hopelessness.* A consequence of entrapment is feeling helpless to effect change, as if there is nothing an individual can do to escape or improve their situation (Maier & Seligman, 2016). This can manifest in low self-efficacy and feeling powerless. When this persists over an extended period, an individual's hopefulness about overcoming depression tends to reduce. This can be compounded by failed attempts at improvement, such as ineffective treatment or misguided advice. It is well known that high levels of hopelessness reduce self-care and increase the risk of self-harm and suicide (Hawton, Comabella, Haw & Saunders, 2013). Under these conditions, the need for timely and effective psychological therapy is pressing, and this is what we will turn to in Chapter 6.

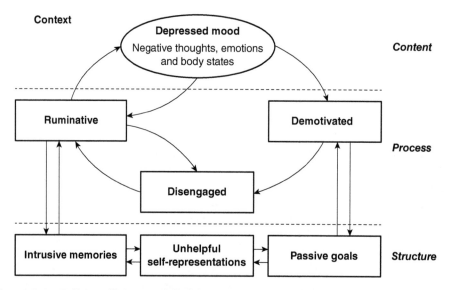

Figure 5.6   Self-regulation model of depression

Treatment Components and Processes

The aim of this chapter is to introduce CBT for major depression based on the self-regulation model. The emphasis is on *treatment components and processes*, some of which are core for all clients and others are optional based on need. Because of the heterogeneity of depression it is not possible to illustrate all components in this chapter. We introduce core aspects of the assessment and acute phases, with optional components and continuation sessions covered in subsequent chapters.

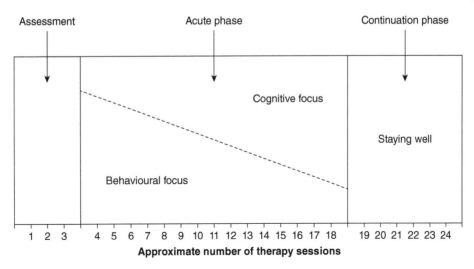

Figure 6.1   Usual treatment phases using the integrated approach

Treatment Phases

Like most courses of CBT there are three main phases: a period of assessment and treatment planning, an acute phase when the active components are delivered, and a continuation phase to limit the risk of relapse. Figure 6.1 represents this diagrammatically with an approximate guide to the number of therapy sessions received by most clients. In clinical practice the assessment phase is usually 2–3 sessions; the acute phase is typically 12–18 sessions (but it can be as few as 10 or as many as 50 when treating severe chronic cases), and the relapse prevention phase is usually 2–6 sessions, again depending on need. Most clients receive between 18–24 sessions in total; some less, some more (Barton et al., 2008).

Like other CBT treatments, the frequency of sessions is greater at the start, ideally twice-weekly in the first month, reducing to weekly, then fortnightly. The acute phase is usually delivered over 3–4 months. Sessions in the relapse prevention phase are usually monthly, so the total elapsed time from the start of assessment to follow-up is between 8 and 12 months for most cases. It is best for clients to be registered with a service long enough for relapse, if it occurs, to be accommodated within one course of treatment. This is preferable to clients needing to be re-referred and incur the risk of a delay. Part III of the book will explore how these, and other treatment parameters, need to be adjusted depending on the depression sub-type, e.g. early-onset, highly recurrent, chronic and persistent.

The other feature to note is the balance of focus between behaviour and cognition within the acute phase. For reasons that will become clear, a behavioural focus tends to be greater in the initial sessions and, as the client's mood improves, a cognitive focus is greater in later sessions. This is the typical pattern but exceptions are not uncommon,

Table 6.1 Treatment components across therapy phases

Phase	Components	Core/Optional
Assessment	Risk assessment	Core
	Clinical assessment	Core
	Alliance building	Core
	Treatment rationale	Core
Acute	Risk assessment	Core
	Approach motivation	Core
	Behavioural engagement	Core
	Reflective processing	Core
	Memory integration	Optional
	Self-organization	Optional
	Goal-organization	Optional
Continuation	Risk assessment	Core
	Staying well	Core

as we will explore throughout the remaining chapters. The core and optional treatment components are listed in Table 6.1.

These components map closely onto the self-regulation model introduced in Chapter 5 (see Figure 5.1). The aim of treatment is to target motivation, action, reflection, memories, self-representations and goals, to re-configure them in a way that restores euthymic mood. The main point to emphasize is this: these components form an *integrated* therapy, not a *modular* treatment. They are not independent modules delivered in sequence. They are interacting components that target different aspects of the maintenance of depression. The selection of components is guided by the emerging case formulation and they combine, in an integrated way, based on that formulation.

Acute phase *core* components map onto the *process level* of the self-regulation model: this is received by all clients and is the main focus of this chapter. For some clients, working at this level automatically reconfigures underlying memories, self-representations and goals. They change *indirectly* through their interaction with the process level, and do not need direct targeting. As we will see from Chapter 7 onwards, in more difficult-to-treat and complex cases, memories, self-representations and goals often complicate the path to improvement. As cases become more recurrent, chronic or complex, the optional components are more likely to be needed, but when and how they are delivered can vary considerably across cases.

We will illustrate this by describing the first part of Chloe's treatment in this chapter. She received a total of twenty therapy sessions, in two phases. The first phase, of fourteen sessions, focused primarily on the core components of *approach motivation, behavioural engagement* and *reflective processing*. Over a 4-month period this resulted in a significant improvement in Chloe's mood, helping her return to work full-time and feel more secure about her parenting skills. In the 6 months following these sessions, for the most part Chloe maintained this improvement, but from time to time she experienced depressed moods that were difficult to overcome. Additionally, she began to experience more intrusive memories of the birth trauma. In Chapter 12 we will describe the additional six sessions Chloe received to complete her treatment. In that phase, the focus was on the structural level of *memory integration, self-organization* and *goal-organization*. Chloe needed a sustained period of improved mood to be able to process the traumatic memories that had precipitated her depression. As we will describe in Chapter 12, the additional sessions had a different focus, and also formed part of her relapse prevention.

Assessment and Treatment Planning

Three of the four components in the assessment phase are no different to any other course of CBT: *risk assessment, clinical assessment* and *alliance building*. We will summarize them briefly here, and devote more space to introducing the *treatment rationale* based on the self-regulation model.

Risk assessment

All contacts with depressed clients need to have some level of risk assessment. This is the reason it is a core component within assessment, treatment and continuation phases. As is well known, major depression confers an increased risk of self-neglect, self-harm and suicide. Approximately 50% of clients with major depressive disorders are affected by suicidal thoughts, plans or intentions, though it is a smaller proportion that go on to attempt or complete suicide (Hawton et al., 2013). Consequently, most standardized depression measures include a risk-related item. When clients complete these items, it is important to pay attention to their responses. A client may choose to disclose suicidal thoughts or plans in a standardized measure, and it can increase risk if the assessor or therapist fails to notice or pay sufficient attention. It is always best to discuss concerns about risk. There is no evidence that discussing risk makes it more likely to happen; on the contrary, the opportunity for the client to openly discuss suicidal thoughts or impulses can contribute to the *reduction* of risk.

The presence of *thoughts* about death and suicide is not the same as suicidal *intentions*, *plans* or *actions*. It is quite common for depressed clients to have fleeting or intrusive thoughts that others would be better off if they were dead, or it would be best if they didn't survive an accident, or fail to wake up. These thoughts can be very troubling for clients and therapists, but *on their own* they do not indicate high risk. In this situation it is best to monitor the thoughts regularly: whether they change and how they affect the client's mood and behaviour. Support the client to deal with the thoughts as thoughts, without assuming they are desires or intentions.

It is more concerning if clients are behaving impulsively, engaging in risky behaviours, abusing substances, have decided a suicide method, set a date, made a plan or formed a clear intention to die. In those situations risk assessment and reduction need to be a high priority, irrespective of the stage in treatment. In Chapter 8 we will explore how the integrated model can *complement* standardized risk protocols. Therapists should always follow the policies and procedures governing risk assessment in their host organization. There is not sufficient space in this book to cover all relevant aspects of this topic in detail; instead we will illustrate how the self-regulation model can enhance standard risk assessments, in Chapter 8.

Clinical assessment

In Chapters 2 and 3 we outlined the main features of assessment for CBT; the integrated model shares most of the same tasks. The therapist needs to find out about the current depressive episode: precipitators, contextual factors, moderators, course, severity and functional impairment. As will become apparent in Part III, it is also important to find out about clients' prior history of depression: therapy has a different emphasis if it is a first-onset compared with a recurrent or chronic disorder. It is also helpful to ask about past treatments to consider how best to deliver this course of therapy, and whether other interventions need to be combined with CBT (e.g. anti-depressant medication, social support, family interventions, etc.).

A brief diagnostic interview can be conducted to confirm the client has a major depressive disorder (Spitzer, Williams, Gibbon & First, 1992) and it is helpful to assess severity and functional impairment with a standardized measure such as the Beck Depression Inventory (BDI-II; Beck et al., 1996), Hamilton Rating Scale for Depression (HAM-D; Porter et al., 2017) or Patient Health Questionnaire (PHQ-9; Kroenke & Spitzer, 2002). This can inform treatment planning; it also provides a baseline to assess subsequent change. As will become apparent in Part IV, there is a range of biological, psychological and social factors that can interact with depression and create complications within the treatment, most notably comorbid disorders. These also need to be assessed, though some complexity factors may only become apparent later in the treatment process. Most of the initial assessment is the therapist finding out information from the client and, if approached insensitively, this can create quite an interrogative style. It is therefore helpful to ask questions in a way that encourages clients' *reflection* on the information being shared, so that the client and the therapist structure the information together, and begin a process of *clinical formulation*: making sense of the precipitation and maintenance of the client's problems.

Alliance building

The assessment phase is a two-way process with the client and the therapist assessing each other. The therapist assesses the client's problems, needs and suitability for CBT. The client assesses the therapist's genuineness, trustworthiness and the credibility of the proposed treatment. The desired outcome is an emerging 'us-ness' based on mutual trust and collaboration. Collaboration is the hallmark of the therapeutic alliance in CBT: it is essential from the first session to foster a culture of co-working and task sharing (Lorenzo-Luaces et al., 2016). As we introduced earlier in Figure 1.2, there is both a *personal* and *task-related* aspect, to enable the appropriate balance of support and change. The distinction between personal bond and task engagement is not trivial and finding the optimal balance can take a lot of therapeutic skill. It also varies across clients. As we will find out in later chapters, sometimes clients have a preference for a strong personal bond and the focus on task needs to increase; conversely, some clients are comfortable with information, advice and techniques and a greater focus on personal bond is required.

Because depressed people tend to represent others as *separate, critical* or *un-interested* (see Figure 2.3), the process of forming a therapeutic alliance needs to disconfirm client expectations, or concerns, that this how the therapist will behave. With this is mind, the therapist needs to create an atmosphere of connection, compassion and curiosity:

- *Connection.* Engage and involve the client as an equal partner in the therapy process. Signal your willingness to participate and work together.
- *Compassion.* Offer empathy with the client's suffering. Communicate your desire to work together to overcome it, not to pass judgement or make criticisms.
- *Curiosity.* Ask helpful questions to reflect on what is maintaining the client's difficulties. Express the importance of understanding what is keeping the client's problems going, to find out how to overcome them.

Since depression is associated with pessimism and hopelessness, it is also important to communicate realistic hope about therapy being helpful. The key word here is *realistic*: what is over-ambitious for some clients is under-ambitious for others and, as we noted in Chapters 2 and 3, hoped-for progress depends on the client *engaging* in treatment, not passively waiting for the therapist to initiate improvements. It is therefore helpful to enquire about the client's previous experiences of therapy, and broader healthcare, because these can shape tacit expectations and implicit goals. This may seem to be an obvious point but, in line with the self-regulation model, depression tends to provoke avoidance, withdrawal, and submissiveness. These can undermine clients' engagement in the therapeutic process, and therapists, whether they are aware of it or not, can be pulled into *over-compensation*. This can result in therapists taking too much responsibility for change, providing excessive reassurance, or offering false hope that sets up unrealistic expectations of change. Alternatively, instead of over-compensating, sometimes therapists *mirror* clients' pessimism and passivity, and the treatment becomes under-ambitious, support-oriented and insufficiently focused on change. The therapeutic process is needed to *find out* how much improvement is possible, and that can never be known at the outset.

To enable a course of therapy to progress, client and therapist need to have *sufficient agreement* about the client's problems and treatment goals. Notice that by this point in the process the dialogue is not just *eliciting information* about difficulties, it is co-creating a shared understanding, or *formulation*, of how those problems developed, what is maintaining them, and what can be done by way of improvement. If there is a significant difference of opinion about the client's problems, or the destination of treatment, this is likely to have a wrenching effect on the process. In Figure 6.2 we have represented *problem agreement* and *goal agreement* as two of the *outputs* of the assessment process needed to initiate a course of treatment. The third element is a sufficiently strong *personal bond*, manifesting as mutual trust within the client and therapist's personal relationship.

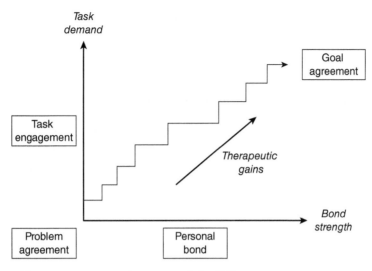

Figure 6.2   Key parameters and outputs of the CBT assessment process

The fourth element is sufficient *task engagement* in overcoming problems and moving towards goals. This is where the treatment rationale is pivotal, because it informs the emerging formulation, and it shapes expectations about which tasks will be needed to effect change. There has to be sufficient agreement what those tasks will be, and they need to be manageable for the client at each stage in the process. The personal bond has to be strong enough to match the demands of the current task; process problems are likely to result if it is not. Conversely, successfully completed tasks can help to strengthen the personal bond and an upward spiral can be initiated. When these four conditions are met (*problem agreement, goal agreement, personal bond, task engagement*), the likelihood of therapeutic gains and a response to treatment is much greater.

Treatment rationale

The self-regulation model is used to socialize clients to CBT, formulate the precipitation and maintenance of the depressive episode, and provide a rationale for change. There are three key elements within the rationale: mood fluctuations, downward spirals and upward spirals. Figure 6.3 is a helpful way to illustrate fluctuations in mood. Most clients recognize the difference between normal moods, a process of worsening (*the downward spiral*) and feeling stuck and unable to change. However, clients vary in the *pattern* of these fluctuations. For example, some people become stuck in mild or moderate depression.

Others have more rapidly oscillating unstable mood. It is helpful to individualize the diagram to develop a shared understanding of clients' mood variations.

We also use Figure 6.3 to achieve two further tasks: firstly, to explore whether depression was *intended*. We ask whether the client expected or intended to become depressed. Clients with recurrent or chronic problems sometimes expect to become depressed, but it is rare for a client to intend or plan to become depressed, even if they believe it is somehow their fault. This creates a less self-blaming explanation that depression is an *unintended accident*; circumstances produced a downward spiral of mood that was unintended and difficult to reverse (Teasdale, 1997). From the first session we are seeking to increase the client's reflective capacity to view depression as an unwanted state they have accidentally fallen into, and are having difficulty overcoming, rather than it being self-induced – 'it's all my fault'; or inevitable – 'this is just how I am'.

Secondly, we introduce CBT as a treatment intended to produce an upward spiral that leads to improvement and, hopefully, a sustained recovery. It is important that the upward spiral is clearly labelled in Figure 6.3 and CBT is identified as a way out of depression, not just a way of understanding how it happened. If the client accepts that their mood fluctuates, and depression is unintended, the next step is finding out about the processes that cause mood to deteriorate and improve: the downward and upward spirals. Figure 6.4 is used to introduce the CBT understanding of these processes. This is based on simplified versions of the self-regulation models, introduced in Chapter 5.

At the outset of treatment, when the client's personal experience is mapped onto it, Figure 6.4 usually has the right amount of information. Figures 5.2 and 5.3 can be incorporated later in treatment, if needed, to provide more detail, but it is not usual to share them at the outset, because they contain more information than is

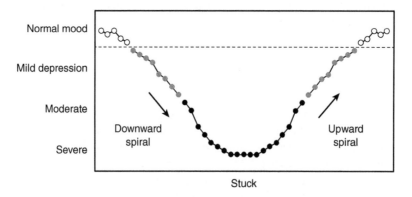

Figure 6.3   Mood fluctuations from normal mood to severe depression

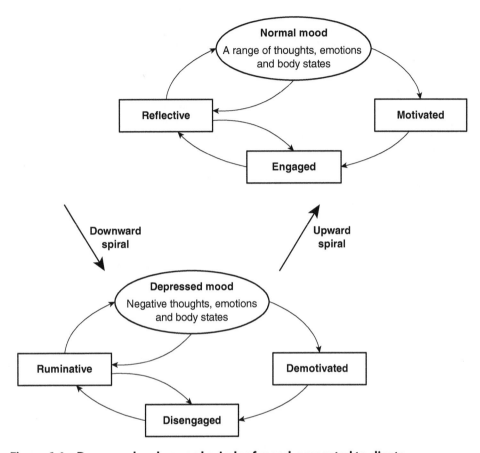

Figure 6.4   Downward and upward spirals of mood, presented to clients

helpful at that stage. Instead it is helpful to ask the client to reflect on a specific occasion when their mood was depressed: through guided discovery, find out if negative thoughts, emotions, body states, demotivation, disengagement and ruminative processing accurately describe the client's experience. Then ask about a contrasting occasion when the client's mood was euthymic, or at least less depressed: again, use guided discovery to explore thoughts, emotions, body states, motivation, engagement and reflective processes. It is important to connect the upward spiral explicitly to the downward, in other words, make it clear that the aim of CBT is to help clients enhance their motivation, engage in actions differently, and reflect on their experiences in a new way. The emphasis is on learning a *process of self-regulation*, rather than directly challenging thoughts or beliefs.

Treatment Rationale: Key Points

- Moods are constituted by thoughts, emotions and body states – during depression they become negative and unpleasant.
- An unintended downward spiral occurs when depressed mood suppresses a person's normal motivation. They feel less interested and enthusiastic, and instead feel like avoiding, escaping or hiding from others.
- When feeling demotivated, people tend to disengage, withdraw and become less active.
- In a disengaged or disconnected state, their mind tends to become preoccupied with analysing what is wrong: this can lead to unhelpful rumination, including an internal self-critical dialogue.
- Repeated cycles of being *demotivated*, *disengaged* and *ruminative* keep depressed moods going, and maintain a downward spiral of depression.
- The way to improve mood is to restore normal motivation, increase engagement, and become more reflective.

Case Illustration | Chloe: assessment and treatment planning

Chloe had been depressed for 3 years prior to her CBT assessment. This was the first time she had suffered a major depressive episode. She had been disappointed by two previous mental health assessments since being diagnosed with post-natal depression (PND): one had resulted in a plan to 'wait and see' on the basis she might recover spontaneously. The other had been a brief structured intervention that did not enquire about the onset of her difficulties. Chloe had researched CBT and was motivated to engage in it, feeling somewhat desperate after 3 years of depression.

A strong personal bond was formed, with the therapist enquiring about the nature and history of Chloe's difficulties and seeking to individualize the treatment to her needs. The assessment screened for Post-Traumatic Stress Disorder (PTSD) and although Chloe described her son's birth as traumatic, and regularly thought about what had happened, these were normal autobiographical memories, not flashbacks, intrusions or nightmares. Chloe was not hyper-aroused or avoiding situations out of fear these events would recur. Chloe and her therapist agreed she had experienced a trauma and it had precipitated a major depressive episode, with the following specific problems: self-criticism, procrastination, upsetting memories, an over-busy mind and difficulties engaging in tasks. The agreed treatment goals were: (a) improve mood, (b) successfully return to work – Chloe was in a phased return after sick leave,

(c) come to terms with the pregnancy and birth experience, (d) improve her relationship with her son, (e) make a full recovery. Chloe acknowledged occasional suicidal thoughts on her PHQ-9 questionnaire but she qualified them as passive and not particularly distressing. She had no ideas about methods, plans or intent and no expressed wish to die; on the contrary she wanted to recover from depression to get back to normal family and working life. This was unchanged throughout her therapy. Her PHQ-9 total score was 19, indicating moderately severe depression.

Chloe recognized the downward spiral as an unintended and unexpected period of depression. She had been anxious throughout her pregnancy and attributed some of her difficulties to that. She recognized other features: changes in motivation (much less interest), behavioural disengagement (much less active) and rumination (very busy mind with lots of memories and several trains of thought). She felt encouraged by the treatment rationale and fed back after the first session: *'I found the session very useful and have begun to feel for the first time in years that I might actually recover.'*

Acute Phase: Core Components

The primary aim of the core treatment components is to overcome the downward spiral, by targeting various aspects of the maintenance cycle shown in Figure 5.3. These components – *approach motivation*, *behavioural engagement* and *reflective processing* – can be *distinguished* but not *separated*, by which we mean they are highly interactive: changing one invariably has a knock-on effect on the others. Nevertheless, they have a different focus and emphasis.

Approach motivation

There are three elements that are targeted for change:

1 Paying attention to needs and desires

We encourage clients to pay attention to their emotions and body states. These are often negative and unpleasant, so it is understandable when people place attention elsewhere and try to distract from their feelings, for example, through rumination. However, this can have the unintended consequence of *disattending to the somatic cues that signal needs.* Recall that one of the fundamentals of self-regulation is learning to notice and satisfy needs and desires. Most needs are expressed in some kind of affective or somatic experience, and we use a modified version of Maslow's Hierarchy of Needs, presented in Figure 6.5, to help clients reflect on these (Maslow, 1943, 1954). The link between *affective signals* and *needs* can be illustrated with the simple example of hunger. Hunger manifests, not as an abstract concept, but through bodily sensations. Somatic cues generate the impulse to source food, linked to the basic need to eat to store energy. These need to be noticed and enacted, serving the higher goal to survive.

In normal mood, this chain of events is largely automatic, but notice there are several steps in the process: (a) goal to survive; (b) need for energy and food; (c) somatic signals of hunger; (d) attention paid to somatic cues and motivational impulses; (e) impulses are acted on; (f) the need is satisfied. This is a good example of approach motivation: impulses towards desired states. Now imagine how this process can be adversely affected by depression. Firstly, the goal to survive may be weaker and more passive than usual. Secondly, there could be less attention paid to somatic cues, since feelings and body states are generally unpleasant and may be avoided. Thirdly, approach impulses may be weaker than usual, because the individual's appetite is suppressed. Fourthly, even if some appetite is present, rumination can interfere with translating these impulses into action. Consequently, the task of engaging in healthy eating may not be as simple as scheduling regular meals – though that could be a helpful place to start. Increasing behavioural engagement, as we will see in the next section, can depend on strengthening goals, increasing attention to somatic cues, and linking needs to actions.

In depression, attending to needs and desires needs to be re-established through changes in cognitive processing and voluntary actions. Because approach motivation is suppressed, we cannot assume that these changes will occur automatically. As we explored in Chapter 3, Behavioural Activation (BA) targets the behaviour, in this case eating. This is a very important step in the cycle, but it is not the only step. The self-regulation approach additionally targets underlying goals (which we will explore in later chapters), increases attention to emotions and body states, and provides a map to link feelings to needs – the Modified Hierarchy of Needs. The same principles apply to all feelings and needs, so that clients become more aware of how to translate feelings into helpful motives and actions, e.g. thirst-water, exposure-shelter, tired-rest, and so on. The main modification to the hierarchy is to have *attainment* (achievements, ambitions, projects, goals, etc.) presented as a more basic need than *relationships* (connection, belonging, trusting, etc.). This was on the basis of repeated feedback from a large number of clients that relationships were generally more important and fulfilling than projects and achievements. It also reflects a shifting emphasis from need to desire across the hierarchy: food, water and shelter are essentials, whereas meaningful projects and relationships tend to be deeper desires that contribute to fulfilment.

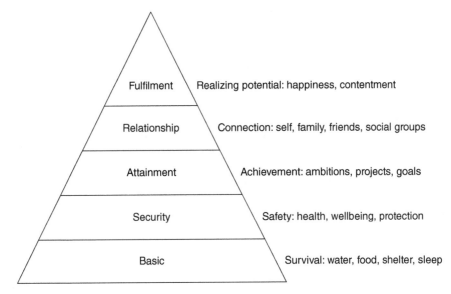

Figure 6.5   Modified Hierarchy of Needs

Note also that a good-enough relationship with oneself is included as a relational need. We will return to this in later chapters when we consider the role of self-compassion and acts of kindness to oneself.

These principles also apply to the other levels in the hierarchy, for example, when people feel frightened they need security and the courage to deal with threats, assuming the threats are real. When people feel bored they need stimulation; when they feel lonely, they need companionship; when they feel shame, they need respect, and so on. We will see in the following sections that depressed people tend to question high-level needs in an abstract way, such as why they are unhappy or keep having failed relationships. This is usually mismatched to what would be most helpful, at least at the start of treatment, which is greater emphasis on behaviours that support basic needs. Fulfilment and happiness are unlikely to be attained without regular meals and sleep, shelter, security, some kind of project or goal and, most importantly, a sense of belonging and connection with other people.

2 Engaging with approach impulses

An extension of paying attention to needs and desires is learning to differentiate approach and avoidance impulses. In most circumstances, approach impulses enable effective self-regulation and have a greater likelihood of satisfying needs and desires. The person's orientation is to *bring about what they would like to happen*, rather than avoid or prevent what they do not want. Consequently, working at the process level means encouraging an interactive sequence, as follows:

a. Helping people pay attention to their approach impulses, what they are attracted to and *feel like* doing.
b. Encouraging them to translate approach impulses into actions.
c. Reflecting on the consequences of those actions, in terms of needs and desires.

There are a variety of potential blocks on this process, and one of the most common is when people's behaviour is heavily rule-governed. Their actions are dominated by beliefs about what they should, ought to or must do, and there is a suspicion of attending to needs and desires, as if that would be selfish, wrong or dangerous. This can be magnified when guilt and shame are present. However, obligation is not motivation. In these situations, it is helpful to experiment with the balance of duties and desires; not that real responsibilities are denied or overlooked, but on their own they are unlikely to meet all of a person's needs.

3 Resisting avoidant impulses

There can also be a felt-sense of security associated with trying to avoid bad experiences, such as failure, rejection or disappointment. In the depressed state, it is understandable that people do not want to feel worse, so there can be an aversion to taking risks that could backfire and further reduce confidence, esteem and efficacy. Not all avoidance is dysfunctional. When there is imminent real danger, avoidance is an appropriate strategy. However, in depression the strategy is applied to *hypothetical threats*, in other words, *worries* that certain actions will backfire and lead to bad outcomes. Consequently, many depressed people *feel like* avoiding, escaping and hiding, as if it is a safe and secure option. As we observed in Chapter 3, these strategies can have short-term benefits by temporarily reducing the negative emotions that have motivated them, such as anxiety, guilt and shame.

In BA, this is understood as negative reinforcement; in the self-regulation approach, we understand avoidant impulses as *urges to satisfy needs*, such as relief or protection. If someone is acutely distressed and in mental turmoil, they will probably have a need for peace and relief, and they might try to satisfy that need by taking drugs or alcohol. If someone feels exposed and vulnerable to others, then they probably have a need for security and support, and they might try to satisfy that need by isolating from others and attempting to be more self-sufficient. As we will see in later sections, in this situation we invite clients to reflect on: (a) What were the *intentions* behind avoidant impulses; what needs were they attempting to satisfy? (b) How well did they satisfy those needs? In most avoidant situations, there is a short-term payoff, but depression creates blinkers, and clients do not always notice the unintended consequences of avoidance. They need more feedback loops to self-regulate appropriately. In the above examples, alcohol could bring temporary relief, but mood becomes more depressed soon after; social isolation could reduce the risk of criticism, but increase loneliness, and so on. The goal is for clients to recognize avoidant impulses and learn that, in the medium to long term, it is better to resist them than act on them. It is best to switch mode from avoidance to approach: for example, 'I feel distressed and need some peace; what is the best way to bring that about? I feel exposed and vulnerable and need some support; what is the best way to bring that about?'

Case Illustration | Chloe: approach motivation

Chloe's threat system gradually dampened by progressively resisting impulses to avoid, escape and withdraw from others. Initially this resulted in increased negative affect, for example, anxiety returning to work and re-engaging with social activities. The reduction in avoidant urges was complemented by a gradual increase in approach motivation, for example, feeling attracted to work tasks and gradually feeling more able to notice them and act on them. Chloe's behavioural engagement was based on learning to pay attention to her needs and desires, then acting on them, rather than following a pre-set activity schedule.

Behavioural engagement

As we mentioned earlier, the core treatment components can be distinguished from each other, but not separated. Learning to differentiate approach and avoidance relies on *acting* on those motives, and then *reflecting* on the consequences. However, when depression is very severe, which it sometimes is at the start of treatment, approach motivation can be so greatly suppressed that it is difficult for clients to notice approach impulses and pay attention to them. Impulses towards desired states are likely to be fleeting and mild, so the opportunity to focus the intervention directly on motivation, at that stage, may be quite limited.

The evidence from Behavioural Activation (BA), and activity scheduling in Beck's CBT, is that a behavioural focus is best-matched to client-need when symptoms are severe and functioning is at its most impaired. Clients' reflective capacity can be so impaired at this point that it is difficult for them to decentre and think clearly about mental events. So although negative thinking and rumination are likely to be present, efforts to reflect on the impact of those thoughts, and how the mind processes them, are likely to perpetuate rumination rather than reduce it. Cognitive processes *are* contributing to the maintenance of severe depression, but attempts to change them *directly* are likely to backfire and have the opposite effect in the early stage of treatment.

When depression is severe, focusing on behaviour has two distinct advantages. Firstly, overt behaviour has a concrete and external manifestation. The severely depressed mind is likely to be stuck in self-focus, highly ruminative, and preoccupied with abstract/conceptual questions: a behavioural focus can initiate a helpful switch in cognitive processing towards more external, experiential and concrete events. However, notice the paradox: by focusing on behaviour, not cognition, a helpful *cognitive* change is initiated by switching into a different processing mode. Secondly, there is no such thing as 'no behaviour'. Sometimes clients create the impression that they are 'doing nothing', implying that not much will be learned by investigating it. On the contrary, clients are sometimes more active than they report, or realize, and much can be learned from periods of relative inactivity, even if it is embarrassing or shaming for clients to report how little they are doing, relative to their normal activities.

Consequently, when depression is severe, the self-regulation approach uses a similar method used in both BA and standard CBT: a Weekly Activity Schedule (WAS) is a helpful way to find out what the client is doing and how those actions link to their mood, and provide a baseline for subsequent change. We use a modified activity record, to keep the task as simple as possible. In our experience, recording activities hourly can be quite demanding for severely depressed clients, as can making ratings of how rewarding or purposeful each activity has been. For that reason, we initially ask clients to record their activities three times each day (morning, afternoon and evening) and make a single mood rating within each of those periods. In our experience, this is usually sufficient to capture *variability* and *fluctuations* in activity and mood.

These fluctuations provide an opportunity to socialize the client further to the downward and upwards spirals (Figure 6.4). This is important because most clients, at least from time to time, make courageous efforts to help themselves feel better and overcome their depression. Some of those efforts can be productive, but difficult to sustain. Other actions may be well-intentioned, but have unhelpful consequences. Either way, we want to normalize the fact that most depressed clients have alternating phases of giving up and *submitting* to their depression (e.g. feeling *trapped, helpless* and/or *hopeless*), then engaging in a variety of coping strategies, either to endure depression or make attempts to overcome it. With this in mind, we encourage clients to reflect on the contrasts between their worst and least bad moods in the previous few days: are there differences in their *actions* during those moods? Did those actions keep them in a downward spiral, or move them towards an upward spiral?

This begins a process of *discriminant learning* between engagement and disengagement, and this usually corresponds closely to the difference between approach and avoidance. We are aiming for the client to learn that being inactive, avoidant, withdrawn, submissive or suicidal is an *understandable* response to feeling depressed, but acting on those impulses will maintain depression, even if they occasionally provide temporary relief. Hence, the rationale is developed to engage rather than disengage, even in the absence of approach impulses. The client has to be prepared to *act against their inclination* if they don't feel like engaging in a behaviour, hence the importance of calibrating the change process to a baseline of current activity.

The self-regulation approach differs from BA and Beck's activity scheduling, in that the aim is not necessarily to become more active, though that is often *part* of what is needed. The aim is to *overcome disengagement* as it is currently manifesting in the client's daily life. Hence, people who are under-active need to gradually increase activity; those who are avoidant need to reduce safety-seeking and test out their fears; people who are withdrawn need to increase social connectedness; people who are submissive need to share power more equally with others, and people who are suicidal need to reflect on what is attracting them to death, and whether there is another way to bring about the benefits that they believe death would afford them (we explore risk assessment and reduction more in Chapter 8). The aim is to engage progressively in approach behaviours that will overcome the particular type of disengagement that is affecting each client, creating a virtuous cycle and an upward spiral of mood.

Approach behaviour is also more likely to satisfy clients' needs and desires than avoidance. For example, people who are:

a. under-active: need to develop routines, interests and enthusiasm
b. avoidant: need a normal level of security and to learn how to tolerate uncertainty
c. withdrawn: need connection, relationship and belonging
d. submissive: need respect, fairness and equality
e. suicidal: need reasons to live and a good-enough relationship with themselves.

We encourage clients to engage in these actions *with the intention of satisfying their needs*. This highlights another significant difference between this approach, Beck's CBT and BA. In BA, the activation process is not a behavioural experiment: it is an agreement to enact certain behaviours in an attempt to elicit positive reinforcement. In Beck's CBT, behavioural experiments are used to test out clients' predictions, to find out if their expectations are accurate or negatively biased. Our approach also uses behavioural experiments, but with a focused aim: *to find out if the client can influence their preferred outcome*. So if an unmet need is identified, for example, a client is eating irregular meals, the therapist would seek to help them as follows:

1. Reflect on what the need is (e.g. sufficient food to provide energy).
2. Consider which actions are required to satisfy the need (e.g. regular food three times each day).
3. Explore what the client would like to happen to satisfy the need (e.g. go to the supermarket, stock up on food, eat regular meals).
4. Elicit the client's prediction whether they will be able to influence what they would like to happen (e.g. '90% sure I will eat food more regularly, even if I'm not that hungry').

Finding out whether clients can influence their preferences is intended to increase *self-efficacy*, i.e. clients' felt-sense that they have the power to influence subjectively important outcomes. This strategy is intended to disconfirm pessimism associated with low self-efficacy, helplessness or powerlessness. It also helps to re-calibrate the client's sense of personal influence. Not all outcomes are controllable; there is uncertainty about what will happen in the future, and sometimes people have less influence than they would like. But depressed clients are prone to under-estimate their power and influence and this maintains disengagement. What is essential in this process is *graded task assignment*. Whatever behaviour change is initiated, it is vital to calibrate the change process to current behaviour and initiate small and manageable changes at each step. This process is also *self-compassionate*. Engaging with un-met needs directs clients' attention to their suffering, and the desire for change is doing something about it, to reduce suffering and improve mood. Actions intended to satisfy needs are acts of kindness; they can be the beginning of an improved relationship with oneself.

Case Illustration | Chloe: behavioural engagement

Across the acute phase Chloe made gradual, phased changes to reduce behavioural avoidance and increase engagement. There was progressively less avoidance of pain and medical situations. Chloe recognized that the anxiety associated with these situations was not just the threat of actual pain, but the possibility of memories of past pain being triggered. There was also progressively less avoidance of her son when either he, or Chloe, felt upset. In parallel with reduced avoidance was increased engagement at work, with family and socially. Chloe made a phased return to work, and the fact it was gradual allowed her to take manageable steps and regain a sense of control influencing it. Her experiments confirmed she was able to engage in work tasks more consistently than she expected. Social engagement had a similar quality; gradually doing a little bit more, considering what she would like to happen, noticing mild interest in going to social events, finding out that she could influence the sort of occasion she would like it to be, etc. The treatment strengthened approach behaviour, to counteract avoidance behaviour. Most of Chloe's perceived threats were disconfirmed and she gradually learned that she could satisfy her desires for an enjoyable social life, job and family. Interpersonal engagement with her husband and son gradually allowed more physical closeness, giving and receiving support, particularly in times of upset.

Reflective processing

Discriminating motivational cues and noticing the consequences of actions relies on reflective cognitive processing. As clients' mood begins to improve we encourage them to take notice of the *cognitive processing mode* they are in before, during and after action (Watkins et al., 2007, 2011). The aim is to increase clients' capacity to reflect on a broad range of experiences. This helps to reduce rumination, including inflexible self-focus. One of the main intended outcomes is for clients to recognize when they have fallen into a downward spiral; not just to understand it in theory, but use it as a way of recognizing the process they are in, when they are in it. A key part of this is learning that rumination is unhelpful, and recognizing when it is happening. Over time, reflective processing has a *meta-cognitive effect*. In other words, clients learn to notice their thoughts as mental events, not facts. To enable this there are three main elements that are targeted for change.

1 Attentional flexibility

The aim is to overcome inflexible self-focus. Sometimes attention needs to be directed internally on thoughts, feelings, impulses or body states. On other occasions, depending on the task, an external focus is needed, for example when having a conversation with another person. The goal is *attentional flexibility* and the capacity to modulate between different foci, depending on need. Prior to action, attention usually needs to be directed internally onto motivational impulses, to notice needs and desires. During action, it usually needs to be directed externally to encourage interaction, absorption and 'flow' in the task. After action, there is an option to direct it internally onto memories of the experience, to notice consequences and reflect on what can be learned.

This can be achieved by conducting behavioural experiments, exploring how different attentional foci influence mood, motivation and action.

As clients' reflective capacity increases, they become more able to decentre from their experiences and notice what is happening, both externally and internally. Decentring is encouraged as a way of tolerating difficult experiences, without suppressing or avoiding them. The aim is to increase clients' meta-cognitive awareness of their mental and bodily events, to hold them in mind in a decentred way, to allow them to be experienced and reflected on. Note well: decentring is not avoidance. It is facing and experiencing something from a helpful distance, rather than suppressing, blocking or dissociating from it.

2 Concrete experiences

The main purpose of attending to concrete expereinces is to counteract depressed clients' tendency to process information in an abstract, conceptual or generalized way. Clients are encouraged to notice, engage with and remember concrete, detailed, sensory information (Watkins & Moberly, 2009). This can be facilitated through the type of Socratic questions that are asked during therapy sessions. It is best to ask about *specific examples* of problems, rather general issues. For example, always ground reflections in time and space with questions such as 'where were you?', 'was it morning, afternoon or evening?', 'was anyone else there?', 'can you describe the scene as you looked round', 'do you recall any particular sounds, smells, tastes?'. The same orientation is to be encouraged during behavioural engagement: encourage clients to become absorbed in their activities, paying attention flexibly, but focusing their mind on concrete experiences rather than theoretical questions. This can also be done in behavioural experiments, to find out the differences in mood and memory when the mind is focused on concrete experiences, rather than abstract questions. It is usually best to 'experience the experience', even if it provokes suffering and needs an accepting and self-compassionate response.

3 Answerable questions

To counteract depressive rumination, one of the most helpful cognitive strategies is for clients to ask themselves answerable questions. This contrasts sharply with ruminative questions, many of which are abstract, unanswerable and lack utility even if they are answered. We have already seen that depressive rumination is an attempt to self-regulate in difficult circumstances. Clients are trying to conceptualize the depressed self from within, and unhelpful repetitive thinking is an unintended consequence. One of the most effective strategies to counteract this is for clients to take notice of the questions in their mind: encourage them to decentre from them and reflect on their impact. In-session behavioural experiments are a good way to find out what impact particular questions have: the client holds a question in mind and the experiment is to find out how it is processed over the course of a minute. Is it answered? Is the answer helpful? Does it lead to new questions? Does it provoke learning or decision making? Does it impact on mood? Modifying questions and continuing to experiment with them is a productive way to extend the client's questioning capacity, and learn the difference between ruminative and reflective questioning. Figure 6.6 can be a useful way of illustrating the difference between helpful and unhelpful repetitive thinking. Some reflective processes involve repetition, for example, memory integration and elaboration after traumatic experiences, which we will explore further in Chapter 12. Helpful repetition *transforms meanings* and moves the mind to a different place, whether through a receptive or active process. In contrast, unhelpful repetition turns the mind in on itself and maintains self-devaluation.

When clients gain attentional flexibility, centre their mind on concrete experiences rather than abstract concepts, and have a capacity to ask helpful questions – this creates *mental freedom* about how mental events are processed. The aim is to for clients to develop a harmonious relationship with their mind. Rather than an oppressive, wrenching or conflictual relationship, we encourage clients to accept involuntary events within their mind and body, such as intrusive thoughts, memories and sensations. These are not controllable, so it is best not to try to control them. Instead, it is best to pay attention to them, decentre from them, and *influence how the mind processes them*. It helps clients to realize that they have a choice how to influence the voluntary

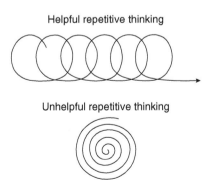

Helpful repetitive thinking

Unhelpful repetitive thinking

Figure 6.6   Helpful and unhelpful repetitive thinking

aspects of the mind. For example, it may be that no process is chosen: the experience or event is simply noticed, and that is all. It could be that a *receptive process* is chosen, for example, allowing the mind to dwell on what is present, allowing associations to form, noticing what the mind does with its contents without an explicit goal ('suspension of ends'). It could be that an *active process* is chosen, for example, forming a goal, strategy, tactic or question to process and transform the event ('strategic thinking'). This type of process is goal-directed: it is aiming to move the mind towards a desired outcome, solution or answer.

Case Illustration | Chloe: reflective processing

Across the acute phase of treatment Chloe's worry and rumination gradually decreased, partly in response to greater behavioural engagement at work, home and socially. One of the key tasks was helping Chloe to have clear goals in the reflections she was undertaking. Questions such as 'why can't I be strong like other women?' led to unhelpful comparisons and counterfactual reasoning; instead Chloe learned to ask 'what made me feel so weak?' This enabled more productive reflection on concrete experiences. It also allowed her to access the emotions accompanying those memories. The question 'is my son really mine?' would result in unhelpful repetitive doubting; instead Chloe learned to ask 'what happened when I was under the anaesthetic?' Again, this enabled more productive reflections on concrete experiences, and it accessed new information and learning. We will return to Chloe's case in Chapter 12 when we consider the links between trauma and depression in more detail. After the initial batch of fourteen sessions her PHQ-9 score had reduced to 10.

Practitioner Tips: Core Treatment Components

- All contacts with depressed clients should have some level of risk assessment, even if it is as simple as asking whether they feel at risk and need help to stay safe. The extent to which risk needs to be focal depends on the client's risk history, recent behaviour and self-reported suicidal thoughts, impulses or intentions.
- During the assessment process, quite a lot of information needs to be gathered and organized to form a treatment plan. As far as possible, make the exchange of information a two-way, collaborative process that encourages shared reflection, and acknowledges that the client will be assessing you, not just you assessing them.
- Communicate realistic hope about the potential benefits of CBT, by working together and sharing responsibility for change. The client will need to opt in and

engage in therapy to find out how much benefit they will receive. This may be difficult initially, since depression is characterized by *disengagement*: hence, early treatment tasks need to be manageable to make it possible for the client to participate.

- Encourage your client to reflect on fluctuations in their mood to help them notice it is not always the same. Draw attention to the relationships between thoughts, emotions and body states to demonstrate that these influence each other and vary over time. Rather than challenge the accuracy of thoughts, help the client notice that when their thinking is more negative, it will tend to depress their mood and lead to negative emotions and unpleasant body states.
- Reflect on specific, concrete examples of occasions the client has felt depressed. Rather than challenging the accuracy of their thoughts, explore whether their mood influenced their motivation (usually to suppress it); then explore whether feeling demotivated affected their behaviour (usually some form of disengagement); then explore whether being disengaged affected their thought processes (usually some form of rumination or suppression). You are trying to help the client reflect on a *maintenance cycle* that keeps them feeling depressed, rather than challenge the accuracy of their thoughts.
- It can also be helpful to reflect on occasions when the client has been feeling less depressed or euthymic. You are trying to help them notice that when they are motivated, engaged and reflective; this will tend to maintain normal (euthymic) mood. In contrast, when they are demotivated, disengaged and ruminative, this will tend to maintain depressed mood. This builds the treatment rationale to learn how to respond differently when feeling demotivated, disengaged or ruminative.
- When clients are severely depressed, in the first instance, it is usually best to work with activity schedules that encourage behavioural engagement, targeted to the particular ways the client has become disengaged. For example, avoidant clients need graded exposure to the tasks they have been avoiding; socially withdrawn clients need gradual re-engagement with other people; submissive clients need a progressive approach towards assertion and power-sharing, and so on.
- As mood begins to improve, encourage your clients to pay more attention to approach impulses, needs and desires. There needs to be a gradual shift from doing what has been scheduled, irrespective of mood, to noticing approach impulses and acting on them. Emphasize the client's needs and desires as the main priority and 'compass' to guide their actions.
- As clients' reflective capacity increases, help them to notice the difference between times when they ruminate in an unhelpful and repetitive way, compared with times when they are able to think clearly, make decisions, reach conclusions, answer questions, and so on. Encourage reflection on where your client places their attention during these times; whether their mind is centred on abstract concepts or concrete experiences; whether they are asking themselves answerable questions. The aim is to encourage mental freedom: choosing how to 'run their head' with flexible attention, an emphasis on concrete experiences and answerable questions.

Summary of Key Points from Part II

- Chapters 5 and 6 have introduced an integrated approach to CBT that has been developed particularly for difficult-to-treat clients who have not responded to established CBT protocols, or not had a sustained response.
- Compared with established CBT, the integrated approach generates more individualized treatment plans based on treatment components relevant to each individual. Some components are core for all clients, others are optional depending on need.
- The integrated approach is based on a *self-regulation model of depression* that understands depression as a deviation from normal self-regulation. Compared with established CBT there is greater emphasis on *self-regulatory processes*, including motivation, goals and self-identity. It is targeting these processes that we believe can help therapy to be effective with more difficult-to-treat cases.
- The self-regulation model describes a number of *vicious cycles* that create self-maintaining loops and can lead to successively worsening downward spirals of mood. In severe depression these cycles can become *inter-locked* analogous to an internal gridlock where the system is stuck and requires external inputs to effect change.
- Treatment is targeted to disrupt these maintenance processes, creating *virtuous cycles* or upward spirals of mood intended to return the individual to normal self-regulation.
- Compared with Beck's CBT:
  - The self-regulation model works less with links between specific thoughts and emotions.
  - The content of negative thoughts is acknowledged, but there is no direct challenge to their accuracy. Instead, we try to help the client take a more reflective position to realize how they are *processing* thoughts in their mind.
  - The aim is to *indirectly* change the content of thinking by influencing: (a) how thoughts are processed in the mind, such as rumination and suppression; (b) greater awareness of the consequences of these processes.
  - Restoring normal reflective, attentional and memory processes is the way of facilitating cognitive change.

- Compared with Jacobson and Martell's BA:
  - The self-regulation model has a greater emphasis on the influence of goals and motivation on action.
  - Contextual factors can be highly relevant for some cases, but less so for others.
  - The key antecedents of action are motivational states, rather than environmental triggers.
  - Consequences of action are very important; but they are viewed as sources of feedback alongside other influences, rather than reinforcement or punishment.

- o Treatment often involves increasing client activity, but there is a greater emphasis on *how* engaged a behaviour is, experimenting with different cognitive processing modes to increase behavioural engagement.

- In subsequent chapters we will apply this framework to different types of clinical cases and focus on particular challenges facing clients and therapists. Part III explores depression sub-types associated with difficult-to-treat cases: early-onset, highly recurrent and chronic/persistent depression. Part IV explores complex cases, including comorbidities with anxiety disorders, PTSD and complex trauma.

PART III
DEPRESSION SUB-TYPES

Part I provided an overview of established CBT and Part II introduced the integrated approach with its emphasis on self-regulatory processes. In Part III we focus on three challenging sub-types of depression that are associated with difficult-to-treat cases: *early-onset*, *highly recurrent* and *chronic/persistent*. The same self-regulation model is used with each of these types but treatment parameters and dynamic focus are somewhat different. The aim of this part is to orient therapists towards the main clinical and contextual issues that have a bearing on these sub-types, so that treatment can be adjusted accordingly.

There are two reasons for prioritizing *early-onset depression*, as explored in Chapter 7. Firstly, people who go on to develop highly recurrent depression are likely to have their first-onset prior to the age of eighteen. We have already seen in Chapter 4 that this subgroup is at high risk of relapse, so they are clearly a priority group. Secondly, CBT for adolescent depression is effective, but not yet as effective as the adult form of CBT. This suggests an opportunity to explore new ways of understanding adolescent depression and potential adjustments to CBT for this client group. There is an obvious need for effective treatment as early as possible in the lifespan, so that CBT can have a potent and prophylactic effect.

Highly recurrent depression, by which we mean three or more major episodes, can be difficult to treat. The reason is, as mentioned in Chapter 4, that maintenance processes become more autonomous when depression becomes highly recurrent. First-onsets are associated with major life stress whereas subsequent episodes, if they recur, do not necessarily have such strong contextual influences. Depressed moods can be activated by relatively mild stress, and this brings particular difficulties for both client and therapist. These clients are also at high risk of relapse, so their priority status is clear. We explore their needs in Chapter 8.

In Chapter 2, we noted that less experienced CBT therapists can find it challenging working with *chronic and persistent depression*. In diagnostic terms, these are clients who have been in a major depressive episode for at least 2 years. In our experience, a diverse range of clients meet this criterion and they can have quite different therapeutic needs. Some clients' depression persists due to unavailable treatment; others because of inadequate treatment; some have received good-quality therapy but were unresponsive to it; others have lifelong depression that has rarely, if ever, been in remission. This is a single diagnostic category with a diverse range of clinical presentations. We consider the various therapeutic implications and treatment adjustments in Chapter 9.

Early-Onset Depression

Early-onset depression refers to young people who experience a first major episode prior to the age of eighteen. They need to be high priority clients, because of the distress they experience during such a formative period of life, and also because untreated adolescent depression can contribute to recurrent difficulties later. At any point in time, between 4% and 5% of adolescents aged 13–18 years are affected by major depression, and young women are more likely to be affected than young men (Thapar et al., 2012). Early-onset depression is associated with never marrying, less adaptive social and occupational functioning, poorer quality of life, greater medical and psychiatric comorbidity, a more negative view of self and life, more lifetime depressive episodes, more suicide attempts, and greater depression severity within recurrent episodes (Jonsson et al., 2011). However, these are *associations*, not *inevitabilities*: if adolescent depression goes untreated the above sequelae are more likely; if it is successfully treated and vulnerabilities are addressed, a more adaptive developmental path can be forged. Hence the pressing need to intervene as effectively and as early as possible in the lifespan (Curry & Wells, 2005).

If you are considering skipping this chapter, because you do not work with young people, please think again. As we discovered in Chapter 4, adults who experienced depression in adolescence are at greater risk of relapse after CBT, even if the current episode is 30 or 40 years post-adolescence. Not surprisingly, therefore, adults with highly recurrent depression are likely to have experienced their first-onset in adolescence (Lewinsohn, Rohde, Seeley, Klein & Gotlib, 2000). The purpose of this chapter is partly to support therapists working with children and young people, but it is also to help adult therapists reflect on the impact of early-onsets in their adult clients, for example, problems with the developmental tasks of adolescence, and vulnerabilities emerging at that time that can be reactivated later. It is not unusual for adolescent phenomena to present in adult clients, and it is helpful for adult therapists to be developmentally aware, with sufficient understanding of those processes. It is also important to emphasize that not all adolescents go on to experience further depressive episodes: the aim is to identify young people at *high risk* of recurrence, and provide therapy early enough, and potent enough, to guide them onto a healthier developmental path.

Adolescent depression is a large topic and we cannot cover all its aspects in a single chapter. We have chosen to concentrate on the treatment of challenging cases, to explore the aetiology and maintenance of early-onset depression, and ways of supporting the developmental tasks of adolescence. We will explore these processes by considering a clinical case, Daniel, a 15-year-old boy who presented with severe depression, suicidal rumination, social anxiety and OCD. He was attending school intermittently, having angry outbursts, but not self-harming or abusing alcohol or drugs. Like many young people, he was not enthusiastic about being referred for help. He went on to receive thirty-seven sessions of CBT over 2 years, mostly individual and some with his parents. He is a good example of the challenges working with adolescent depression: a young person in a downward spiral of mental health, reluctant to receive help, in a family whose conflicts are contributing to the maintenance of his difficulties.

CBT for Adolescent Depression

CBT for adolescent depression is a less developed field than adult depression, and this is reflected to some degree in clinical outcomes (Reinecke, Ryan & DuBois, 1998). A meta-analysis of eleven RCTs (from 1980 to 2006) observed a post-treatment effect size of 0.53, which is clinically significant but somewhat less potent than adult CBT (Driessen & Hollon, 2010; Klein, Jacobs & Reinecke, 2007). The largest trial included in this meta-analysis was the Treatment for Adolescents with Depression Study (March et al., 2004; TADS, 2005), which compared CBT ($n = 111$) with SSRI medication ($n = 109$) and CBT/SSRI Combined ($n = 107$). Twenty-four CBT sessions were offered and a mean of seventeen were received. Combined Treatment was found to be robustly superior to CBT and modestly, and inconsistently, better than SSRI alone. Adding CBT to SSRI minimized suicidal ideation and treatment-emergent suicidal events. When treating severe depression, CBT had a slower response than SSRI or Combined Treatment: more than half the participants had not responded by 12 weeks, with CBT catching up with SSRI by weeks 18–24 and Combined by weeks 30–36.

There have been two further trials of note since the 2007 meta-analysis (Klein et al., 2007). The ADAPT study (Goodyer, Dubicka, Wilkinson, Kelvin & Roberts, 2008) was a pragmatic RCT comparing SSRI medication ($n = 103$) with SSRI/CBT Combined ($n = 105$). There was an 80% response to treatment in both arms, but no difference between SSRI and Combined, and therefore no advantage for augmenting medication with CBT. It is worth noting, however, that although nineteen sessions of CBT were offered, the mean number received was only six. The IMPACT study (Goodyer et al.,

2017) compared a brief psychosocial intervention ($n = 158$), with CBT ($n = 155$) and short-term psychoanalytical therapy ($n = 157$). The CBT participants received a mean of nine sessions. All three treatments achieved approximately 50% reduction in depression symptoms, one year after treatment, and there were no differences between treatments. Prescribing an SSRI during treatment or follow-up did not differ between the groups and did not mediate the outcome.

Overall, there is evidence that CBT for adolescent depression is clinically effective and provides protection against suicidality. However: (a) the effect size is only moderate and less than CBT for adult depression; (b) there is no evidence that CBT is more effective than other therapies; (c) CBT is slower acting than medication for severe depression; (d) CBT's effects appear to be weaker when only a small dose of therapy is delivered (i.e. six or fewer sessions). In the case of small doses, it is not simply a matter of how much therapy is offered; it can be a challenge to encourage young people to accept larger doses of treatment, even when it is in their interests to receive them. This is highly relevant to alliance building and the treatment rationale, which we will turn to later. We believe there is an opportunity, and imperative, to find out if CBT for adolescent depression can be made more potent. The health-economic argument for prioritizing adolescent depression, and treating it more effectively, is clear-cut: the long-term savings on all metrics are vast if young people are able to find a healthier path, not to mention the greater quality of life for those individuals.

First-Onsets across the Lifespan

How, then, can we approach adolescent depression with fresh eyes? One approach is to consider what is known about first-onsets across the lifespan. First-onsets can occur at any age, as illustrated in Figure 7.1. The data represented in this graph come from a large-scale study of depressed adults who were interviewed to find out when they first experienced a major episode (Zisook et al., 2007). The results speak for themselves: people of all ages can fall into major depression, including people in their fifties, sixties and seventies, who have no previous history of mood disturbance. As an illustration we have already described first-onsets earlier in the book: Angela (Chapter 2) and Chloe (Chapters 5 and 6) were in their thirties when they first became depressed. Bob (Chapter 3) was in his fifties. None had a history of depression prior to these episodes.

We are not advocating that adolescent depression is prioritized to the *exclusion* of these later age-groups; on the contrary, as Figure 7.1 illustrates, depression needs to be approached as a lifespan problem. Nevertheless, the pattern of results is clear: more first-onsets occur between the ages of 13 and 18 than at any other time of life, and there is a steady decrease in the likelihood of them occurring thereafter. Early-onset depression presents an opportunity to identify young people at high risk of recurrent

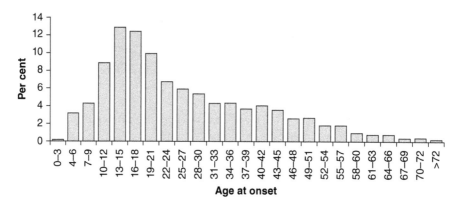

Figure 7.1   Age distribution of first-onsets in a sample of adult major depression (*n* = 4041) (from Zisook et al., 2007)

depression, as early as possible in the lifespan, and arrest progress towards patterns of recurrence and chronicity (Barton et al., 2008).

A key point in understanding the nature of first-onsets is that there is a high probability of *major life stress* precipitating the onset and influencing the subsequent course of the disorder. This pattern is observed in first-onsets across the lifespan. Figure 7.2 summarizes the findings of five historical studies that investigated the percentage of depressive episodes associated with major life stress, as reported in Post (1992). Approximately 70% of first-onsets were precipitated by, or associated with, major life stress. This reduced to approximately 40% in second episodes and approximately 30% in third episodes. As an illustration, recall that Angela's depression was triggered by significant marital problems (Chapter 2), Bob's depression was initiated by work stress and subsequent redundancy (Chapter 3), and Chloe's depression was precipitated by a traumatic experience of childbirth (Chapters 5 and 6). Treatment of early-onset depression has to *address the impact of real adverse events* such as trauma, abuse, neglect, academic stress, bullying, interpersonal conflict and ostracization: these are the common precipitants of adolescent depression. Depressed adolescents are likely to have suffered, or be suffering, the consequences of these types of experiences (Harkness, Bruce & Lumley, 2006; Lewinsohn, Allen, Seeley & Gotlib, 1999; Williamson, Birmaher, Frank, Anderson, Matty & Kupfer, 1998).

Remember: from a self-regulation perspective, depressed moods are a normal consequence of these experiences. It would be surprising if these experiences did *not* provoke at least some self-devaluation and depressed mood. However, *a depressive disorder is not an inevitable consequence of depressed moods*: even in severe or recurrent stress, some young people have the resilience and support available to withstand threats to their wellbeing, and stay out of a downward spiral of mood. It is not just the experience of

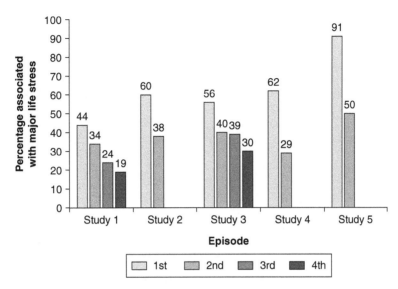

Figure 7.2 **Percentage of depressive episodes associated with major life stress, reported in Post (1992)**

adversity that matters; it is the psychological impact of those experiences, how a young person responds to them and what their caregivers and helpers provide by way of support. What matters is the interaction of life stress with a young person's inner resilience and external support, called *diathesis–stress interactions.*

Diathesis–Stress Interactions

Pre-existing susceptibilities (*diatheses*) interact with stressors (*adverse experiences*) and their interaction triggers the onset of a depressive disorder (Lewinsohn, Joiner & Rohde, 2001). We have illustrated this in Figure 7.3, contrasting diathesis–stress relationships in first-onset versus recurrent and chronic depression. The relative contribution of stress, life events and adverse experiences is greater in first-onsets, and these need to be a greater part of the formulation and treatment focus. As depression becomes more recurrent or persistent it tends to become more *autonomous* and less contingent on major stress, a phenomenon we will return to in Chapters 8 and 9.

As illustrated in Figure 7.3, the relative contribution of life stress in adolescent depression is high, and this means that young people who are not particularly susceptible can become depressed, in the unfortunate event of severe stress or multiple adverse experiences. The diathesis–stress interactions will be buffered, to some degree,

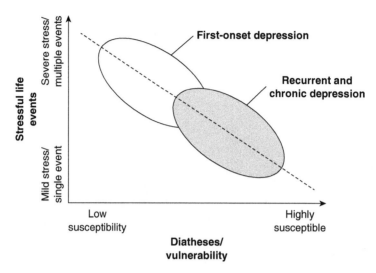

Figure 7.3   Diathesis–stress interactions in sub-types of major depression

by family and social support: so, when a young person falls into a major episode, we are seeking to understand three factors:

a. The nature of the life stress and adversity the young person has experienced: is it minor or major, a single event or recurring, past or current?
b. The young person's pre-existing susceptibility and resilience factors: what is the balance between them?
c. The quality and amount of family and social support: what has been offered and what has been received?

We will explore these issues by considering a clinical case, Daniel.

Case Illustration | Daniel: diathesis–stress interactions in the precipitation of early-onset depression

a. Life stress and adversity

Daniel was the younger of two brothers, whose parents separated when he was very young. He was an emotionally sensitive boy whose mother was over-protective of him, especially in relation to his older brother, who could be verbally aggressive and at times vindictive. Daniel and his mother tried to protect each other from the aggressive older brother and, at times, Daniel would go into the line of fire to protect his mother. However, his mother also had an explosive temper and was controlling and critical of Daniel, some of the time. There was high expressed emotion in the family and a lot of verbal aggression (not physical), which had a sustained and profound impact on Daniel's emotional sensitivities. During his infrequent contacts, Daniel's father expressed high expectations of Daniel's academic performance and communicated disappointment when these were not met. Daniel was intelligent and creative, preferring music and film to more conventional academic subjects.

b. Resilience and susceptibility factors

It was a confusing family situation for Daniel, to have a mother who was alternately protective, controlling and hostile. It created an ambivalent mother–son relationship and an unstable, unpredictable and uncertain home life. The family conflicts produced an environment that led to both *anxious avoidance* and *submissiveness* in Daniel, with proneness to embarrassment, shame and humiliation. Over the previous 5 years he had become more self-conscious in social situations: his social anxiety has become increasingly problematic, leading to intermittent avoidance. In the previous 2 years, he had been bothered by obsessive thoughts, particularly that he might hurt others by saying or doing the wrong thing. Daniel was confused: he sometimes felt *protected* by his mother and *responsible* for her wellbeing. He also felt *disregarded*, *controlled* and *criticized,* and in these mental states his self-esteem and self-efficacy markedly reduced. His internal and external situation had been worsening gradually over several years.

c. Family and social support

When adversity is experienced outside the family, there is a need for strong family relationships to buffer its effects. When the family is the primary source of stress, a young person is reliant on other external sources of support. Daniel had a few close friends at school, but he preferred not to discuss his home life with them. He received some indirect support, feeling better about himself when he spent time with his friends, but this was insufficient to buffer the repeated effects of fraternal and maternal attacks.

Later in this chapter we will expand on how we understand resilience in self-regulatory terms. It is usually the result of secure attachment relationships, strong self-esteem and self-efficacy, and an approach-orientation to daily life. In contrast, young people who are more susceptible to depression tend to have insecure, anxious or disorganized attachments, weaker self-esteem and self-efficacy, and an avoidant-orientation (Lee & Hankin, 2009). If a stressor, or accumulation of stressors, is greater than the resilience (*internal*) and support (*external*) available to buffer it, self-devaluation and depressed mood are much more likely to occur, and will be harder to reverse. We also know that young people with a family history of mood disorders are at greater risk of depression, and this could be explained by one, some or all of the above factors.

Developmental Tasks of Adolescence

The adolescent years of, approximately, ages 13–18 are usually a period of *identity formation* when young people gradually separate from their birth family, become more independent and make the transition from childhood to adulthood (Klimstra, Hale, Raaijmakers, Branje & Meeus, 2010). It is normal in this period to explore different ways of being, have adventures and experiment with new experiences. For most young people it is also a period of decision making about social groups, relationships, education and future employment. Identity begins to be *self-generated*, not just learned or acquired from early experiences. Young people start to make conscious choices about whom they relate to, what they do, and who they are (Crocetti, 2017). They generate *possible selves* and explore them through goal-directed actions. There are *divergent* phases in which multiple possibilities are explored and considered, then there are *convergent* phases in which selections and choices are made. Internalization continues; in fact, it never ceases – but new identities are the product of choice and self-generation. When the process is successfully negotiated, what emerges in adulthood is a balance of *individuation* and *belonging*: differentiating oneself from others with a unique identity and values, at the same time identifying with particular others and forming new attachments outside the birth family. We have illustrated this developmental process in Figure 7.4.

Exploration and decision making in adolescence need to be *scaffolded* – there needs to be a gradual transition from childhood to adulthood, with the right amount and type of support from caregivers. When family involvement is insufficient (*under-scaffolding*), young people are prone to isolation: they may seek guidance outside the family, try to increase self-reliance, or become more withdrawn with insufficient direction and purpose. The latter situation can lead to *identity diffusion* with insufficient decision making, goal setting and an unconsolidated self-identity. When family involvement is excessive (*over-scaffolding*), young people are prone to entrapment: their secure passage to adulthood is organized and insured, but it is overly influenced by the involvement and decisions of others. This can lead to *identity foreclosure*, where uncertainty is reduced by taking early life decisions, sometimes based on a priori theories, expectations or precedents rather than concrete experiences, needs and desires.

These developmental tasks are challenging at the best of times: even resilient young people, with limited stress and strong family support, experience some emotional turbulence during adolescence. Imagine how much more challenging it is for a less resilient young person, like Daniel, experiencing significant stress and not receiving the support he needs to buffer it. Under these conditions, depressed mood is very understandable, and there is a risk of it being maintained if the young person is unable to work against the force of the downward spiral. It is entirely understandable that trauma, abuse, neglect, academic stress, bullying, interpersonal conflict or ostracization have the potential, not just to trigger depressed moods, but also disrupt the developmental tasks of adolescence. Hence, within a course of CBT, the initial focus is overcoming depression, as introduced in Chapter 6, but with young clients there is the additional need to support their developmental tasks, and encourage their family to engage in this process too.

Acute Phase Treatment

Alliance building

The first goal of treatment is to improve mood; the second goal is to support the developmental tasks of adolescence; the third goal is to increase the young person's resilience, so they are protected from depression in the future. The treatment components are the same as in adult depression, but the delivery is subtly different. This is often noticeable in the initial sessions, in two respects. Firstly, because adolescents are legally minors, and have dependent status, they are sometimes beholden to one or both parents to support their travel, attendance and participation in treatment. As in Daniel's case, this can be a complication when parental behaviours form part of the stress that

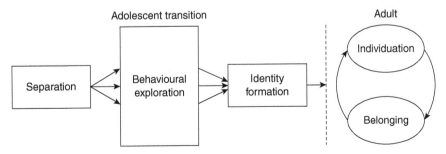

Figure 7.4   Developmental transition from adolescence to adulthood

has triggered the depression in the first instance. In fact, Daniel did not attend his first assessment session, his mother did.

Secondly, young people may not fully understand, or expect, the role of collaboration that underpins the therapeutic relationship in CBT. Collaboration is not just considering the young person's views, it is sharing power with them as an equal partner: neither party dominates, and neither acquiesces. This can be very liberating for a young person, particularly when depressed, but it is unlikely to be their expectation prior to treatment. It is usual for children to have less power than the adults they depend on. In the case of depressed adolescents, it is often true that they have suffered from abuse of power, or lack of respect of their value or rights. Consequently, entering treatment they may be expecting, or fearing, punishment and judgement rather than support and compassion. This was certainly true in Daniel's case.

For these reasons, alliance building and engaging young people in CBT can be complicated and time-consuming. It is not unusual for a young person to take a passive and sceptical role initially, waiting to be convinced by the therapist's integrity and trustworthiness. It can also take time to clarify the therapist's relationship with parents and the rest of the family. What are the boundaries of confidentiality? Will parents be told about the content of therapy sessions? These are important issues to discuss and clarify. In our experience, it is essential that the primary alliance is with the young person and all other alliances, for example with family members, are secondary. The young person is the named client; their needs have to be prioritized and the family system is engaged and disengaged in different phases, depending on the needs of the young person at that time.

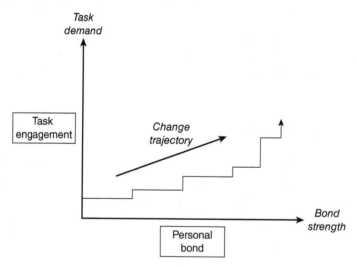

Figure 7.5   Typical trajectory of change in CBT for adolescent depression

In Figure 7.5 we have represented the situation of investing heavily in building a personal bond at the outset of treatment. This can result in a slow initial trajectory towards change, but sometimes this is a necessary step in the process. Recall that in RCTs, young people have received approximately 50% of the CBT sessions available to them: means of 17/24 (TADS, 2005), 6/19 (ADAPT: Goodyer et al., 2008), and 9/20 sessions (IMPACT: Goodyer et al., 2017). We should not be surprised when this pattern is replicated in routine practice. Therapists, and services, need to decide how to respond to cancellations and non-arrivals. Do they signal a lack of commitment, and therefore warrant discharge? Or are they an inevitable consequence of the self-dysregulation of depressed adolescents and, as such, referrals should be kept open, with pro-active attempts to encourage re-engagement? The latter is the ethos of an early intervention service, seeking to maximize engagement, sometimes against the odds, because the long-term benefits of treatment justify the short-term costs of inconvenience and discontinuity. Daniel's therapist adopted the latter approach, tolerating several cancellations and non-arrivals across a 2-year period. This strategy resulted in a dose of thirty-seven sessions being received, considerably more than average levels in CBT trials, and a greater opportunity for treatment to have a potent effect.

Initial formulation and core treatment components

The initial formulation is based on the downward spiral model, as introduced in Chapter 6. The downward spiral is precipitated in the context of diathesis–stress interactions, but at the outset of treatment, it may or may not be apparent what those are. As therapy develops, the life stress that the young person is reacting to usually becomes clearer but, to begin with, the aim is to present depression as:

a. a reaction to difficult experiences
b. in which negative thoughts, emotions and body states have a depressing effect on mood
c. which suppresses normal motivation, leading to disengaged behaviour and ruminative thinking.

In Daniel's case, he had a felt-sense of being worthless and that life was futile; this severely depressed his mood, resulting in extreme tiredness, reduced motivation and strong urges to withdraw from daily life. He continued to eat regularly but slept long hours and spent most of his waking time in his bedroom on the Internet. He was highly ruminative, spending many hours questioning the point of living, leading to pronounced suicidal ideation. In Daniel's case this did not lead to risky behaviours, plans or intent, but it needed careful risk assessment across the treatment phases. Daniel's full case formulation, including the structural level, is presented in Figure 7.6.

As we described in Chapter 6, the process level is the main therapeutic target in the initial stages of treatment. Approximately the first half of Daniel's therapy targeted *approach motivation*, *behavioural engagement*, and *reflective processing*. Behavioural engagement initially focused on self-care, daily routines and pleasurable experiences, especially playing and listening to music, which was Daniel's passion. There were elements of inactivity, avoidance, withdrawal, submissiveness and suicidality in Daniel's presentation; hence, several maintenance processes had to be overcome. There were notable occasions when Daniel was surprised that he was able to influence his preferred outcomes, for example, at family gatherings and band rehearsals, though there remained a significant level of behavioural avoidance, maintained by social anxiety. In Part IV of the book, we address the issue of how to approach treatment when comorbid disorders are present, such as social anxiety and OCD. Comorbidity with adolescent depression is typically 80–90% in clinical services: anxiety disorders, conduct disorder, oppositional defiant disorder, substance use and ADHD are all common co-occurrences. We will not discuss them in detail here, suffice to say that Daniel and his therapist had to attend to how his social anxieties and obsessive thoughts *interacted* with his depression.

Daniel gradually became more aware of his hierarchy of needs, particularly his interest in music and film, and his desire to explore a career in that area. The normal adolescent process of identity exploration had been occurring covertly in Daniel's mind, rather than overtly in the social world, so his abstract existential questioning (e.g. 'what's the point in living?' and 'who cares whether I live or die?') lacked concrete experience and a social context. He was trying to negotiate the tasks of adolescence internally, withdrawn from others and normal social experiences: it was a conscious strategy to protect himself from the risk and suffering of social interaction, to give himself the reflective space to consider the big questions. In Daniel's words, '*I removed myself from external stress (the world) and found another in hyperawareness of internal events (the mind)*'. Daniel learned the unhelpfulness of brooding on these thoughts and became more aware of the limits of mental control and the unhelpfulness of trying to over-control his mind. By the end of treatment he still had tendencies towards social avoidance and rumination, but was much more aware of them and able to notice the boundary between helpful reflection and unhelpful self-analysis.

His parents accompanied him to five of the thirty-seven sessions. This was difficult for Daniel initially, but in time it helped him, and his therapist, to recognize the family dynamics he had been reacting to. This helped Daniel to gain a better understanding of how he had fallen into depression. It also enabled his parents to modify their

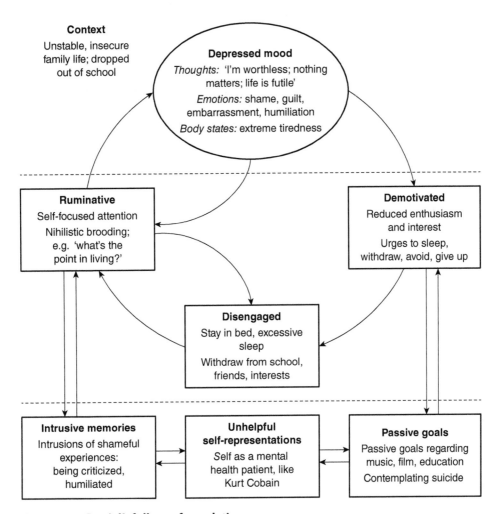

Figure 7.6   Daniel's full case formulation

behaviour, to some degree, so they could become a source of support rather than a source of stress. One year after the end of treatment, Daniel, by then aged 18, had a follow-up in adult services. He had begun college and was playing occasionally in a band. His OCD was in full remission, and his social anxieties were fluctuating. He had residual depression symptoms (PHQ-9 = 14), but they were not stopping him functioning at college and enjoying a satisfying, if somewhat constrained, social life as a member of a music group.

Memories, Self-Representations and Goals

Having explored the core treatment components in Chapter 6, the remainder of this chapter will focus on optional treatment components: *memory integration, self-organization* and *goal-organization*. These aim to encourage changes in the structure of autobiographical memory, self-identity and life-goal subsystems. As we noted in Chapter 5, euthymic mood is associated with the capacity to access memories of specific events and experiences. The aim of treatment is to encourage a well-organized autobiographical memory system; when memories are integrated and well structured, people can access them both thematically and by epoch, for example, *favourite holidays* and *my life in 2005*. A resilient memory system does not only retrieve events, it provides the inputs for *narratives*. It enables people to recount their personal story with specific tales embedded in a larger narrative. When working with young people, it is important to take advantage of the *reminiscence bump* (Thomsen, Pillemer & Ivcevic, 2011). This is the finding that adults recollect more memories from their adolescence than any other period of life. This is the period when concrete experiences are remembered, identities are formed and young people begin to plan for the future. CBT needs to support these tasks, as the main context for helpful thinking and behaviour to develop.

Resilience

Memories are associated with self-representations, grown out of concrete experiences. As we noted in Chapter 5, some self-representations are *learned and internalized* through early attachment experiences, such as being lovable, competent and safe. Others are *constructed* from adolescence onwards, for example, investments in relationships, friendships, body, gender, appearance, nationality, ethnicity, politics, religion, work, career, marital status, parenthood, interests and so on. Resilience can begin to develop during neonatal phases of development. Babies held in safe, predictable environments, who are accepted, nurtured, praised and rewarded, are receiving the precursors of resilience. A process of *internalization* begins, in which memories of these foundation experiences gradually form into self-representations. These are *pre-verbal mental models of the self*, and we propose that they are structured in three interconnected domains:

1. *Relationship and affiliation*. The result of being accepted and nurtured is the internalization that the self is liked and loved and is therefore likeable, lovable and acceptable to others. This is depicted in Figure 7.7 as a helpful early representation: 'lovable'. 'Lovable' is written in quotes for two reasons: early representations are initiated in pre-verbal development and tend to trigger a 'felt-sense' or 'felt-truth' when they are activated, rather than a set

of propositions or clearly defined beliefs. Secondly, the particular content or themes that apply for any individual can vary a great deal, so people may refer to their relational self in a variety of different ways, not just in terms of love-ability. Such representations also form part of the self-to-self relationship, as children become self-aware and develop reflective capacities. This is the precursor to self-care and paying attention to one's own needs and desires. It supports the internal capacity to *self-soothe* during distress, as well as forming trusting, affiliative relationships from middle childhood onwards.

2. *Efficacy and competence.* The experience of initiating cause and effect is essential for a child to develop *self-efficacy*, in other words, learning that he or she can influence internal and external events through voluntary actions. When those actions, or their outcomes, are noticed, praised or rewarded, *competence* can be internalized: the self is capable of completing tasks and producing results to an acceptable standard. This helps to develop confidence about goal-directed tasks and expectations of success. In Figure 7.7 this is depicted as a helpful early representation 'competent', but, as before, the specific content will vary a lot across individuals.

3. *Security and independence.* Secure and sufficiently predictable early experiences become internalized as the self's *safeness* and this enables gradual exploration of the world at greater distances from caregivers. We view this domain as the primary consequence of early attachment relationships. When they are secure, children internalize that it is *they* who are safe and can deal with hazards that occur, not just the result of being in secure situations in the presence of a caregiver. Gradual exploration away from caregivers helps to increase a growing sense of independence – not isolation or alienation – but a felt-sense of *self-reliance,* in the context of belonging with others, even when they are not visible or physically present.

Notice that within the self-identity system, links are made across these domains: feeling safe and secure is the platform for building relationships and engaging in tasks and goals. Being liked and respected helps to maintain a sense of security, as does being effective and competent engaging in tasks. This is the precursor of *self-organization* and what emerges during adolescence is a process of separation, exploration and identity-formation that enables a unique self-organization to develop. Helpful early self-representations provide the internal structures to approach the tasks of adolescence.

Vulnerability

The helpful representations in Figure 7.7 depict an ideal childhood, a highly resilient individual and, most likely, a smooth transition to adult life. Even for young people with stable and happy childhoods, life is not always so smooth or ideal: caregivers make mistakes and children have upsets, disappointments and frightening experiences as well as acceptance, praise and safety. Worse than this, as we have already noted, some children experience extended periods of trauma, abuse or neglect, and these can have a significant and damaging effect on their wellbeing and self-identity. The unhelpful representations in Figure 7.7 depict the other extreme, of a damaging childhood and an individual left vulnerable to depression. Instead of acceptance and nurturance, the child experienced rejection and neglect; instead of praise and reward, the child experienced criticism and punishment; instead of safety and predictability, the child experienced danger and chaos. If these experiences become the norm, *internalization* will occur in which the child feels disliked and unwanted, rather than liked and loved; incompetent and useless, rather than competent and effective; weak and vulnerable, rather than safe and independent.

If these, or similar, unhelpful representations begin to affect the self-to-self relationship, this will be emotionally painful, distressing and potentially depressing to a young person. Self-representations such as these do not provide a strong platform to approach adolescent transition. On the contrary, they are likely to generate anxiety about rejection, failure and one's ability to cope with independent life. It is much harder to negotiate a process of separation from caregivers if attachment relationships have been insecure, anxious, ambivalent or disorganized. Separation and individuation rely on behavioural exploration, and if a young person's felt-sense of safeness is under-developed, this can result in avoidance and passivity, and lead to insufficient breadth of concrete experiences.

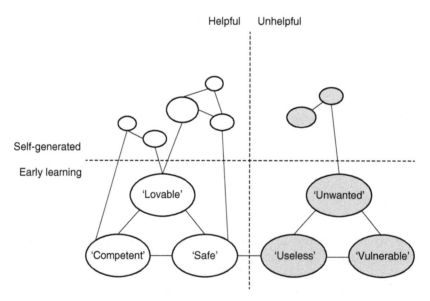

Figure 7.7   Resilient and vulnerable aspects of self-organization

Strengths and weaknesses

Of course, most young people have a combination of helpful and unhelpful self-representations. Those who are depression-prone will have relatively more of the unhelpful type, whereas those who are resilient will have relatively more of the helpful type. As we have already outlined, during depression, helpful representations are disrupted or deactivated, and unhelpful representations are formed or activated, and the likelihood of those phase shifts occurring is a consequence of their interaction with life stress and the buffering effect of social support. With this in mind, we have hypothesized about Daniel's self-organization and represented it in Figure 7.8. Self-representations that are internalized and well-established are enclosed by continuous lines, whereas unconsolidated identities, such as *possible selves*, are enclosed by dotted lines. The size of each node represents how core, important or central it is within self-definition, and the connecting lines represent associations between nodes.

Daniel had positive early experiences of being protected and nurtured by his mother. This helped him, inconsistently, to develop a felt-sense of safeness and

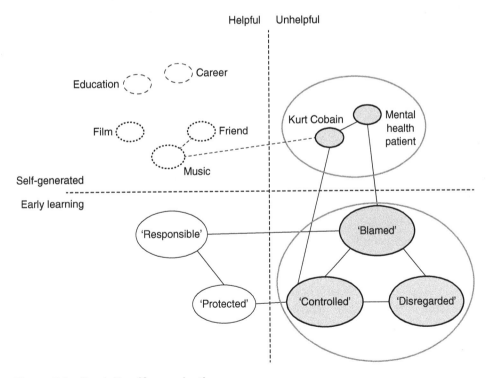

Figure 7.8   Daniel's self-organization

security. However, the protection was coloured by inconsistency, unpredictability and confusion: this left Daniel feeling controlled and manipulated. He also internalized a representation of responsibility which had both a helpful and unhelpful range. In its helpful range, Daniel was sensitive to and protective of others' needs, including his mother, friends and other family members. In its unhelpful range, Daniel would easily feel blamed and guilty about negative events, such as family conflicts. These conflicts were very aversive for Daniel and his needs were overlooked and neglected during these periods. Consequently, he internalized a representation of being disregarded by others.

Euthymic mood relies on sufficient helpful representations being activated, and sufficient unhelpful representations (if they exist) being deactivated. One of the ways of strengthening helpful representations is for *self-generated* identities to become associated with helpful early representations, for example, *protection* and *responsibility* creating a basis for Daniel's emerging identity as a *musician, film fan* and *friend*. In fact, in Daniel's case these were unconsolidated as identities: he engaged in *activities* related to music, film and friendship, but he had not yet *internalized* them as self-representations. His unhelpful representations of being *disregarded, controlled* and *blamed* were dominating his identity and interfering with the tasks of adolescence: separation, behavioural exploration and identity-formation. Specifically, Daniel's fears of rejection, humiliation and negative evaluation from others were manifesting as social anxiety, and limiting his engagement with new experiences.

The gradual increase in social anxiety and depressed mood over a 2- to 3-year period culminated in Daniel dropping out of school aged 15. This was the tipping point: his unhelpful self-representations became fully activated, represented in Figure 7.8 as the circled nodes, and a downward spiral of mood occurred. The phase shift into unhelpful self-representations elicited associated memories, predominantly of feeling humiliated in response to verbal attacks at home. Daniel's emerging identities as a musician, film fan and friend were deactivated and instead he began to identify strongly with being a mental health patient, specifically the singer Kurt Cobain, who shared Daniel's interest in music, suffered from severe depression and eventually took his own life. In this mental state, Daniel's life goals concerning music, film and education became passive, and instead he began to ruminate about suicide as a means of escape from the misery he was experiencing.

Daniel's identity formation was taking place covertly in his mind rather than through behavioural exploration and concrete experiences. In this situation, the experience of *being depressed* can be internalized and become part of self-definition; self and depression become *fused* or *enmeshed*. Rather than being a person of value, who is temporarily depressed, the client experiences themselves as worthless, useless, disregarded and unimportant, and depression is appraised as a *consequence* of being that way. In this situation, it will be very difficult to develop a good-enough relationship with oneself. When self and depression become fully fused, the depressed state becomes self-defining; people identify with it as their true self, and this is one of the greatest risks of adolescent depression: *identification with being depressed*.

Case Illustration | Daniel: self-organization

To mitigate the risk of *self-depression fusion*, Daniel's therapist guided him towards behavioural engagements that had the potential to strengthen helpful selves, and indirectly weaken unhelpful selves. The aim is to take advantage of *plasticity* in the self-regulation system during adolescent development, encouraging consolidation of helpful self-representations, such as *musician*, *film fan* and *friend*, at the same time disrupting and deactivating unhelpful identities, such as *Kurt Cobain* and *mental health patient*. The best strategy is not to direct too much attention to unhelpful selves, because any form of reflection, and especially rumination, has the potential to consolidate these nodes and the connections between them. Focusing attention on needs, desires and approach impulses will guide a young person towards the life they *would like to have*. Being a mental health patient and committing suicide was not a *desire* for Daniel, and in light of this he gradually became more oriented around his music, friends and film interests.

Once mood is somewhat improved, it is good to encourage the formation of *approach goals*. Adult clients are already likely to have life-goals, and be disengaged from them, whereas adolescent clients are more likely to need to form life-goals, not least because a period of depression can disrupt the normal identity-formation process. Hence, it is helpful to make goal-organization an explicit and structured process in treatment, introducing the idea of a goal hierarchy with a desired outcome at the top, and various sub-goals beneath it, then concrete steps beneath the sub-goals, and so on. This framework is depicted in Figure 7.9.

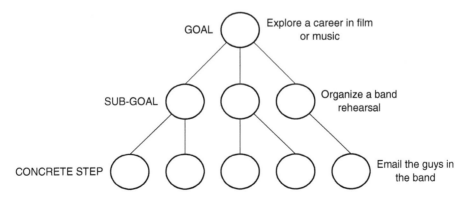

Figure 7.9   Example of an approach goal hierarchy

This can help a young person to learn a method of *planning*: engaging with manageable, concrete steps that are small sub-goals, enabling progress towards a higher-order goal. This is also a way of encouraging *exploration* rather than *foreclosure* or *diffusion*; a step could be finding out some information about a college course, or going to visit a potential new employer. Try to encourage steps that are rooted in concrete experiences, rather than abstract ideas.

Case Illustration | Daniel: goal-organization

In Daniel's therapy his interest to develop a career in the music or film industry was affirmed by his therapist as something to explore in a concrete and experiential way. Behavioural engagement, for example, a band rehearsal, created *new autobiographical memories* which consolidated Daniel's *self-representation as a musician*, which further strengthened his *goal to explore a career* in music. Hence, the structural level of self-regulation became more adaptive and resilient, through the tasks of adolescence being supported in treatment.

Practitioner Tips: Early-Onset Depression

- Identify young people at high risk of relapse and recurrence, particularly those who have suffered trauma, neglect or abuse. Offer longer courses of therapy as needed, treating their depression thoroughly and building as much resilience as possible.
- Give time and care to the process of forming a therapeutic alliance; share power and collaborate with the young person as an equal partner in their therapy.
- As far as possible, respond to cancellations and non-arrivals in a proactive way, reaching out to the young person and encouraging their engagement. This will often be needed to deliver a standard dose of 16–20 sessions to treat a major depressive episode.
- Most adolescent depression is precipitated by life stress, such as trauma, abuse, neglect, academic stress, bullying, interpersonal conflict or ostracization. Therapy should explicitly address the psychological impact of these real adverse events.
- Support the developmental tasks of adolescence, such as separation from the birth family, behavioural exploration and identity-formation. Encourage family awareness of the need to provide a helpful type and amount of support during the transition to adulthood.

- Try to reduce the risk of *self-depression fusion*, when young people identify with being depressed and internalize it as a self-identity. Encourage the development of helpful self-representations that contribute positively to self-esteem, maintain self-efficacy, and enable a young person to interact in ways that satisfy their needs.
- Encourage engagement with possible selves and life-goals that connect the young person to their longer-term future. Provide an explicit framework for exploring needs and desires, and encourage planning through manageable concrete steps that build up to sub-goals and goals.

Highly Recurrent Depression

Epidemiological studies suggest that 10–20% of adults experience a major depressive episode at some time in their life, but a smaller proportion present to mental health services or receive psychological therapy (Kessler & Bromet, 2013). Many adult first-onsets make a natural recovery, engage in self-help, receive counselling and/or anti-depressant medication, and these inputs are sufficient for them to return to normal functioning and stay well in the future. In mental health services, most cases of major depression are recurrences because they are the people for whom the above interventions are insufficient, and depression then becomes a recurring problem.

In this chapter we focus on the needs of people with highly recurrent depression, by which we mean three or more previous episodes. We have already seen in Chapter 4 that this group is at high risk of relapse: they often have an unstable response to treatment and/or residual symptoms. People with highly recurrent depression are also likely to have had their first-onset during adolescence, hence the links between Chapter 7 and this chapter. In the absence of effective treatment, the vulnerabilities presenting in early-onsets can be carried forward and compounded by successive depressive episodes. There is a high probability these clients will have suffered some form of childhood abuse, neglect or trauma and the experience of successive depressive episodes can have a further 'scarring' effect. This is the hypothesis that major episodes themselves have a detrimental psychological impact that increases the risk of future depression (Rohde, Lewinsohn & Seeley, 1990).

The integrated model outlined in Chapters 5 and 6 can be applied to any case of depression, including highly recurrent, and the purpose of this chapter is to outline the adjustments made to treatment to accommodate the needs of this client group, particularly those with unstable mood. Specifically, we will consider the following treatment components: *treatment rationale*, *risk assessment*, *self-organization* and *staying well*. A clinical case, Evelyn, is used to illustrate key points.

Treatment Rationale

For many people with highly recurrent depression, minor challenges or setbacks can reactivate depressing thoughts and emotions that were present during previous depressive episodes (Teasdale, 1988). The clinical case we will consider, Evelyn, experienced this as an unpredictable 'plummeting' in her mood. Evelyn was a 53-year-old married woman with two grown-up daughters from a previous marriage. She first presented to mental health services aged 42 following a serious suicide attempt, after the breakdown of her first marriage. In the following 11 years she received various courses of anti-depressant medication, counselling and one course of CBT. These had a limited effect and by the time of her referral to the Newcastle CBT Centre, Evelyn had developed a pattern of highly recurrent depression. On reflection, Evelyn recognized she had suffered from depression intermittently as a teenager and young adult but had perceived it as unhappiness rather than a treatable mood disorder. By the age of 53 she had experienced at least seven recurrences and her depression had developed an autonomous quality that could be triggered in the absence of major life stress (see Figure 7.3). Evelyn's PHQ-9 score at assessment was 19, indicating moderately-severe depression.

Within the treatment rationale, the *autonomy* of these processes is emphasized. This is the key piece of psychoeducation for clients with highly recurrent depression, to help them understand why their mood can dip unpredictably and inexplicably: successive depressive episodes create a 'depressed mode' of thoughts, feelings, body states and memories that can be reactivated by small setbacks, minor stress or negative emotions (Teasdale et al., 2001). This process is called *cognitive reactivation* and it is analogous to *kindling*; in other words, the threshold for these processes to be reactivated reduces with repeated activation of the relevant neurological pathways (Post, 1992). Consequently, the extent of mood change the client experiences can be disproportionate to the event that triggered it, assuming a trigger can be identified. Evelyn recognized this process very clearly and an example from her, and her husband's, diary is given below.

Case Illustration | Evelyn's diary: example of cognitive reactivation

'Difficult day. Sad, tearful, angry and frightened all at the same time. Really upset with how easily my brain just switched from OK to depressed in an instant. Scared that, once again, all the positives of the last 5 months can be wiped out just like that.

(Continued)

(Continued)

Couldn't be bothered with anything or anyone – wished I wasn't here, period. Felt trapped and resentful.'

Husband's diary of the same day

'Difficult weekend. She flipped on Friday as she went for her shower – from jokey and happy to a starry-eyed stranger who is sadly familiar. I am terrified for her (not too strong a word). She managed to put on a face when with people but withdrew instantly when we were on our own. I don't know what to do!'

During assessment, to represent the 'plummeting' process, the graph representing Evelyn's mood was drawn as a steep and sudden downward spiral (see Figure 6.3). To minimize these sudden mood shifts, Evelyn would try to spot potential triggers and seek to avoid them. This reflected her long-standing tendencies to use distraction and emotional avoidance as coping strategies. Evelyn would also ruminate about what had caused a depressed mood, when one occurred without an obvious reason. Since negative emotions can reactivate depressive processes in this way, there is a logic behind trying to avoid them. But as we have seen in previous chapters, in the long term an avoidant orientation increases the risk of depression. Negative emotions are normal and common, so it was impossible for Evelyn to avoid them altogether. Instead she would suppress them and try to ignore them, which would sometimes leave her emotionally impacted, with unprocessed personal memories.

The treatment rationale for highly recurrent depression is to encourage clients to *accept* that depressing thoughts, emotions, body states and memories will sometimes be switched on unpredictably, and not to go to great lengths to avoid this happening. Instead, clients are encouraged to develop the skills and efficacy needed to stay out of a downward spiral when depressed moods have been triggered. Hence, a clear differentiation is made between a *depressed mood* (a temporary affective state) and a *mood disorder* (being stuck in depression and unable to reverse it). People can learn to pay attention to their moods and respond to them differently, and this enables them to self-correct and be relatively short-lasting. This is illustrated in Figure 8.1. There is usually a delay before the upward spiral takes effect, but the key learning is engaging with the upward spiral and noticing that it helps to reverse depressed moods.

The rationale is as follows: for some clients their particular 'depressed mode' of thoughts, feelings, body states and memories is so well developed that going to great lengths to avoid it being reactivated is unlikely to be successful in the long term, not least because the more autonomous it becomes the wider range of internal and external cues that can trigger it. Consequently, strategies to *avoid* triggers, although they may sometimes work in the short term, can maintain an avoidant orientation in daily life that leads to *self-limitation*, e.g. not socializing in case a depressed mood is triggered, or avoiding relationships in case of interpersonal conflict. Rather than centring on approach motivation and paying attention to needs and desires, avoiding triggers can push an individual into an avoidant mode of functioning that maintains the setting conditions for future depression.

A key part of the treatment is supporting and encouraging the client to respond differently when they feel depressed: learning the difference between the downward and upward spirals; paying attention to needs and desires; engaging in actions intended to satisfy needs; reflecting on the consequences of actions rather than ruminating about causes, and so on. The aim is to help the client develop the efficacy and confidence to stay out of a downward spiral when a depressed mood occurs. Notice also that compared with first-onsets, and perhaps earlier recurrences, contextual factors are usually a less focal part of the treatment. We say 'usually', because there will be particular circumstances when major events or severe stress have occurred. Highly recurrent depression can be maintained without such events, but that does not mean they never happen. When they occur they need to be formulated like any other case, in terms of their impact on downward and upward spirals.

Overall, the treatment goals for highly recurrent depression require a subtle combination of acceptance and change: (a) *acceptance that depressed moods sometimes happen*: they are generally unpredictable and can't always be avoided; (b) *learn how to respond so that depressed moods are reversed and time-limited*: the client needs to learn that their response to the mood influences its trajectory. This is a subtly different rationale to aiming for a sustained recovery following a discrete depressive episode. Sustained recovery should never be ruled out or dismissed: but in the case of highly recurrent depression, it is usually best to start with goals focused on *improvement* and find out how much progress can be made. A full recovery is a possibility when there is sufficient progress.

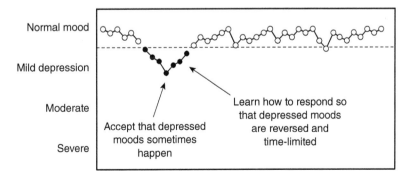

Figure 8.1   Treatment rationale for highly recurrent depression

In Evelyn's case four treatment goals were agreed: (1) faster recovery from depressed moods; (2) longer periods between depressed moods; (3) less severe symptoms during depressed phases; and (4) fewer residual symptoms after depressed phases.

Evelyn initially received 24 therapy sessions over a 10-month acute phase, this dose and time-course reflecting the entrenched nature of her mood disorder. The downward spiral model was used to help her understand the reactivation process, and she recognized a recurring pattern of being demotivated, disengaged and ruminative when her mood plummeted unpredictably, as illustrated in Figure 8.2.

As we have already outlined in Chapters 6 and 7, this formulation is used as a basis for *approach motivation, behavioural engagement* and *reflective processing* in the first phase of treatment. In Evelyn's case this was framed as a way of responding when her mood became unexpectedly depressed:

- Accept you are in a depressed mood rather than analyse why.
- Pay attention to what you *feel like* doing:
  - ○ Resist impulses to avoid, escape or hide.
  - ○ Trust impulses to engage with your needs and desires.

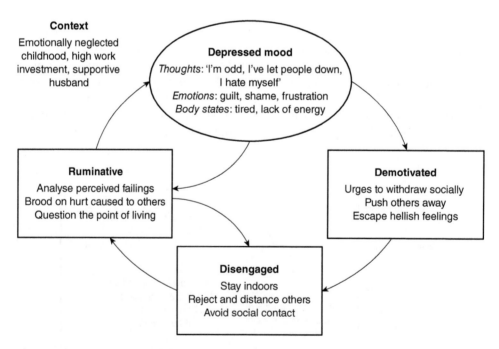

Figure 8.2   Evelyn's downward spiral formulation

- Stay engaged with plans and activities.
- Remain connected with other people.
- Place at least some of your attention externally, not just on your thoughts and feelings.
- Try to notice the consequence of your actions, rather than analyse yourself or your life.

Evelyn also used the upward spiral as a way of approaching situations that she was dreading or worried about. For example, if she was predicting that an event would go badly, she learned to ask herself what she would *like to happen* in that situation, then engage in actions to influence her preferred outcome. She would be encouraged to approach the situation as an experiment to find out how much influence she could have. It is important to use this strategy in a consistent way over several situations, not just as a one-off technique. Evelyn learned that, in general, she had more influence over her preferences than she expected. However, her preferred outcome did not always happen, and sometimes what she had been fearing or dreading did happen. However, she learned that seeking to bring about preferred outcomes usually improved her mood, whereas dreading unwanted outcomes would tend to keep her feeling depressed and anxious.

Risk Assessment

In the first phase of Evelyn's treatment, risk assessment played a prominent part. In the 19 months preceding her CBT, Evelyn had kept a daily mood diary using a 0–10 scale: 0 = very severe depression; 10 = feeling OK. This was used as a pre-treatment baseline and it is illustrated in Figure 8.3. With scores of 6/10 or more, Evelyn felt life was bearable and worth living, but any less than 6/10 she felt unmotivated and was prone to becoming socially withdrawn. Scores of 4/10 or less were associated with suicidality, both rumination and considering action. As Figure 8.3 illustrates, Evelyn experienced cyclical periods of depression that would last several months. These did not have a seasonal pattern and in between times she would feel reasonably OK, work long hours running her business, and enjoy holidays with her husband. There was a lot of variability within phases, so in the depressed phase there would be occasional OK days and in the OK phase there would be occasional depressed days. As indicated in Figure 8.3, in the previous 19 months there had been at least six occasions during which Evelyn had been affected by significant suicidality.

The first point to emphasize is, all practitioners are strongly encouraged to follow the agreed risk procedures within their healthcare organization. The following guidance is intended to *support* and *augment* those procedures, but it should never replace them. We cannot envisage a scenario in which there would be a conflict between the two, but in the event that this should happen, we encourage practitioners to prioritize their organization's agreed procedures.

Within the integrated approach, suicidal risk is formulated *within* the downward spiral model, therefore it is viewed as a constituent part of the therapy. Suicide is understood as a lethal form of disengagement. When people attempt to kill themselves there is usually an extended process that starts with a momentary thought (e.g. 'I wish I wasn't here') and over time this deepens and grows into beliefs, images, intentions, plans or actions. The process involves a range of thoughts, emotions, body states, motivations and behaviours unfolding over time.

Suicidal thoughts are typically self-attacking such as 'I don't deserve to live' or 'others would be better off without me', however from another perspective these are attempts at self-help. For someone enduring intense depression, the prospect of suicide can be strangely comforting, particularly if they feel hopeless about improvement or recovery. It is a perceived means of stopping something unbearable, or escaping a trapped situation: it is a fall-back, a last resort if depression continues and nothing else leads to improvement. In those states the prospect of suicide can be soothing, but for many people it is also conflictual, distressing and frightening. Not many people have an ambition for suicide; they do not grow up with a desire to end their own life. On the contrary, depression is an accident and when people feel trapped in it they want an escape route; they want a release from misery and a resolution to problems that appear insurmountable and unending. Suicide attempts, without the full intention of dying, can also be acts of communication and cries for help.

Not surprisingly there is usually some ambivalence and motivational conflict about suicide; some approach impulses and some avoidance. This can manifest as an internal struggle about whether to engage with suicidal impulses or resist them, and this can be highly ruminative. People may have moral or ethical concerns; they may be afraid of pain or unintended disability; they may be concerned about unwanted effects on

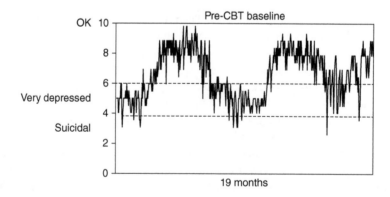

Figure 8.3   Evelyn's daily mood ratings in the 19 months prior to CBT

others, and so on. Hence for many depressed people, death becomes a *passive goal*: they are comforted by the thought of not waking up tomorrow or dying in an accident, but they do not form an intention to die or make plans to end their life.

Risk is considerably higher when people engage in preparatory behaviours: for example, exploring methods, obtaining the means, forming plans, setting a time or date, engaging in risky behaviours, behaving impulsively, using substances, and so on. These are engaged behaviours but they serve the *higher-order goal to disengage*; hence we understand them as part of a withdrawal process. When there are signs of heightened risk it is important that safety becomes the priority for that session. Even if other plans were in place, treatment can only benefit clients who are alive to receive it. It is important to continue to work collaboratively with the client; to view safety as a fundamental part of the therapy rather than a separate procedure. There are various steps to address suicidality effectively.

1 Ask questions about suicidal thoughts, impulses and plans

If there is a long history of suicidality it is likely some of this information will already be shared, in which case focus on recent changes in suicidality, including any contextual or internal changes that have increased the likelihood of thoughts becoming actions. In the vast majority of cases this information will map onto the downward spiral: depression is deepening and having a self-destructive effect on the client. The therapist's role is to help the client recognize that engaging with these thoughts and impulses is maintaining and deepening their depression. To return to health the client needs to resist these impulses, engage with other thoughts and feelings, and seek alternative solutions to problems that appear insoluble. In a proportion of cases this rationale will be sufficient to help the client decentre, reflect on the downward spiral and motivate them to re-engage with the upward spiral. The key point is the client needs to commit to staying safe and accept whatever support is needed to achieve that.

2 Learn how to respond to suicidal thoughts and impulses

Even if suicidal thoughts and impulses are unwanted it doesn't mean that they will not recur. As we have already outlined, a proportion of memories and thoughts are intrusive and uninvited, so the client needs to be prepared for them to come back. If a client has already recognized it is unhelpful to engage with these thoughts and impulses, we can have some hope they will have the same appraisal at a later date, but we should not assume it. Clients' appraisals of suicidal thoughts in the therapy room may or may not generalize to other situations, so we need to prepare the client for feeling tempted to engage with suicidal impulses at a later point.

The most helpful response to suicidal thoughts and impulses is to notice they are present and *relate to them as events in the mind or body*. It will not help to push them away or suppress them, because a rebound effect is likely. It is also unhelpful to act on them or ruminate about them. What matters is how clients respond when the thoughts or impulses are present. Are they able to notice the thoughts and not engage with them? The aim is reflective processing and mindful awareness rather than rumination or thought suppression. Are they able to feel impulses and not act on them? The aim is to attend to approach impulses, rather than urges to avoid or escape. It is worth testing this out in a behavioural experiment, to find out if the client is able to tolerate suicidal thoughts or urges. If the client is able to tolerate them and agrees to others being informed, such as the family doctor, this level of assessment and intervention is appropriate for the presenting risk. The next therapy session should be scheduled soon and there should be a review of suicidal thoughts and impulses: did they recur and how did the client respond to them? Did the client access additional support if it was needed?

3 The intervention needs to be stepped up if clients are ambivalent about staying safe

If suicidal thoughts and impulses are mapped onto the downward spiral and the client's response is to the effect 'it doesn't matter if this makes me more depressed; I won't be alive to feel it', then risk is very high and requires further attention. There are two main aspects. One is for third parties to become actively involved, such as family members, the family doctor, crisis team and other health/social care professionals. The risk needs to be shared so that others are alerted and engaged in supporting the client through this period. Request your client's consent for others to be involved and do all you can to maintain a strong therapeutic alliance. However, if the client does not consent, there is a duty of care to inform others when risk is very high. A therapeutic rupture may result, but that needs to be balanced with the presenting risk.

The second aspect is to engage with the upward spiral in the therapy session, in other words: turn attention to what the client needs and desires, engage in actions that will satisfy needs and reflect on the consequences of actions, rather than their causes or meanings. One way to do this is to take seriously the client's suicidal intention or plan, to better understand their motivation and what they hope it will achieve. Figure 8.4 presents a structure for doing this. This was completed with Evelyn in an early therapy session when she was ambivalent about resisting suicidal impulses.

It is best to start with the *intended consequences* of suicide: what does the client hope it would it achieve? In Evelyn's case, when she was severely depressed, she felt powerless to overcome hellish feelings and the main attraction of suicide was a way of ending those feelings. There was also some anticipated relief in no longer being herself. Notably, however, she only experienced these impulses when her mood was severely depressed, so they were mood-state dependent. Evelyn would start to consider methods of suicide and her attention would narrow around the expected benefits. Some client's expectations are unrealistic, for example, imagining suicide will create a blissful feeling of calm or serenity, when in fact it would result in the permanent cessation of all experience.

The second aspect to consider is *unintended consequences*. This is very important to cover because clients' attention can otherwise narrow around desired outcomes and fail to consider the full reality of suicidal actions, including: what can go wrong during suicidal acts; whether it would be painful or painless; whether it would be quick or slow; whether there is a risk of illness or disability; if completed, how the body would appear afterwards, who would discover it, when and how loved ones would find out, the emotional impact on family, friends and colleagues, etc. In Evelyn's case, the primary protective factor was her knowledge of how devastating the experience would be for her husband, who was very loving and devoted. This was not a straightforward deterrent, however, because during severe depression Evelyn sometimes felt frustrated that her husband's presence blocked her from ending her life. She would try to hide this from him, creating a cauldron of intense emotions: guilt at the effect of her depression on him, yet also a brooding resentment that his presence prevented her escaping life through suicide.

The third aspect is designed to further broaden attention, to consider *reasons for living* that are not just based on avoiding the unwanted consequences of suicide. In this respect Evelyn could bring to mind aspects of work that gave her satisfaction, plus the knowledge that she and her husband sometimes enjoyed good holidays, though it was difficult for her to remember specific occasions when she was severely depressed. On their own these were not powerful deterrents from suicide, but they reminded Evelyn she did not always feel severely depressed, and there was a strong likelihood these feelings would lift and improve as they had on all previous occasions. In the first phase of treatment Evelyn doubted that severely depressed moods would ever lift, but she gradually learned these moods were time-limited and reversible.

The fourth aspect is focusing on *alternative actions* to suicide: are there other ways of dealing with challenges that don't involve killing yourself? The aim is to harness broadened attention regarding unwanted consequences and reasons for living, to plan alternative behaviours that are concrete and imminent. Ideally, alternative actions will achieve some of the desired consequences of suicide, without the

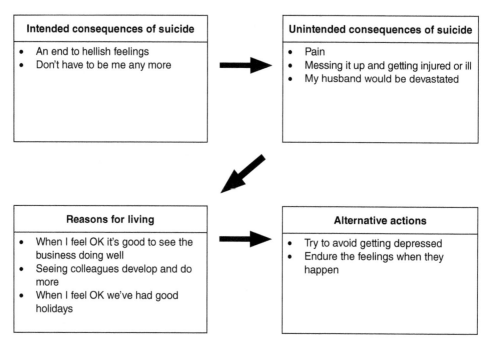

Figure 8.4 **Reflection on suicidal thoughts, impulses and plans**

suicide; for example, giving Evelyn alternative ways of coping with hellish feelings, and helping her to feel better about herself and her life. Framed as un-met needs, this is a way of switching from avoidance/escape to approach: an alternative to 'ending hellish feelings' could be noticing and reversing depressed moods more effectively; an alternative to 'not being you' could be investing more in the aspects of yourself that you do like and respect.

Initially, Evelyn viewed alternative actions in terms of avoidance and endurance: trying to stop getting depressed and putting up with it when it happened. Gradually she began to recognize that her methods of avoidance and endurance, although they may occasionally have short-term benefits, were contributing to triggering and maintaining depressed moods. For example, Evelyn's way of enduring severe depression was to stay in bed and be rude to her husband as a way of distancing from him, so she could endure the feelings on her own and minimize her guilt about its indirect effects on him. Over time she began to recognize this created isolation and angry rumination, maintaining her depression rather than reversing it.

Hopefully these more detailed reflections, summarized in Figure 8.4, are sufficient for clients to decide to keep themselves safe. If that is achieved, the guidance from point 2, above, is followed with a focus on how to respond to suicidal thoughts and impulses when they occur. However, if the detailed reflections in Figure 8.4 do not have the desired effect and the client it is still tempted by suicidal urges, or feels unable to resist them, it is essential to alert other professionals and family members to create a co-ordinated response to manage the risk. Increase the frequency of therapy sessions and ensure the client has a clear plan of who they are due to meet when, and how to ask for more help if they need it. It may also be necessary for the client to be assessed under the Mental Health Act by a duty psychiatrist, particularly if they have imminent plans to end their life. It is incumbent on all therapists working with major depression to be familiar with the relevant procedures in their organization for this eventuality.

Self-organization

Over the first sixteen sessions, Evelyn gradually became less avoidant and started to handle suicidal ruminations differently. There was a small but significant change in her belief that depressed moods were unending and outside her influence. She began to approach dreaded situations with a greater sense of purpose, learning that she sometimes had more influence in those situations than she realized. However, it was very difficult for Evelyn to accept the unpredictability of her moods. At the start of treatment, Evelyn's moods triggered and reversed unpredictably, as if they were liable to semi-automatic switching. A common pattern was intense guilt and self-blame in response to others being disadvantaged or unfairly treated, for example, family members, employees or customers. Evelyn was also prone to feeling odd, different and disconnected in social situations; however, this did not happen all the time. She was highly socially skilled, a strong leader in the workplace, and not usually anxious around other people. It remained a matter of extreme frustration to her that these mood changes were so unpredictable and she was unable to gain control over them.

To understand the switching process better, Evelyn and her therapist turned their attention to the structural level of memories, self-representations and goals. The extended formulation is illustrated in Figure 8.5. In terms of self-representations from *early learning*, Evelyn was a highly intelligent, emotionally sensitive girl raised by parents who were unhappily married but stayed together out of loyalty to their vows and their daughter. Evelyn felt close to her mother when she was younger, but less so as she approached adolescence. Regrettably, her parents enacted their conflicts through heated and unresolved arguments throughout Evelyn's childhood. They were less intelligent than Evelyn, and unaware of the damaging effects of their behaviour on her wellbeing. Evelyn grew up dreading her parents' arguments and felt emotionally drained by the atmosphere of conflict and hostility in the family home. She developed a felt-responsibility to try to improve the situation. She often felt unhappy and only later realized she had been depressed at least some of her childhood, feeling responsible for her parents' unhappiness and ultimately helpless to prevent it.

Evelyn did not suffer abuse or trauma but her emotional needs were overlooked and neglected when her parents' attention was focused on their resentment of each other. Evelyn worked hard at school, sometimes compulsively, and was successful in her exams. This gave her a distraction from home life and a level of efficacy and self-esteem. It was the main vehicle for her adolescent transition. Distraction also became a frequently used coping strategy. She did well at university, studying agriculture, and

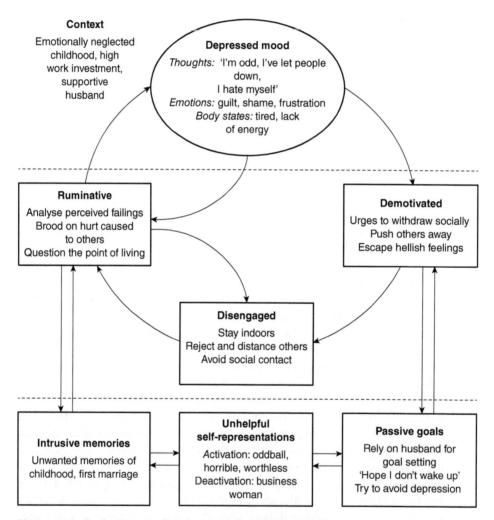

Figure 8.5   Evelyn's extended downward spiral formulation

in the following years built up a highly successful market gardening business that employed several hundred staff. Her main *modus operandi* was to invest heavily in work, where her attention was more externally focused, and she was able to feel productive and useful at least some of the time. Reminders of her childhood and conflictual first marriage could be distressing for Evelyn, particularly the feeling of being disconnected and ill-fitting in the world, which dominated her adolescence. Her guilt at the effects of the first marriage on her grown-up daughters could also be overwhelming and provoke a phase shift in self-identity.

The emerging self-identity formulation is presented in Figure 8.6. Evelyn internalized a felt-sense of *independence* and *responsibility* as a young child that had an adaptive range: it enabled her to organize her life outside the family and be highly engaged in educational goals, so much so that she became known in her high school as the person who would help with other people's homework. This led to success at university and in her subsequent career, leading to a self-representation as a *successful business woman*. Notice, however, that Evelyn's idiosyncratic self-organization represented this in terms of her responsibility to her staff and customers, not her abilities in building a successful business. Evelyn could grudgingly acknowledge she was an educated and capable person, but these were barely admissible *facts* rather than *self-representations*: they were not how she represented herself.

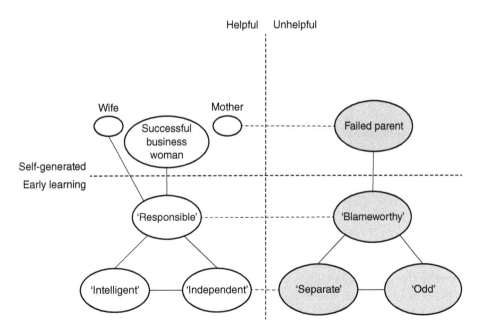

Figure 8.6   Switching conditions between helpful and unhelpful self-representations

Conversely, her adverse early experiences resulted in internalizing a felt-sense of being *blameworthy* for the family conflicts and being unable to resolve them. This was the unhelpful consequence of having such a strong sense of responsibility. Similarly, the unhelpful consequence of being independent was a felt-sense of *disconnection*, *separateness* and *oddness* that was upsetting and distressing for Evelyn. When these representations were activated she would experience a plummeting of mood, followed by intense guilt and self-loathing. They would also activate a representation as a *failed parent* that had developed during her first marriage.

Consequently, Evelyn and her therapist realized that the switching in her mood could be understood in terms of whether helpful or unhelpful nodes were dominant. In terms of Evelyn's inner experience, her felt-sense of being blameworthy, separate and odd was powerful and self-defining. She compensated this felt-sense by being a successful business woman. This helped to make sense of Evelyn investing heavily in her work, and her preference to distract herself from reflecting on her past, feelings or current self. Work-related activity had the potential to deactivate 'blameworthy, separate and odd' and activate 'successful business woman'. When Evelyn was able to maintain that pattern of activation, it helped to ward off depression and generate euthymic mood. However, there were several difficulties maintaining her preferred self-identity:

- *Multiple cues.* There were a large number of internal and external cues that would activate 'blameworthy, separate and odd', including social situations, mistakes, memories and other daily events. This made it unfeasible to avoid these representations from being activated at least some of the time, and usually unpredictably.
- *Internal connections.* Evelyn's helpful representations were thematically linked to the unhelpful nodes, the best example being responsible/blameworthy. Consequently, inferential activity in a helpful domain could easily lead to unhelpful structures being activated.
- *Over-investment in work.* Evelyn's investment in being a successful business woman was wholehearted and time-consuming. She did not have interests outside of work, had no close friends, and her only social life was organized by her husband as joint activities. Consequently, when the business was going well, Evelyn's mood tended to be OK – but feeling OK was fragile and highly dependent on events at work, not all of which were under her control.
- *Self-depression fusion.* A major complication was Evelyn's strong identification with the depressed state when she was in it, as if severe depression was her true self. Even when her mood was OK she was prone to believing she was pretending life was worth living by having a successful business. In the depressed state, Evelyn viewed her business as a mere coping strategy; a temporary illusion warding off the inevitability of returning to the full truth of self-loathing.

The formulation of Evelyn's self-organization led to two main therapeutic strategies; firstly, encouragement to *diversify* outside of work and construct new self-representations. This was fully supported by Evelyn's husband, who was concerned how engrossed and stressed Evelyn could become when work was particularly busy. The aim was to create new memories and self-representations through a process of *diversification*, analogous to the identity formation process during adolescence. Secondly, when a client identifies so strongly with the depressed state it can be helpful to build an alternative explanation of how they have come to dislike themselves so much. This can be done using a Theory A/B format, as below.

Competing Theories about Evelyn's Self-representations

- Theory A: I'm a disconnected and odd person who lets other people down, and I feel depressed because this is just how I am. No matter what I do I can't change myself. I distract myself by over-working and trying to do good, but sooner or later I return to feeling depressed, because this is what I'm like and I hate it.
- Theory B: My parents had relationship problems throughout my childhood and this had a deep effect on me. When they were preoccupied with resenting each other, my needs were overlooked. I did not receive sufficient attention, understanding or compassion and this made it difficult to develop compassion for myself. Instead I internalized the atmosphere of hostility at home and was left feeling overly responsible for my parents' conflicts. I am *not* odd or unacceptable to others: these are normal self-doubts young people go through, but I didn't have the parenting I needed, so I internalized these ideas as if they were true, and now they sometimes *feel true*. My heightened sense of responsibility leads me to be overly self-blaming and this becomes self-attacking when I feel depressed.

When in euthymic mood Evelyn was able to decentre and recognize the truth in Theory B, however even then she would experience some guilt as if she was blaming her parents and not taking sufficient responsibility for her own problems. The main problem was what happened when her mood became more severely depressed. In that mood-state, Theory B would appear to be a flimsy set of excuses, and Theory A would *feel* true. This fusion of self and depression could provoke a pronounced downward spiral, and it took several months for Evelyn to respond differently when her unhelpful self-representations were activated. Therapy did not stop these activations occurring, but Evelyn gradually began to respond differently when it happened. It can best be described as *trying to suspend belief in Theory A*: remembering Theory B, resisting impulses to avoid and withdraw, staying engaged in plans and activities, and focusing on present experiences rather than analysing self, depression and life.

The net effect of these changes is illustrated in Figure 8.7 which shows the progression of Evelyn's mood diary over the acute phase. By the end of twenty-four sessions across 10 months, Evelyn's PHQ-9 score had reduced to 2 which was a clinically significant improvement. However, the pattern of *mood variation* was as important as her symptoms at any point in time. The data suggested improvement in key areas. Evelyn was achieving faster recovery from depressed moods, had less severe symptoms during depressed phases, and fewer residual symptoms following them. However, the pattern of recurrence had become *more* frequent, not less, even though Evelyn's functioning during depressed moods was better than before. Compared with the pre-CBT baseline, the number of days with mood ratings less than 6 was significantly fewer and there were no days with ratings of 4 or less.

Evelyn's observations about the change process were helpful in making sense of the data. She reported using the scale differently since the start of CBT. As she described it, although the numbers on the graph had changed she did not feel much subjective change in the *emotions* she experienced during depressed moods. When she felt guilty she felt just as guilty as before, and so on. However, she reported ruminating less about negative feelings and not letting them get in the way of her plans to the same extent. She described less self-loathing and a greater belief that depressed moods would reverse. Her appraisal of the value of these changes depended on her

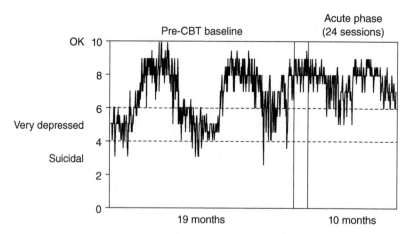

Figure 8.7 Mood changes and fluctuations across the acute phase

mood. During periods of depression, Evelyn would doubt there had been any change, or at least not one that was meaningful to her. When her mood was OK she would agree there had been significant improvement, though it remained a disappointment to her that CBT did not prevent depressed moods recurring: this remained difficult for her to accept.

Staying Well

In Chapter 4 we considered methods for preventing relapse and staying well. Notice that Evelyn had several of the key features of clients at greater risk of relapse:

- *Significant childhood adversity* – neglected emotional and support needs.
- *Early onset of depression* – first major episode before the age of 18.
- *Highly recurrent depression* – multiple previous episodes.
- *Unstable remission* – response to treatment, but with intermittent symptom reversals and residual symptoms.

It was therefore important to prioritize Evelyn for continuation therapy, so she moved into a 21-month continuation phase, with approximately monthly booster sessions. Her depression was not in remission by the end of the acute phase but we were able to use the principles of Continuation Cognitive Therapy (C-CT), as summarized in Chapter 4, to help her maintain her treatment gains: consolidate and generalize learning; pay attention to setbacks and signs of relapse; learn how to reverse cognitive reactivation when it occurred.

In Chapter 4 we reported Angela's stress test and her robustness to cognitive reactivation. In Evelyn's case, naturalistic stressors regularly triggered mild depression and cognitive reactivation occurred on an approximately monthly basis. Consequently the therapeutic focus was to help Evelyn reverse the effects of reactivation when it occurred: to resist impulses to avoid, withdraw, escape or disengage; turn attention to present needs and desires; engage in behaviours to satisfy those needs; reflect on the consequence of actions rather than ruminate about meanings and implications.

In Evelyn's case, staying well was complicated by her memory for therapy sessions; it was very difficult for her to remember details. Long-term depression (recurrent or chronic) can impact negatively on cognitive functioning and in Evelyn's case her memories for certain events were over-general and lacking specificity. Consequently, in the absence of booster sessions she was largely reliant on *implicit* CBT knowledge and *automatic* processes to help her stay well. Given her risk profile, there was likely to be a gap between the challenges produced by cognitive reactivation, and her capacity to stay well through implicit knowledge.

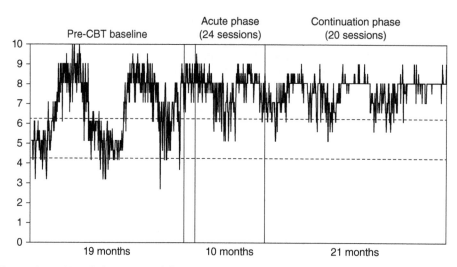

Figure 8.8   Mood changes and fluctuations in the continuation phase

This is indeed what happened. After regular therapeutic contact in the acute phase, Evelyn's memory of what she had learned decayed significantly and this enabled downward spirals to take hold and maintain depressed moods. The function of monthly booster sessions was to strengthen and maintain Evelyn's *memories of CBT*, otherwise she would forget what she had learned and be less well placed to respond to cognitive reactivations. The ultimate aim is for continuation sessions to be temporary, not permanent: in other words, CBT remains time-limited. The aim was for Evelyn's learning to deepen and memories to strengthen so she could self-regulate effectively without regular therapeutic input. As sessions became less frequent, Evelyn was able to keep her mood in the 'OK' range most of the time without therapeutic support. She had gradually internalized the CBT and could access the learning when it was most needed. Her daily diary illustrates this enduring effect, depicted in Figure 8.8.

Practitioner Tips: Highly Recurrent Depression

- In highly recurrent depression, minor stress can be sufficient to trigger depressive episodes, through a process of *cognitive reactivation*. Mild negative affect (NA) can activate depressing thoughts and memories from previous depressive episodes: this is why mood can be reactive and unstable. Try to help your client *accept* that this will happen from time to time. Rather than trying to avoid it, learn how best to respond so that depressed moods are reversed and time-limited.

- Major life stress is less likely to be the treatment focus, because depression can be precipitated without it. However, life stress sometimes occurs, and when it does contextual factors need to be incorporated in treatment in the usual way.

- During heightened risk of suicide, clients' attention tends to narrow around the *intended* consequences of death, that is, the perceived advantages of not being alive. In this situation, try to: (a) broaden clients' attention to consider *unintended* consequences; (b) find alternative ways of achieving the perceived advantages, that don't involve self-destruction. For example, if suicide is attractive because it would put an end to mental turmoil and escape a bad relationship, explore other ways of finding mental peace and resolving relationship problems.

- When mood has improved, and clients are more reflective and less ruminative, work together to map out their unique *self-organization*, that is, the various self-representations they have internalized at different points in the lifespan. It will help self-regulation to have an explicit map of different self-states. It can also help to uncouple *self-depression fusion*, in other words, identification with the depressed state. Encourage reflection on how unhelpful self-identities became internalized; this can give clients an alternative explanation why they sometimes dislike themselves and become depressed.

- Sometimes clients over-invest in one preferred self-identity to deactivate other self-representations that have a depressing effect. There is a logic to this strategy, but it can narrow attention in the over-invested area and lead to secondary problems. When this occurs, encourage *diversification* so that the client has a broader range of helpful identities.

- People with highly recurrent depression are at risk of relapse and recurrence, particularly if they: (a) have an unstable remission with residual symptoms; (b) suffered trauma, neglect or abuse in childhood; (c) experienced an early-onset depression during adolescence (see Chapter 7). It is essential to provide booster sessions to high-risk clients, to help them consolidate and generalize their learning. Memory for the therapy can be incomplete and implicit, so continuation should aim to make their learning more explicit. Clients need *accessible memories* of treatment that they can use to stay well when faced with challenges and setbacks.

9

Chronic and Persistent Depression

People with chronic and persistent depression form a heterogeneous group who have been in a major depressive episode for at least the past 2 years. As one might expect, when an individual has been in depression for a long period of time, it is much less likely that they will *suddenly* return to euthymic mood and normal functioning. Most people with chronic depression can recover, or at least make significant improvements, but as illustrated in Figure 9.1, the trajectory of change is usually slow, gradual and stepwise compared with non-chronic depression. This has implications for parameters such as the dose of treatment and frequency of therapy sessions (McCullough, 2003).

A recent meta-analysis of psychotherapy for chronic depression, including CBT, found larger effects in studies providing a greater number of therapy sessions, with at least eighteen sessions needed to treat adequately. Studies providing over thirty sessions

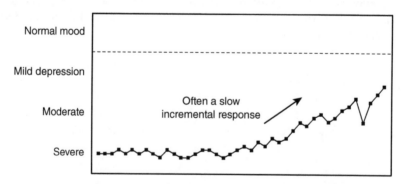

Figure 9.1   Typical treatment response to CBT for chronic depression

found larger effects (Cuijpers et al., 2010). In Chapter 8 we saw how recurrent depression can have a reactivating, oscillating pattern with individuals switching between different mood-states. These features can also present in chronic depression, but the more common pattern is a stable depressed state with individuals enjoying few, if any, periods of wellness and euthymic mood (Barnhofer, Brennan, Crane, Duggan & Williams, 2014). Recurrent depression tends to be associated with unstable or reactive mood, whereas persistent depression is associated with overly stable mood-states that have the appearance of being 'stuck in a rut' (Moore & Garland, 2003). They tend to be relatively unresponsive to external and internal change. Some clients will have periods of overly stable mood, then periods of reactive mood, but it is more common to have one predominant type. As we noted in Chapter 2, less experienced therapists sometimes struggle treating chronic depression: it can be frustrating and dispiriting when the change process is difficult and slow. The aim of this chapter is to explore how to adapt treatment to meet these clients' needs, including adjustments to service parameters and the optimal therapeutic approach.

Chronic Sub-types

Twenty per cent of major depressive episodes develop a persistent and chronic course and risk factors for this include: family history of mood disorder, history of childhood abuse, early-onset depression and high levels of comorbidity (Garcia-Torro et al., 2013; Holtzel, Harter, Reese & Kriston, 2011). Not surprisingly, when clients have been depressed for a long period of time they tend to experience self-depression fusion, helplessness and hopelessness (Riso & Newman, 2003). Nevertheless, people with persistent depression do not form a single homogenous group. It is helpful to consider different patterns of chronicity, and in our experience four questions are important to ask clients in the assessment phase:

1. When did the current episode of depression begin?
2. Looking back on your life, have you had periods of wellness when you were not depressed?
3. Which treatments have you received?
4. How helpful have those treatments been for you?

Before embarking on a course of CBT it is highly advisable to find out the answers to these questions. They will help to inform the treatment parameters and therapeutic approach most likely to be helpful in each case. In our experience, the answers to these questions reveal three main chronic sub-types that require a subtly different treatment approach: *recent chronicity*, *prior wellness* and *lifelong depression*. These have different courses and mood patterns across the lifespan, as illustrated in Figure 9.2.

We want to stress that these are patterns and are not meant to exclude particular variations or hybrid forms. For each individual it is good practice to map out their unique depression history, although it can be difficult to obtain a fully accurate picture by only asking your client. As we have already observed, depression exerts a negative cognitive bias and has an obstructing effect on access to specific autobiographical memories. Without intending it, depressed clients can under-represent periods of wellness in their life, because memories of those times are less available during depressed moods. It is therefore helpful to ask specific questions about different phases of life, and triangulate the answers with clinical records and family member accounts.

Some clients will have experienced long-term mild depression, called dysthymia, with major episodes superimposed. This is sometimes called 'double depression'. We don't directly address dysthymia in this chapter but it is important to be aware of it as a risk factor for major depression. Other clients will have experienced recurrent episodes that gradually become more persistent and chronic. Others will have sustained periods of wellness with chronic episodes interspersed, and so on. What matters is to identify the relevant features for each case and respond to them as needed.

Recent Chronicity

It might appear paradoxical to describe depression as both chronic *and* recent, but we are referring to people who have only recently met diagnostic criteria for chronic depression. Their depression is 'technically' chronic. In relation to the overall lifespan, 2 years is not a long period of time, though it is likely to *feel* a long time for the

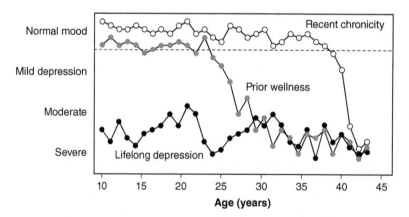

Figure 9.2   Examples of common sub-types of chronic and persistent depression

person stuck in depression. A person who has been depressed for 2 years has a different change potential compared with someone who has been depressed for 20 years. The prognosis and treatment approach are substantially different. Two years is probably a small percentage of their whole life: 7% in a 30-year-old, 5% in a 40-year-old, 4% in a 50-year-old, and so on. In other words, it is not necessary *at this stage* to assume that recently chronic cases are treatment-resistant or have complex psychopathology. Either of those may be true, but it is too early to say. Something is causing their depression to persist, and it is important to find out what that is and tackle it.

As would be expected, people who have been depressed a long time are likely to have received a variety of treatments, both pharmacological and psychological. However, this is not necessarily true for recently chronic clients. One explanation for the persistence of their depression is that they have not yet received the treatment they need. Some of this group will have relatively straightforward problems that will respond to a standard course of CBT, if or when it is provided. Others may have unusual or complicating factors that are contributing to the persistence of their difficulties. We have represented these possibilities in Table 9.1 in considering answers to two key questions: (1) Has an adequate course of CBT already been provided? (2) Could unusual or complicating factors be contributing to the persistence of the depression?

Many recently chronic cases will respond to an evidence-based therapy, such as CBT, but they may be unaware of it, have been told it is unavailable in their locality, or are currently waiting to receive it. Until an adequate course of therapy has been provided it is premature to conclude that something unusual or complicated is maintaining their depression. Even if this is strongly suspected, for example the presence of trauma, childhood abuse or physical health complications – it doesn't follow that an established CBT protocol will not help. In fact, all available evidence suggests that standard CBT

Table 9.1   Decision tree for recently chronic cases

		Has an adequate course of CBT already been provided?	
		No	**Yes**
Could unusual or complicating factors be contributing to the persistence of the depression?	**Probably no**	Provide an established course of CBT and monitor the outcome	Provide an alternative treatment or different type of CBT
	Probably yes	Find out how much an established course of CBT helps	Adjust CBT for persistent or complex cases

protocols *can* help in the treatment of chronic and complex cases. Complexity is the focus of Part IV of the book and we will explore there what is meant by a complex case and how best to approach treatment when complexity is present.

Within this sub-group there can also be people who have received inadequate treatment, for example, polypharmacy or sub-therapeutic doses of medication or CBT. In the mind of the client, these could have the appearance of a full course of treatment. An intervention *informed* by CBT is not the same as a full course of cognitive-behavioural *therapy*. Low-intensity cognitive-behavioural interventions can be extremely effective treating mild or moderate depression, but they are unlikely to meet the needs of people with chronic, severe depression. There is potential harm if clients conclude that neither medication nor CBT worked for them when, in fact, there are several major classes of anti-depressant medication, and multiple ways of adapting CBT based on client need.

Recently chronic clients need hopeful therapists who encourage engagement with a full course of CBT. Sustained recovery is a realistic goal. To encourage client engagement it is usually best to start with the modest aim of improving mood and achieving a reduction in depression symptoms. This can feel more realistic to clients who, by now, tend to feel helpless and hopeless about change. When some improvement has been achieved then aim for further improvement, and so on, so there is a stepwise graded approach to finding out how much improvement is possible. The main difference compared with non-chronic depression is the greater likelihood of slow and gradual change so, on average, clients need a longer period of time to overcome the depressed state, not just a greater number of sessions. It is essential to make those expectations explicit during treatment planning, for example, to ask how soon the client is hoping to feel better, what it will be like for them if progress is slow to begin with, and so on.

Although more time and a greater number of sessions are usually needed, it is best not to have a vague or open-ended therapy contract. What works best is to offer blocks of sessions with proximal goals, for example, offering around ten sessions initially to find out what progress can be made. Link this to very concrete goals, such as improved self-care, going out of the house more often, and so on. Then review and consider further blocks of sessions to find out what further progress can be achieved. Clients should be made aware that full recovery is possible, but usually requires longer-term treatment. In all other respects treatment can be approached in the normal way.

We have already considered a recently chronic case when we described Angela in Chapter 2. After 4 years of depression she had a partial response to anti-depressant medication but no prior CBT. She was successfully treated in a standard course of Beck's CBT, although it is worth revisiting Figure 2.2 to consider the change trajectory in her symptoms. For the first fifteen sessions there was no symptomatic reduction, and it was only thereafter her mood began to improve. This is a good example of the 'stuckness' of chronic depression and the time it can take to return to wellness, even in the absence of marked complexity. It also highlights the need for realistic expectations so that clients and therapists do not become dispirited when progress is slow initially.

Prior Wellness

Angela spent 4 years in depression and was able to return to euthymic mood after a standard course of CBT. Unfortunately, some chronic cases do not return to wellness, and for them depression becomes a normal way of life. These people have typically been depressed for 5–10 years and sometimes substantially longer. In such cases *resignation* and *mental defeat* are commonplace: depression can become a dominant, oppressive force in their life that weighs heavily and limits their enjoyment and functioning. There is little, if any, respite from it. Typically there are intermittent periods of help-seeking interspersed with phases of hopelessness about change.

Nevertheless, a sub-group of chronically depressed people have had previous phases of wellness earlier in their lifespan, and this is an important factor in their prognosis and treatment. For example, recall Bob whose treatment we described in Chapter 3. He had been depressed for the past 12 years but had no history of depression, or other mental health problems prior to this. Twelve years is a long time to be stuck in depression, and maintenance processes can become very habitual and entrenched over such a long period. However, the history of prior wellness suggests two factors worthy of consideration:

1. The person had, and perhaps still has, a capacity for adaptive functioning and euthymic mood.
2. Whatever their susceptibilities to depression, they did not trigger depressive episodes earlier in the lifespan.

These facts signal hope: it is worth finding out how much improvement is possible and whether the person can return to a non-depressed state. This does not mean they are likely to recover quickly; but it means recovery is *possible*, precisely because there are psychological states that previously existed and could be *recovered* or *rediscovered*. This is the main reason for differentiating *prior wellness* and *lifelong depression*. As we will see later, when a person has lifelong depression, and no periods of prior wellness, the challenge is to help them create a *new state* of wellbeing and euthymic mood. It is not something they return to or recover; it is the emergence of a new way of being. For some people this *is* possible, though of course it is not easy to achieve. In contrast, prior wellness suggests recovery is a concrete possibility, even if it is not easily won.

In Bob's case, we realized later that he did not receive the time or treatment dose he needed to make a full recovery. Looking back at Figure 3.3, across the sessions there was a gradual reduction in symptoms, but his therapy finished before finding out whether further improvement was possible. This is confirmed in Figure 3.6: there were small, gradual improvements in positive and negative affect during the acute phase and those encouraging trends continued in the continuation phase. Notice, however, that there was no further improvement in positive affect after the therapeutic contact ceased.

These mistakes helped us learn to be more hopeful with chronically depressed clients, while also being honest with them, and ourselves, about what is involved in achieving improvement or recovery. Like a pearl of great price, significant improvement in chronic depression is not likely to happen quickly, easily or cheaply – but it is possible. People need to decide if they are prepared to commit to that therapeutic journey, and services need to decide if they have the resources to support it. The alternative is inaccurate and sometimes damaging pessimism that chronic depression is inevitably untreatable: that people need to accept they have a lifelong condition and cope with it and manage as best they can. Sadly, this is *sometimes* true – but it is a conclusion that should be reached *after* all treatment options have been exhausted, not at the point of assessment and formulation.

People with long-term depression are likely to have an extensive treatment history and, by implication, have been 'resistant' to those therapies. However, even for this group it can be surprising which treatments have *not* been offered for an adequate period at an adequate dose. Such clients are often called *treatment-resistant,* because no matter which variation of therapy is offered they seem to be resistant to benefiting from it. This situation can perpetuate long-term stuckness, in which depression is seemingly impervious to all attempts to improve it. Treatment-resistant depression is difficult to understand. It is hard to know whether the resistance is a property of the client, the depression, or the therapies they have received. In this situation it is easy to lapse into lazy thinking that these clients don't want to get better, aren't sufficiently motivated, don't adhere properly to therapies or have 'secondary gains'. Something is maintaining their depression: whatever that is, it will not be helped by subtly pejorative attributions from health professionals. In our experience, clients do not intend or plan to get depressed, and they would gladly opt for sustained recovery if they could imagine it, and had sufficient belief that a treatment could help them achieve it. We are seeking to engage with the part of the client that is 'fed up with being fed up', to offer realistic hope in a treatment that could have a significant and lasting effect.

It is also true that clients sometimes fear change and have difficulty tolerating the uncertainty of what will happen if they attempt to improve their mood. The prospect of improvement can be strangely threatening because it can be hard to imagine, and might not last. It could feel even worse, in the longer term, to experience improvement that was not sustained; to have hopes raised then dashed. Consequently, when depression becomes a stable and almost permanent state there can be an *illusion of security* associated with it. It becomes familiar: processes and structures that are well established can be difficult to dis-establish, even when they are a source of misery. People can become emotionally attached to their depression, as if it is a friend or valued possession. Their self-identity can become fused with it. Certainty, even a miserable certainty, can feel preferable to the uncertainty and unfamiliarity of wellbeing. Clients with treatment-resistant depression therefore need their therapists to consider, in a thorough and reflective way, what additional factors could be contributing to the maintenance of their disorder, including fear of change.

Case Illustration | Frank: chronic depression with prior wellness

Frank, who was aged 44 and married with a grown-up son, was referred to the Newcastle CBT Centre with a 19-year history of panic disorder with agoraphobia, Generalized Anxiety Disorder (GAD), social anxiety and depression. He had developed panic attacks in his mid-twenties with no previous mental health problems. He started avoiding situations out of fear he would have further panic attacks. His avoidance increased and he eventually lost his job. Frank retreated from normal life, became increasingly worried and preoccupied about panicking and being seen by others. As his negative affect increased (e.g. anxiety, embarrassment, shame) he became more avoidant and his positive affect decreased. His motivation to find other work and maintain a social life gradually became suppressed. Anxious avoidance interacted with depressive withdrawal and Frank became reclusive. Within a year of losing his job he rarely left his house and had only occasionally done so in the previous 18 years. Prior to his referral, Frank had received six courses of counselling, clinical psychology or psychotherapy including a recent thirty-session course of CBT for panic and depression. These therapies had minimal benefit: his depression and anxiety disorders were 'treatment-resistant'. His pre-treatment PHQ-9 score was 22.

It is common for people with highly chronic depression to have raised levels of *avoidance*. Frank's depression was the consequence of long-standing anxiety disorders, where the associated avoidance is a known risk factor for depression.

Multiple comorbidities can also increase case complexity, a phenomenon we will explore in detail in Part IV. Suffice to say, complex cases do not need complicated treatment. They need simple treatment carefully targeted on the factors maintaining their problems. As with many comorbid cases, Frank did not need separate treatment for panic disorder, agoraphobia, GAD, social anxiety and depression. His treatment focused primarily on the *functional links* between depression and agoraphobia, the rationale being that avoidant behaviours, designed to prevent panic and social embarrassment, were also maintaining his social withdrawal, and these were core to maintaining a range of his other problems. This is described within the downward spiral model in Figure 9.3.

Frank felt ashamed of himself and very guilty about not contributing to his family's finances. He perceived himself to be inferior and useless. He had an impoverished self-identity enmeshed with the family home where he had spent that last 19 years. He felt embarrassed that he had no stories to tell other people about his day: nothing new happened in his life. His main goals and motivation were avoidant: panic, other people, embarrassment, thinking and remembering. He would alternate between over-thinking through worry and self-critical rumination, then have long periods of distraction and cognitive avoidance, aided by alcohol.

The main therapeutic strategy was to overcome avoidance and increase approach behaviour, seeking to reduce avoidance motivation and negative affect, while simultaneously stimulating approach motivation and positive affect. This was done in three ways:

1. Establish concrete approach goals; Frank's desires; how he would like to live.
2. Pay attention to approach impulses and increase behavioural engagement with these goals. This strategy enabled simultaneous exposure to feared stimuli and situations.
3. Reflect on the emotional and interpersonal consequences of engaging in these new behaviours.

Frank was able to generate four approach goals and these formed a natural hierarchy: (a) go out of his house without fear; (b) go out for a coffee or meal; (c) train to be a painter/decorator; (d) get a job as a painter/decorator.

In contrast with previous therapies, a slow rate of change was anticipated and accepted by both Frank and his therapist. Frank had received behavioural treatment in the past, and it had focused on activating key behaviours, such as going out of his house, but did not pay sufficient attention to the *emotions* this provoked in him. Frank had endured the distress that was triggered, rather than learning to feel differently when being out. The strategy in this approach was to engage in small behavioural changes, initially with the aim of Frank's negative affect decreasing (e.g. anxiety) and his positive affect increasing (e.g. comfort). These emotional changes

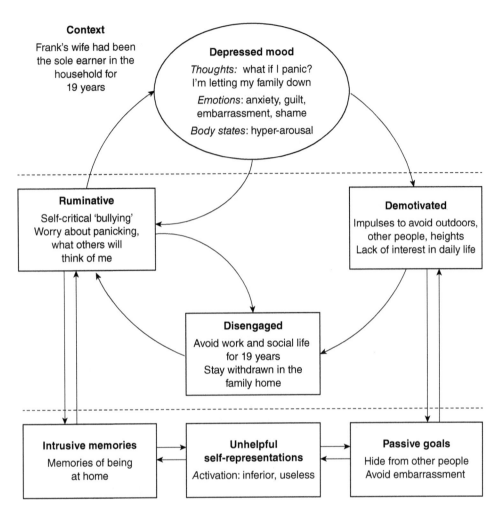

Figure 9.3   Frank's downward spiral of depression and agoraphobia

were deemed equally important as the behavioural change. Avoidance and approach systems both received attention, to reflect the fact that an anxiety disorder and mood disorder were both being treated. Importantly, behavioural changes were calibrated to Frank's *current* behaviour: the initial steps were small deviations from what he was already doing. They were directed towards the agreed goals, but the starting point was always current behaviour; this made it less likely that the task would inadvertently be overly demanding.

The first agreed goal was for Frank to be able to go out of his house and feel comfortable doing it, i.e. not just endure it or have less fear – but also have some positive feelings. In each case the sequence was the same:

a. Frank would remind himself of his goals and why he was doing this behaviour, turning his attention to approach impulses.
b. He would engage in the behaviour as fully as possible, i.e. without safety-seeking strategies, such as distraction or avoiding eye contact.
c. He would attend to his emotions and body states while engaging in the behaviour, monitoring negative affect (to give it time to decrease) and positive affect (to give it time to increase). This increased the likelihood of concrete processing.
d. Afterwards Frank would reflect on the various consequences of his actions, to make his learning explicit.

This process had all the key features of the upward spiral, with exposure therapy for agoraphobia embedded within it. Crucially, Frank stayed long enough in situations for his anxiety to habituate, and he repeated tasks often enough for positive affect to develop. His post-action reflection also maximized opportunities for disconfirmation of his expectations, for example, that he would be asked by others why he wasn't at work, wouldn't be able to cope with the feelings, and so on.

Figure 9.4 summarizes the behavioural changes across the first year of Frank's therapy, showing the graded tasks that he approached at each stage. A slow pace was established with lots of repetition of the target behaviours. The aim was to conduct full and thorough exposure to feared situations and to only move onto the next step when the last one had become comfortable, not just tolerable. The first 4 months focused on Frank stepping a few yards out of his front door into his garden, then holding his head high when he did this, then walking in the local street, and so on.

As might be expected, at various points progress was slowed by barriers to change that Frank sometimes felt were insurmountable, for example, worry about being stopped and asked questions, self-critical rumination, intense shame and severe anxiety symptoms. The strategy was to attend to these factors if and when they created a block on progress, and do enough work on them to enable the change process to continue. We will return to this therapeutic strategy in Part IV. The main challenges to progress are shown in the lower half of the diagram in Figure 9.4. As the figure suggests, the trajectory of change was often 'three steps forward, two steps back'. In our experience, this type of change pattern is to be expected when treating persistent depression; the important factor is tolerating setbacks and appraising them as opportunities to learn something new, for example, about the context, or the effect of the client's behaviour.

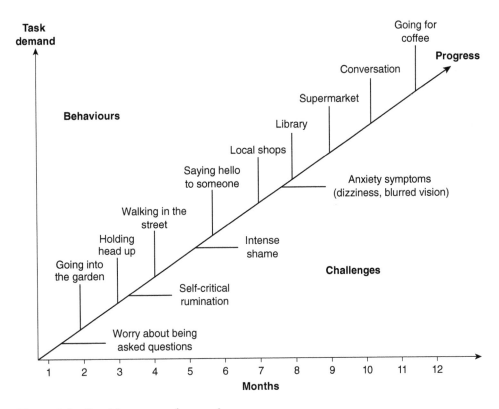

Figure 9.4   Frank's progress in year 1

After 12 months of treatment, and thirty-six therapy sessions, Frank's PHQ-9 score was 9, and he had achieved his goal to go out for coffee on his own. For Frank this was a huge step forward in his life, and he needed time to process the positive shock of having achieved it. In terms of the self-regulation model, memories and self-representations were not *direct* targets for change but they changed indirectly as a consequence of changes in motivation, engagement and reflective processing. Frank had new autobiographical memories to emotionally process. He was laying down new general knowledge, for example, about coffee shops and his local area. There was also the beginning of a new identity of himself as a normal person. Thinking back to Chapter 7, we can think of the change process as a second adolescence: separating from his physical home, exploring the local environment, forming a self-identity, and so on.

After the first year of therapy, Frank felt able to confide in his therapist how severe his depression had been in the past, including severe suicidality. Out of shame, Frank had hidden many of these details from previous therapists, and the depressive aspects of his problems had largely been overlooked. This indicated a strong therapeutic alliance in the current treatment: there was increasing client disclosure as progress was made approaching more demanding, but always manageable, tasks.

Although Frank had a strong internal felt-sense of being inferior and useless, this had not been internalized during his *early* development. He was able to explain to his therapist that he was depressed because of his situation: he wouldn't expect to feel inferior and useless if he had a job and could contribute to the family finances. In other words, the felt-sense of being useless was contextual (outside-in) rather than an unhelpful sense of self from childhood. Consequently, the generation of new helpful self-identities, such as *student, wage earner* or *painter/decorator* could be sufficient to provoke a shift in self-identity. This is the critical point in terms of prior wellness. Frank had a 19-year history of panic disorder with agoraphobia, social anxiety and depression, but his underlying susceptibilities were primarily to anxiety, not depression. Frank did not have early-onset depression, nor were his self-representations from early learning depressiogenic in nature.

In spite of long-term chronicity, Frank went on to sustain significant improvements in his mood. He received a further twenty-four therapy sessions in year 2 with the behavioural changes and challenges summarized in Figure 9.5. By the end of year 2 his PHQ-9 score was 13. The goal to train as a painter/decorator meant that Frank had to face further fears, including a previously undisclosed height phobia that required 4 months of treatment. As he approached the goal to apply for college courses, his worry and social anxiety became more pronounced and this needed additional attention. By the end of year 2, he felt well enough to apply for a place in college, and he met with a student support officer to find out what would be involved and make plans.

In year 3, Frank was progressing independently and only needed monthly booster sessions with his therapist. His progress is summarized in Figure 9.6. He had successfully adjusted to life at college and was enjoying feeling part of the social group as well as being highly engaged in the training course. At the end of year 3, Frank's PHQ-9 score was 13. Notice, however, that the downward spiral did not disappear. Throughout the 3 years of treatment there were periods of stuckness when worry, self-critical rumination and severe anxiety would be reactivated and progress would stall. There was also a huge developmental 'catch-up' task for Frank, in terms of learning about daily life, social relationships, the pressures of college deadlines, the risks of giving up benefits and taking on a student loan, and so on. At no point did Frank find this process easy; he sometimes found it scary and hopeless and was tempted to retreat back into his former hiding. But overall, the satisfaction and positive affect he received was strong enough to maintain his courage and motivation towards what he most desired: to have a paid job of work and provide for his family.

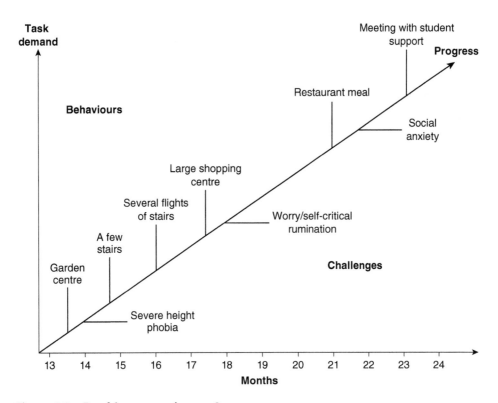

Figure 9.5   Frank's progress in year 2

At the time of writing, in 2018, Frank has successfully completed college and is now looking for a job. He received a courage award from his college and attended a case conference with his therapist at the Newcastle CBT Centre to describe his treatment and answer questions. He went from having no story to having an extraordinary story. Of course, not all clients have such a positive outcome after 19 years of chronic anxiety and depression – but Frank's case shows what is *possible*, particularly when clients have had periods of prior wellness.

We are imagining some readers baulking at the thought of approximately eighty therapy sessions over 3 years. How many services can offer that! Unfortunately, not many. But consider the health economics. The sessions Frank received at the CBT Centre were considerably fewer than the six previous therapies combined, and the 3 year investment in change was 15 years fewer than the period of time he had been inactive, anxious, depressed, claiming sickness benefit and reliant on his wife to provide for their family. Treatment has resulted in Frank, now aged 48, looking forward to a normal life. Aside from the quality of life for him and his family, how much social and healthcare resource has been *saved* in the future by giving him

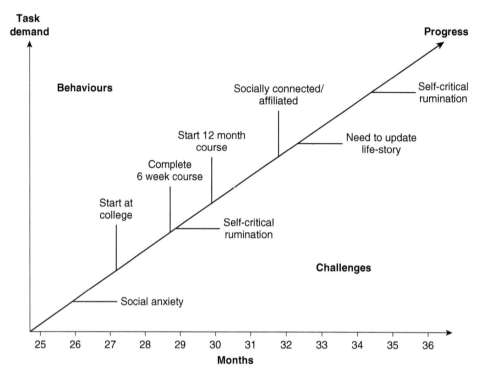

Figure 9.6   Frank's progress in year 3

the treatment he needs now? We will return to this and other service issues in the synthesis in Chapter 13.

Lifelong Depression

The final sub-type, and in many ways the most challenging, is people who have lifelong depression with few, if any, periods of euthymic mood. As we mentioned previously, these people do not *recover* in the literal sense of returning to a previous state of well-being. The aim is to help them overcome depression sufficiently to *discover* a more satisfying way of living – possibly for the first time. As we move from considering recent chronicity, prior wellness and lifelong depression, the balance of acceptance and change tends to alter subtly but significantly. In all cases we want clients to make as much progress as possible, but the aims have to be realistic. False hope can be just as damaging as no hope. For recently chronic cases, sustained recovery is the clear target, even though it is approached in a graded way. For clients with treatment-resistant depression and prior wellness, the first target is improvement and full recovery is explored as a possibility. For people with lifelong depression, the primary target is to find out whether a more satisfying way of life is possible.

In some cases this can mean discovering and sustaining euthymic mood. What is most likely is maximizing those aspects of life that can be changed, accepting what cannot, and learning the difference between the two. Recall Evelyn in Chapter 7: she learned to accept that depressed moods were reactivated from time to time. They were not predictable and she could not prevent or control them. She intensely disliked this situation and wished deeply that it was different – but trying to control the uncontrollable was frustrating and ultimately futile. The depressiogenic response was to become *resigned* that what she wanted was not possible. The therapeutic response was to *accept* what was not possible, and instead seek to be powerful elsewhere.

This is the framework to have in mind when working with people with lifelong depression. It is not credible for them to be offered 10–12 sessions of CBT with a recovery goal – they are unlikely to have a concept of what recovery is. That type of offer would demonstrate a lack of understanding on therapists' part and would be likely to strain alliance building. A more credible offer is to explore *variability* in the client's mood to find out what happens when their depression is less severe; to explore whether there are fleeting moments of pleasure, enjoyment or other positive emotions that could be reflected on and understood in more depth. For clients where depression is the rule and all else is the exception, the therapeutic strategy is to explore the exception, not the rule. Little is gained by spending repeated sessions exploring depression and how bad it has been. Instead, the counter-intuitive strategy is to focus on the *upward spiral* to find out if there are times, however short-lived, when life is more rewarding. If those moments exist – and they usually do – they could provide an opportunity to explore what motivation, action and reflection accompany them.

Case Illustration | Gemma

Gemma was aged 40, single and worked as a medical consultant in a local NHS Trust. She had lifelong persistent difficulties with depression going back to middle childhood. Her mother had suffered severe recurrent depression and there had been periods of separation early in Gemma's life. Gemma's mother focused the family's attention on her own difficulties and this resulted in Gemma internalizing that her

(Continued)

(Continued)

needs didn't matter, in comparison with her mother's. Her mother's responses to Gemma's needs were often dismissive or critical, with a lack of awareness of the effect this had on Gemma. The mantra to put other people's needs first connected with the family's religious values in which self-sacrifice was reified and self-care or self-development were associated with selfish indulgence.

This situation catastrophically worsened when Gemma was aged 10: her father – who had been a quiet, loving and moderating influence – contracted a serious illness and became severely disabled with a shortened life expectancy. This situation exacerbated the pre-existing family dynamics, with Gemma and her brother expected to subjugate their needs even further to help their mother care for their father. This situation was expected to be a short-term adaptation to a family crisis. Thirty years later, Gemma's father was still living in the family home with severe and worsening disabilities and her mother as his main carer.

In that time, there had been no change to the prevailing family expectation that Gemma should devote her life to supporting her mother with her father's care. This situation had a profound effect on Gemma's emerging self-identity as an adolescent, and it complicated the normal processes of separation, individuation and peer-group belonging. Gemma managed to leave home, study medicine at university, form friendships and develop a successful career – but with near-constant severe guilt that she should subjugate herself more fully to her parents' needs, a view intermittently reinforced by forceful maternal criticism. In fact, as an adult Gemma provided her parents with monthly financial support, medical advice, made regular visits home, and was available most days for emotional support. This was rarely, if ever, sufficient to satisfy her mother's felt-sense of entitlement to Gemma's support.

What neither parent realized was the acutely depressing effect of Gemma's guilt, and her felt-sense of being a selfish person who ought to be doing more for others, not more for herself. Gemma had good personal hygiene and usually ate regular meals, but that was the extent to which she could consistently attend to her own needs and desires. For example, it was a struggle for Gemma to buy herself a cup of coffee: this would trigger ruminative self-criticism that she was wasting money that could be spent on her parents, or others who were more in need than herself. Her self-criticisms bore a striking resemblance to the maternal criticisms she had experienced throughout her life.

Consequently, Gemma developed a lifelong struggle with depression that varied over time but was always present to some degree. She lived most of her adult life with moderate symptoms that would occasionally become milder and occasionally more severe. At various points she had considered suicide, and been close to acting on two occasions. Nevertheless, she learned how to function well as a doctor, in spite of these symptoms, and was highly respected in her profession. When her depression was more severe she had sought help and had received one course of long-term dynamic psychotherapy and one brief course of CBT, both of which had helped at the time, but neither had a lasting effect. At the time of her referral, Gemma was receiving pharmacotherapy from a specialist affective disorders service. Her downward spiral formulation is shown in Figure 9.7, representing periods of severe depression. At the start of treatment, her PHQ-9 score was 23.

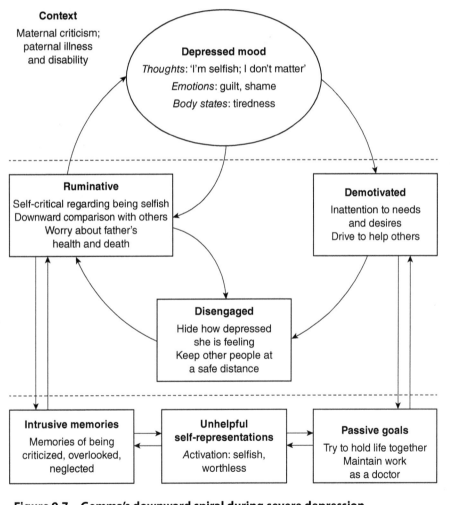

Context

Maternal criticism; paternal illness and disability

Depressed mood

Thoughts: 'I'm selfish; I don't matter'
Emotions: guilt, shame
Body states: tiredness

Ruminative

Self-critical regarding being selfish
Downward comparison with others
Worry about father's health and death

Demotivated

Inattention to needs and desires
Drive to help others

Disengaged

Hide how depressed she is feeling
Keep other people at a safe distance

Intrusive memories

Memories of being criticized, overlooked, neglected

Unhelpful self-representations

Activation: selfish, worthless

Passive goals

Try to hold life together
Maintain work as a doctor

Figure 9.7   Gemma's downward spiral during severe depression

Focus on the upward spiral

As a focused piece of therapeutic work within a longer-term treatment, Gemma and her therapist decided to spend 3 months focusing almost exclusively on *positive affect*. To form a baseline, Gemma kept a daily diary for 3 weeks in which she recorded her levels of happiness (mean = 5/100), contentment (mean = 6/100), sadness (mean = 84/100) and anxiety (mean = 93/100). She also made a daily conviction rating in the following statements: 'I can recover from depression' (6/100); 'I have things in the future to look forward to' (5/100); 'I can build a more satisfying life' (6/100). These results were consistent with Gemma's severe and chronic depression.

The next step used the Positive And Negative Assessment Schedule (PANAS; Watson, Clark & Tellegan, 1988) to present Gemma with a list of positive emotional and affective states. Gemma's task was to select a small number that she currently experienced and/or that she would *like* to feel more intensely and more regularly. Notice that the emphasis was on positive affect and seeking to stimulate the approach system. Gemma chose the following positive affective states: *concentrating, relaxed, kind to myself, confident, joyful*. These terms were then included in a daily diary. Gemma's task was not initially to make any changes in her behaviour; rather to pay more attention to her feelings, and at the end of each day make a note if she had experienced any of these positive emotions. The aim was to encourage a concrete processing mode, and try to enhance the specificity of Gemma's autobiographical memories. If she experienced the positive emotions, she made an intensity rating (0–100) and included some notes about the situation and what she was doing at the time.

This strategy was intended to help Gemma place more attention on positive affective states, learn more about the actions and mental states associated with them, and create an opportunity to engage more fully in those states. Figure 9.7 presents the mean intensity ratings for three of the positive emotions (Gemma rarely experienced the others). As would be expected in a severely depressed person, the rates of positive affect were generally low, however they were not zero. In the first couple of weeks Gemma was pleasantly surprised how consistently she was able to *concentrate*, particularly in her workplace. The average ratings for *relaxed* and *kind to myself* were low initially, but they tended to occur intermittently to a significant degree rather than at a low level every day. It was also a surprise to Gemma that she experienced these feelings from time to time. The method helped her to pay attention to and remember those experiences in a different way.

As each week progressed, Gemma and her therapist paid close attention to the situations and behaviours associated with these emotions. There were no obvious effects across situations, but certain behavioural patterns became more apparent. To Gemma's surprise these tended *not* to correspond to the coping strategies she believed she should use when she felt down, in particular, rigorous exercise. Gemma was a member of a local gym and would aim to go there 3–4 evenings each week with the explicit aim of helping her mood. On reflection, she realized her motivation for the gym was often duty-based, not desire-based: obligation rather than motivation.

Instead, what emerged out of the diaries was that she tended to experience positive emotions when she was *communicating with other people* and *behaving compassionately to herself*. Figure 9.9 illustrates the number of communicative behaviours associated with positive emotions across the treatment, including discussing, listening, watching, reflecting and so on. After 3–4 weeks, the correlation between positive affect and communication was becoming more apparent, and this became the basis for paying more attention to communicative impulses (*approach motivation*) and *behavioural engagement*. Even when she wasn't feeling motivated to do so, Gemma would maintain greater contact with friends and trusted colleagues, in particular scheduling more social engagements at the weekend. In particular, she was encouraged to pay attention to approach impulses to connect with others; to recognize times she *felt like* making contact with others and encourage herself to do so. As can be seen visually in Figure 9.7 this led to an increase in communicative behaviours from around week 9 of the 12-week intervention, and an associated increase in positive affect observed in Figure 9.8. In spite of the chronic nature of Gemma's depression, there were some aspects of the upward spiral being woven into her daily life.

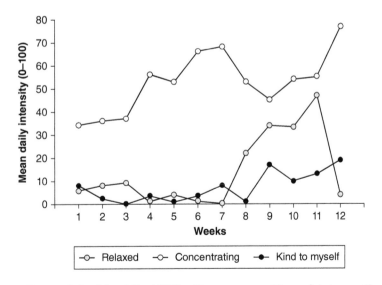

Figure 9.8   Gemma's Positive Affect (PA) ratings across a 12-week intervention

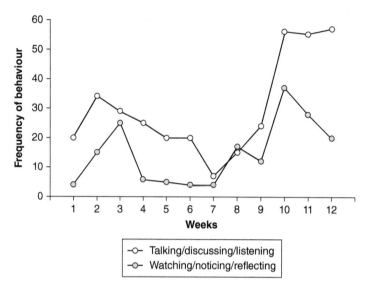

Figure 9.9   Gemma's communicative behaviours associated with Positive Affect (PA)

The other finding was the helpful role of self-compassionate behaviours, illustrated in Figure 9.10. These took longer to notice within the therapy because they occurred with a lower frequency than communication. Nevertheless, by week 9 Gemma was recognizing the value of regular meals, rest, gentle exercise and other 'concessions' to herself, such as buying a favourite picture and a radio she had liked for several months. These were huge steps for Gemma to take because they were disobedient to her self-representation to give to others, not herself. In the short term they activated the unhelpful self-representation *selfish*. A complication was self-critical rumination that she was being selfish, indulging herself in this way: this was a prominent theme in therapy sessions, with the diary evidence available to help Gemma remember that no one was hurt or harmed by her looking after herself, and attending to her needs and desires. On the contrary, she benefited and everyone else in contact with her was likely to benefit too.

We have included this example to demonstrate a way of working with lifelong chronic depression that is focused and time-limited. Twelve sessions was *not* sufficient to meet Gemma's full therapeutic needs; in fact, in her case it was twelve sessions within a longer course of over forty sessions. Nevertheless, this approach can go some way to encouraging the development of approach motivation, behavioural engagement and reflective processing. It can also create new autobiographical memories that have the potential to develop helpful self-representations: this process is likely to be slow, but it is *possible*. The key difference in treating lifelong depression

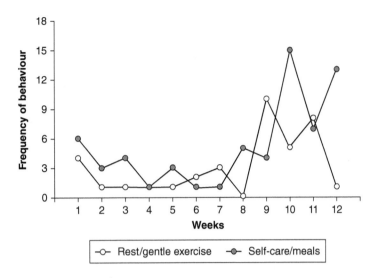

Figure 9.10   Gemma's self-compassionate behaviours associated with Positive Affect (PA)

is, the self-representations that are needed are often those that were not internalized in early childhood. In Chapter 7, Daniel was encouraged to engage with friends, film and cinema. In Chapter 8, Evelyn was encouraged to diversify socially, so she wasn't over-invested in her work role. In contrast, Gemma was attempting to develop a capacity for self-care that ideally begins to form at the toddler stage of development. In Gemma's case, there was a pressing need for a more caring and compassionate relationship with herself, in addition to stronger emotional attachments and connection to others. This is Gemma's feedback on the 12-week intervention, to illustrate the therapeutic impact from the client's perspective.

Case Illustration: Gemma's feedback on the 12-week intervention

- 'The focus on positive emotions and communicative behaviours helped me to remember what I had done, which was and still is important to me. It allowed some

(Continued)

> (Continued)
>
> recall in what otherwise felt like a fog of nothingness. As my mood improved, the details and colour of the diaries changed.'
> - 'Writing entries for myself meant that they were real experiences I'd had, not just ideas for discussion.'
> - 'Reviewing the diaries with my therapist meant that, although I may have felt guilty at having some time with friends and be afraid of getting better, there was an external voice reflecting my experience back to me. This gave credibility to my experience and feelings, which I guess I haven't had from my family so much.'
> - 'Seeing the overall track of emotions and behaviours, with the undulations but steady rise, also helped me to visualize the longer-term outcome and goals; plus that setbacks or a bad day is OK.'

In the following 14 months, and a further eighteen sessions, Gemma continued to attend to her self-care and open herself to increased communication and connection with other people. This was an extremely unsettling and turbulent process for her. Approximately 3 years after her first CBT session, she took the risk of inviting a group of colleagues to her home for a party – the first time she had done so in her adult life. Within a few weeks of that she had formed a relationship, her second serious relationship. Within a few weeks of that, she had made a trip abroad to have a holiday with friends from university. In the following few months, and for the first time in her adult life, Gemma's depression was in remission (PHQ-9 score = 1). She had found out that a more satisfying way of life *was* possible, and moved into the continuation phase of learning how to stay well.

Practitioner Tips: Working with Chronic Cases

- Assess clients' history of depression thoroughly to differentiate cases that are *recently chronic*, from those with *prior wellness*, from those with *lifelong depression*.
- Also assess clients' history of receiving treatments. They may be referred with *treatment-resistant depression*, in which case it is helpful to review which treatments have been received and how the client responded to them. This can inform the approach that is most likely to be helpful in the current course of therapy.
- In recently chronic cases (i.e. major depression for not much longer than 2 years) there might not be anything unusual or complicated maintaining the disorder. It could have persisted because of delays accessing treatment, rather than case

complexity. In this scenario, therapy will not need much, if any, adjustment compared with non-chronic depression. A standard course of CBT should be offered with a goal for sustained recovery.

- Depression that has persisted for several years will, on average, need more sessions and a longer period of time to change, compared with non-chronic depression. Progress is likely to be slow, with alternating phases of progress and setbacks.

- When clients have had periods of prior wellness earlier in the lifespan, it is important to be hopeful about recovering previous functioning. The goal should be to *find out* how much improvement is possible; this cannot be known at the outset, so uncertainty needs to be tolerated. Entrenched patterns of disengagement and avoidance will take time to overcome, so it is important not to mistake *slow* progress for *no* progress. The strategy is to target small changes initially, calibrated to current functioning.

- Clients with lifelong depression also need hopeful therapists. The goal is to find out whether new ways of functioning can be established. Downward spirals of mood need attention, as in any other course of CBT, but it is important to focus sufficiently on upward spirals, in other words, find out about times when the client is *less* depressed and has moments of *positive affect*, even if these are occasional and fleeting. The strategy is to amplify these moments: increase behavioural engagement around them, and try to build helpful self-representations that were not internalized in early development.

Summary of Key Points from Part III

- The self-regulation model and integrated treatment can be adapted for a broad range of depressed presentations. In Part III, we have explored three sub-types that can be difficult to treat and are at heightened risk of non-response, relapse and recurrence: *early-onset*, *highly recurrent* and *chronic/persistent*.
- Part II illustrated the core treatment components given to all clients: *approach motivation*, *behavioural engagement* and *reflective processing*. Part III has introduced the optional components that are usually needed to treat more difficult-to-treat cases: *memory integration*, *self-organization*, *goal-organization*.
- With more difficult-to-treat cases, it is essential to conduct a thorough depression history, to establish a clear timeline of prior depressive episodes and periods of wellness. This should include an assessment of previous treatments, to learn what has been helpful in the past and identify alternative treatment options.
- It is essential to be developmentally aware. A high proportion of adults with highly recurrent or chronic depression suffered trauma, abuse or neglect in childhood, and experienced a major depressive episode prior to becoming an adult. Time-limited periods of uncertainty, confusion and depressed moods are normal in adolescence, but if these persist and do not self-correct, it is vital that young people are offered help to come out of depression, so that depression is the exception, not the rule.
- Therapists working with adolescents should, as far as possible, keep reaching out to young people, even if there is weak or intermittent engagement in treatment. Depression is a disorder of motivation, so if young people are unmotivated about treatment, this may be due to their depression, not their unsuitability for therapy. To make it more likely they will receive an optimal dose of treatment, pay particular attention to the process of forming a working alliance, and take care that young people are the primary clients, with clear boundaries between them and the systems in which they are embedded. Stay mindful of their developmental tasks: separation, exploration and identity-formation, and support them to learn the difference between good and bad risks.
- The role of context varies greatly across cases. In early and first-onsets it is highly likely that depression has been a reaction to major life events or adverse situations. These could be one-off events, but more often they are evolving situations or multiple events that have had a cumulative effect, such as oppression, neglect or abuse. When misfortune and adversity is real, not imagined, it is essential to acknowledge the reality of clients' experience and help them survive and out-grow it. CBT is not pretending that negative events were positive: it is learning to respond to adversity in an adaptive way,

so that self-respect and good self-regulation are restored or established, in spite of adverse experiences.

- As depression becomes more recurrent or chronic, context is less likely to be the primary maintaining factor. This does not mean it should be ignored, but contextual changes are unlikely to be sufficient *on their own* to bring a client out of depression. Consequently, greater attention needs to be paid to *intrapsychic processes* and *interactions with the environment*. For example, a change of partner, job or country could form *part* of a recovery from depression, but intrapsychic processes such as rumination, intrusive memories, self-devaluation and goal passivity need proportionally more attention as depression becomes a more persistent or recurrent problem. The inner environment needs proportionally more attention as depression becomes recurrent or persistent.

- Highly recurrent depression is associated with *unstable mood*, and the goal of treatment is to stabilize euthymic mood by helping clients respond differently to their affective and mental states. Counter-intuitively, the goal is not to avoid depression. It is to accept that depressed moods happen from time to time, sometimes unpredictably, and to respond to them in an engaged, compassionate and mindful way, so they are time-limited and do not deteriorate into a major episode. Some awareness of triggers can be helpful, but not if it results in a strategy to avoid triggers at all costs. It is better to focus on *how best to respond to depressed moods*, whatever their causes. Through this approach, clients become less anxious about becoming depressed, because they learn how to reverse depressed moods when they occur. Depression then has a less limiting and contingent effect on their lives.

- Chronic and persistent depression is associated with *overly stable mood*. Clients who have been depressed for several years often feel *stuck*, as if nothing sparks their interest and lightens their mood. The goal is to invest in gradual change and accept it is likely to be slower than the client would like. Calibrate change to current behaviour and functioning, aiming for small increases in motivation, engagement and reflection. It is essential to focus on increasing positive affect (PA), not just decreasing negative affect (NA), even if PA is occasional and fleeting at the start of treatment. This can be achieved by repeating behaviours until PA is achieved, placing greater attention on PA, and making it the primary focus of diary recording. Differentiate between: (a) clients who have only recently met criteria for chronic depression, (b) clients with prior periods of wellness earlier in the lifespan, and (c) clients with lifelong depression. These clients need different goals: (a) to recover, (b) to regain previous functioning, and (c) to establish new patterns of self-regulation.

- All depressed clients need hopeful therapists: the skill is learning what to put one's hopes in. Hence it is essential to have realistic goals, even if these are modest at the outset of treatment. It is better to achieve a modest goal than fail an ambitious one: modest goals can lead to progressively greater ambitions as treatment proceeds.

PART IV
COMPLEX CASES

As we have seen throughout the previous chapters, CBT for depression can be a highly effective treatment but therapists find it difficult to deliver the therapy when cases are challenging, unusual or complex. 'Complex case' is a widely used phrase, but it tends to have different meanings in different contexts and, at worst, this creates confusion and inconsistency. The aim of Part IV is to define 'complex' in the context of major depression, and consider how to understand and treat complex cases, using the integrated approach.

Chapter 10 explores what complex depression is and considers ways in which CBT can be adapted to treat it. We propose a biopsychosocial model: complexity results from depression *interacting* with a range of biological, psychological and social factors. The presence of these factors is not necessarily complicating, because a standard course of CBT can still be effective, for example, when clients have physical illness, comorbid disorders or social problems, such as unemployment. However, sometimes these factors interact in ways that impede working alliances and/or modify the usual maintenance of depression. When the interactions are problematic, the proposed strategy is three-fold: firstly, provide a *disorder-specific* treatment and, as far as possible, *tether* it to an agreed treatment target, keeping therapy simple at the point of delivery. Secondly, if this approach is not effective, target *trans-diagnostic* processes that maintain multiple disorders. Thirdly, if this approach is not effective, develop a *bespoke* individualized formulation that targets unusual, unpredictable or unstable interactions between the client's problems.

Chapter 11 applies these principles to the treatment of mixed anxiety/depression. Anxiety disorders are very common comorbidities of major depression, yet there is relatively little guidance how to adjust treatment for depression under comorbid conditions. The chapter explores *functional links* between depression and anxiety, that is, processes that feed off each other and are mutually maintaining. The processes that maintain depression can have additional influences from anxiety disorders, for example, threat appraisals influencing helplessness, worry influencing rumination, avoidance influencing withdrawal, and so on. Disorder-specific treatment can be effective when anxious processes are *sympathetic* to changes in mood, and virtuous cycles are formed in which depression and anxiety improve together. For more complex cases, trans-diagnostic processes may need to be targeted. In a minority of cases, these approaches will not work because the interactions are unpredictable or atypical, and a bespoke treatment is needed.

Chapter 12 extends this approach to consider depression following trauma. Depressed mood is a very common co-occurrence of PTSD. In many cases, depression does not need separate treatment, because although it influences re-experiencing, avoidance and hyper-arousal, standard treatment for PTSD is sufficient to overcome depressed mood. However, there are a number of post-traumatic phenomena that precipitate more complex and persistent depression, that do require direct intervention. The chapter considers depression that persists after PTSD has been successfully treated, the complicating effect of repeated trauma, and depression in the context of developmental trauma. Therapists need to pay particular attention to clients' self-organization, and the effects of traumatic memories on their self-identity. In cases of developmental trauma, emotions and body states can be dissociated, and unhelpful self-representations, that have been compartmentalized or 'dormant', can be reactivated. Treatment needs to connect clients with their concrete experiences and integrate unhelpful self-representations, rather than suppress them.

10

Biopsychosocial Interactions

Defining Complexity

Approximately 90,000 people enter psychological therapy in Improving Access to Psychological Therapies (IAPT) services across England every month, many of them affected by depressive disorders (IAPT Executive Summary, 2016). A proportion of clinical presentations within mental health services has always been complex. Even if that proportion is unchanged, since IAPT has made psychological therapies more available, the overall number of clients with complex needs is much greater (Clark, 2011). CBT therapists, particularly those working at Step 3, are working with what are regarded as complex cases – for example, clients with trauma histories and personality problems – and a number are known not to respond to disorder-specific protocols (Goddard, Wingrove & Moran, 2015).

NICE guidance for the treatment of complex depression identifies a group of clients who are expected to receive treatment at Step 4 in the stepped care system:

> Complex depression includes depression that shows an inadequate response to multiple treatments, is complicated by psychotic symptoms, and/or is associated with significant psychiatric comorbidity or psychosocial factors. (NICE, 2009)

Most therapists would expect a client with depression who also manifests psychosis, other comorbidities, psychosocial stress and/or an inadequate response to previous treatments to be a challenging case. Such cases would typically be described as 'complex' but the above guidance doesn't really *define* what complexity is. Nor does it distinguish personally demanding or technically difficult cases from those that are genuinely complex.

Arguably, the absence of an accepted definition of complexity has led to its over-use in some circumstances. When the concept is over-used there are various conse-quences: firstly, 'complex' can become a post-hoc attribution for treatment failures, producing an empty explanation of why CBT was ineffective with particular cases, and probably concealing a lack of understanding of why treatment did not work (Tarrier & Johnson, 2015). Treatment failures may or may not be attributable to complexity, but this can only be established in prospective clinical tests, not post-hoc rationalizations. Secondly, 'complex' becomes a proxy or collective term for a range of depressive fea-tures that have precise clinical meanings, many of which we have already covered in previous chapters: for example, severe, high-risk, treatment-resistant, recurrent, chronic/persistent (Garland, 2015). These features create difficulties for therapists, and clients, but they are not necessarily *complicated*. Thirdly, 'complex' can be used to justify drift from evidence-based protocols on the assumption that such cases are unlikely to respond to standardized treatments (Waller & Turner, 2016). The impre-cise or over-use of 'complex' has raised concerns that therapists deviate unnecessarily from treatment protocols when faced with what they appraise to be complex cases, whether or not true complexity is present.

We propose that complexity is a valid clinical construct that can be clearly defined and does not need to be based on post-hoc rationalizations or imprecise clinical terms:

> 'Complexity consists of biological, psychological and social factors interacting to impede the working alliance and/or modify the usual maintenance of a disorder.'

Simple and Complex Systems

Simple systems have only a few moving parts and generally behave in predictable ways, whereas complex systems have *multiple moving parts* and sometimes behave unpre-dictably. Real-life challenges often have multiple parts woven together, which Rittel & Webber (1973) called 'wicked problems', to describe the messiness of these situations. This is our starting point in considering how complexity manifests in depression. When the NICE definition is reconsidered, a client whose depression is in interac-tion with psychosis, other comorbidities and psychosocial stress can be seen to have difficulties with 'multiple moving parts'. The treating therapist is not only presented with depression – there are several other factors to consider. It would be a significant-enough challenge if these were separate independent problems, for example if psycho-sis, other comorbidities and psychosocial stress had no impact on the maintenance of depression. In practice, problems of this type tend to interact and influence each other.

If we adopt a pragmatic strategy to use the simplest possible intervention that has a good probability of being effective, there may be cases with 'multiple moving parts' that nevertheless respond to *disorder-specific* protocols. There are good reasons to take this view seriously. For example, consider a recent randomized controlled trial of CBT for moderate/severe depression (DeRubeis et al., 2005). Approximately 60% of clients in the CBT arm responded to treatment, which is the usual level of response for major depression. Across the whole trial, 72% of clients had Axis I comorbidity (mostly anxiety disorders) and 48% had Axis II comorbidity. Comorbidities were not directly treated, yet therapy was still effective. 'Non-depression' factors, such as comorbidities, do not *necessarily* prevent disorder-specific protocols from working. We can choose to focus on the positive aspects of these findings: 60% responded without specifically attending to other disorders. Or we can choose to focus on the negative aspect: 40% did not respond and now need further treatment. The question then arises: which factors negatively impacted on these clients' outcomes? For example, in this trial, clients with comorbid social anxiety were less likely to recover from depression.

Sometimes non-depression factors are *not* complications; they co-exist with depression and are either unaffected, or benefit indirectly from its treatment. In other situations non-depression factors *are* complications; they impede the development of working alliances and/or modify how depression is maintained. In the first case disorder-specific protocols should proceed as usual. In the second case, treatment may need some kind of adjustment or adaptation. The challenge for therapists is how to tell the difference between the two, and what adjustments to make when complications are proving to be problematic.

Biopsychosocial Factors

We have approached this issue pragmatically and empirically by recording and mapping the non-depression features of successive depression cases over several years' clinical work. The result is presented in Table 10.1. We have found that non-depression factors tend to fall into biological, psychological and social categories, and Table 10.1 lists the most common factors we have encountered in our clinical practice. It is important to note, the examples listed are not exhaustive or exclusive; rather they are *representative* of common biopsychosocial factors. They vary in their amenability to change, either spontaneously or through treatment, with some more mutable than others. Depending on the service and case-mix there may be particular biological, psychological and social factors not listed here, and therapists are encouraged to extend the map to include factors that present in their particular service. The key point is this: these factors are not features or symptoms *of* major depression.

They are not a constituent of the mood disorder, but they have the potential to co-occur and interact with it, and their presence may or may not have a complicating effect. This contrasts with sub-types and features of depression such as severe, high-risk, treatment-resistant, recurrent, chronic/persistent, etc. These are features *of* the mood disorder. They can create difficult technical and personal challenges, for both client and therapist, but they are not necessarily complications with 'multiple moving parts'.

In this taxonomy, there are at least eight types of biological, psychological and social factors that have the potential to interact with depression in a complicating way. Of course, since these are *types* of factors, there is an even larger number of *specific phenomena* that fall within these categories. Cases vary in how many of these factors are present, and during assessment we attempt to identify them in a systematic way. We use a diagrammatic version of Table 10.1, shown in Figure 10.1, circling the factors present for any particular case. Mutability is a spectrum, with less mutable factors located on the outer rings, and more mutable factors on the inner rings. In general, factors near the centre can be solved and overcome, whereas factors near the outside can possibly be influenced but not always solved. The advantage of a diagrammatic map is having a spatial representation of the particular factors present for an individual case. The explicitness of this process helps in assessment, formulation and treatment planning.

Figure 10.1 illustrates the biopsychosocial factors present in the case of Chloe, who we introduced in Chapters 5 and 6. The main biological factors were her chronic and acute illnesses: Chloe had a history of serious cardiac problems and post-partum medical complications that required surgery. The main social factor was the

Table 10.1 Common biopsychosocial complexity factors associated with major depression

Mutability	Biological	Psychological	Social
High	Acute illness	Anxiety disorders	Interpersonal problems
Moderate	Somaticization	Trauma/PTSD	Family problems
	Medically unexplained symptoms	Psychosis/Mania	Social problems
		Body/Eating disorders	Work/Education problems
	Sleep disorder		
Low	Brain injury/Stroke	Cognitive problems	Housing problems
	Chronic fatigue/Stress	Personality problems	Healthcare factors
	Physical disability	Developmental problems	Economic factors
	Chronic pain/Illness		Cultural factors
		Chronic addiction	

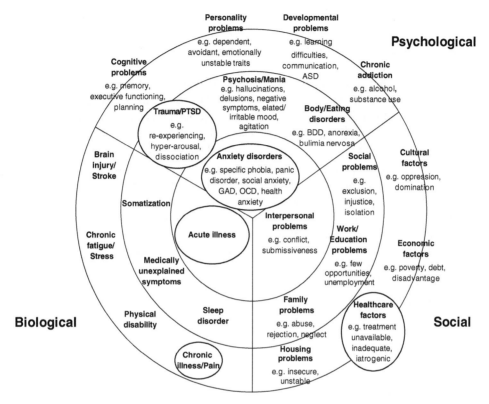

Figure 10.1   Biopsychosocial factors associated with Chloe's depression (see Chapters 5 and 6)

healthcare system: psychological treatment had initially been unavailable, with watchful waiting occurring over an extended period, contrary to NICE guidance. There were also two psychological factors: significantly heightened anxiety, equating to sub-clinical features of GAD, and the traumatic birth experience.

At this stage in the mapping process these are biopsychosocial factors, not complications (Tarrier & Johnson, 2015). The aim of assessment is to identify the factors that interact in a complicating way, even if they are few in number. The number of biopsychosocial factors is therefore *not* a sensitive measure of complexity, because it is the nature of their interaction that determines whether or not they have a complicating effect. However, the presence of multiple factors is a good indicator of the need for care co-ordination. Cases with multiple problems are not necessarily complex, but their treatment can become complicated if there is insufficient care planning and co-ordination between healthcare professionals. Clients may need biological and social interventions concurrent with their CBT; in the case of moderate or severe depression, clinical guidance recommends providing CBT in combination with anti-depressant medication (ADM), and encourages engagement with available sources of social support.

For clients with multiple problems, there is an obvious question: whose job is it to co-ordinate the overall package of care? A number of arrangements can work well. Sometimes the client's General Practitioner (GP) is best placed to overview the care-plan, and it is sufficient for different professionals to be kept informed of each other's work. However, as the number of biopsychosocial factors and interventions increases, there is an advantage in having a named care co-ordinator working within special-ist mental or physical health services. This does not have to be the CBT therapist; in fact, there are distinct advantages in it not being the CBT therapist. There is a poten-tial risk that care co-ordination becomes conflated with the tasks of therapy: time and resources that could be spent providing CBT are devoted to care co-ordination instead. In the worst-case scenario, this can become a complication within the CBT, if the treatment becomes diffuse and interrupted by broader healthcare problems. The complication in this situation is not that the client has multiple problems; it is the absence of separate care co-ordination.

Macro Formulations

Even when care co-ordination is held elsewhere, when clients have multiple prob-lems there is a risk of CBT becoming diffuse and disorganized. The CBT therapist needs to be aware of the range of biopsychosocial factors affecting the client; but it does not follow that they all need to be addressed explicitly in therapy. It is helpful during the assessment process to use the biopsychosocial map to generate hypothe-ses about the case. This produces what we call a *macro formulation*, in other words an *overview of the major factors that could be linked to the client's depression*. Figure 10.2 provides an example, taking the factors identified in Figure 10.1 and hypothesiz-ing how they might interact with depression, and each other. In Chloe's case, the therapist formed a hypothesis that her early experiences with cardiac ill-health had an unhelpful psychological impact and increased her susceptibility to anxi-ety and depression. As we will explore in Chapter 12, this hypothesis turned out to be accurate, enabling Chloe and her therapist to undertake a further piece of work integrating her traumatic memories, once her mood had improved and sta-bilized. Notice, however, that the macro formulation did not form the main basis of early-phase treatment, as outlined in Chapter 6. As you will recall, the early therapeutic work focused on approach motivation, behavioural engagement and reflective processing. These targets emerged from a *micro formulation* of Chloe's depression, in other words, *cognitive and behavioural processes that maintain specific problems.*

This illustrates one of the dilemmas working with cases with multiple problems: whether to pursue a *macro* or *micro* therapeutic strategy. A macro strategy aims for a broad-based clinical formulation that encapsulates the full range of the client's problems. It has the advantage of breadth: non-depression factors are incorporated, and the therapist is well-placed to intervene if and when they become complications. A micro strategy aims for a highly specified formulation of one of the client's presenting problems, such as their depression. It has the advantage of depth: maintenance processes are formulated in a high level of detail, and the therapist is well placed to initiate a process of change.

When working with clients with multiple problems, the art of therapy is maintaining the balance between the two. When a micro strategy is adopted, therapeutic attention is tightly focused on an identified problem and, at worst, this can create blinkers to other important phenomena. A restricted field of vision, and insufficient reflective distance, can result. When a macro strategy is adopted, there is a risk that a comprehensive formulation becomes an end in itself, rather than a catalyst for change. Time spent conceptualizing the whole case could be devoted to active experimentation with one of the client's problems, thereby promoting a process of change. Over-commitment to either approach can be a barrier to change. If the macro level is neglected, non-depression factors can complicate treatment without the therapist noticing. If the micro level is neglected, formulation can become an end in itself. The suggested balance is to adopt a *micro approach with macro awareness.* In other words, focus in detail on agreed target problems, but maintain a broad awareness of non-depression factors that could complicate the therapy. The biopsychosocial map helps to maintain that broader awareness.

As we have stated, the presence of multiple biopsychosocial factors does not, in itself, constitute complexity. The question is then: under what conditions do multiple factors lead to *complications*? Our answer defines complexity with respect to the process of treatment, not just attributes of the client. Biopsychosocial factors become complications when their interactions *impede the working alliance* and/or *modify the usual maintenance of a disorder.* We will explore each of these in turn.

Working Alliances

As we introduced in Chapters 1 and 6, the therapeutic alliance in CBT is very important: it is the bedrock of collaboration that enables a shared process of reflection, experimentation and change. There are two related aspects: (a) the personal bond; (b) engagement with goals and tasks. The *working alliance* is the

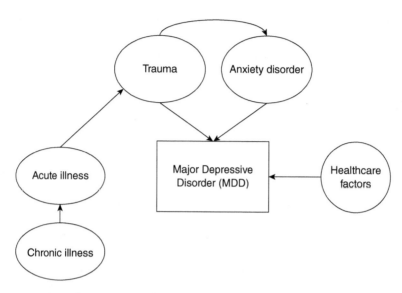

Figure 10.2 Hypotheses about Chloe's macro formulation

interaction of the two. The bond is the personal relationship between client and therapist expressed in mutual trust, felt-connection and 'us-ness'. When the bond is strong, there is a high level of disclosure from client to therapist, and a similarly high level of confidence in the treatment process. When goal/task engagement is strong, there is a high level of agreement about the aims of therapy and shared participation in the tasks needed to achieve them. As we outlined in Chapter 1, as the personal bond strengthens it usually facilitates engagement with more demanding tasks. When those tasks are completed, and assuming they lead to useful learning or symptomatic relief, this further strengthens the personal bond, and an upward spiral (or virtuous cycle) develops.

Biopsychosocial factors create complications, *in so far as* they impede the development of mutual trust and collaboration, and/or they obstruct engagement with the tasks that are likely to be of greatest benefit. This definition is not primarily concerned with characteristics of the client; it is concerned with the client's problems in *relationship* to their context, the therapist and the healthcare system. Consequently, rather than judging clients to be more or less complex, we try to detect and formulate *specific complications* that emerge in relation to the treatment of particular clients' problems. The therapist's task is to understand and respond to particular complications, to unblock the path to effective therapy.

Personal bond complications

We will illustrate a personal bond complication from Daniel's treatment, described in Chapter 7. As you will recall, Daniel's family was a major source of the on-going stress that had contributed to his depression. His relationship with his mother was a significant part of his difficulties, and he was initially reliant on her to transport him to therapy sessions. In one sense it was helpful that Daniel's mother was present at clinic, because it enabled her to attend some of the sessions. This created more therapeutic possibilities, and gave Daniel's therapist a clearer picture of the family dynamics. However, it created a complicated situation for Daniel and his therapist in which to form a personal bond. To obtain the benefit of an empathic and supportive therapist, Daniel had to open himself to the risk that another adult would undermine him in the presence of his mother. Initially Daniel was very anxious that the therapist would ally with his mother, and become part of the 'others' that criticized and ridiculed him. The therapist was unaware of the extent of Daniel's concerns, although he was mindful of the types of fears that might be present in a 15-year-old boy with social anxiety, in a novel social situation.

The stuckness that developed was overcome within approximately four sessions, but during this time Daniel did not speak very much in sessions, and his therapist was unsure why, other than that it was probably linked to his social anxiety. Client and therapist were stuck in a situation with *insufficient bond to engage in tasks that could strengthen their bond*. Gradually, Daniel's anxieties were disconfirmed: he learned that the therapist prioritized his needs and held a boundary around confidential information. This took a lot of skill from the therapist, to make it clear that Daniel was his main client, but also maintain a secondary alliance with his mother that would be helpful in engaging the wider family system. The therapist was correct that the stuckness was linked to Daniel's social anxiety – fears of negative evaluation from others – but he did not realize, until later, that the presence of Daniel's mother, even sitting in the waiting room, had such an inhibiting effect on Daniel's ability to collaborate.

Task engagement complications

We will illustrate a task engagement complication from Evelyn's treatment, described in Chapter 8. Evelyn and her therapist had a strong personal bond, but at one point in treatment they had a difference of opinion about the next stage in therapy. The therapist had formed the hypothesis that Evelyn's investment in work was partly helpful and partly unhelpful. It was beneficial in so far as it could help her feel better about herself: productive, supportive of others, developing a strong business, and so on. However, it appeared unhelpful that Evelyn would sometimes work to distract herself from upsetting thoughts and memories, and stay late at work to the detriment of her sleep patterns. Evelyn's husband was also concerned that she would work late, and he believed this triggered 'mini burn-outs' that would precede phases of more severe depression. Evelyn felt that her therapist, and husband, were failing to understand how helpful work was to her, because it was one of the few activities that would invariably have a beneficial effect on her mood. She were very reluctant to go down a path that could lead to her work being questioned, or threatened, so there developed a stuckness about whether, and how, to approach these issues. The personal bond was sufficiently strong to tolerate this difference of opinion; it was not a therapeutic rupture, but it created a temporary impasse in terms of the next steps in treatment.

Later in the process, the therapist was able to reflect that, at that point in treatment, he had not appreciated the extent to which Evelyn relied on her work to maintain a sense of meaning and purpose. From Evelyn's point of view, even if she did distract herself and over-work on occasions, this was a price worth paying to have a role in life that could take her away from being herself. The complication was Evelyn's over-investment in work *interacting* with the therapist's eagerness to challenge unhelpful habits. The therapist's oversight was not realizing that Evelyn needed to increase her range of helpful behaviours first, before being prepared to reduce those that were partly unhelpful. Framing the proposed task as a 'review of work behaviours' elicited a defensive response; whereas 'increasing mood-enhancing behaviours' might have been accepted as a secure path that did not threaten established ways of coping.

In both of the above examples, the client had a definite part in the complications, but it was more subtle than Daniel *being* a complex case because of his family's conflicts, and Evelyn *being* a complex case because of her over-reliance on work. A much more dynamic, less blaming and less pejorative nomenclature is needed, where the 'case' is not just the client; it is everything and everyone involved with the client, including the healthcare system.

Modified Maintenance

The second type of complexity is when biopsychosocial factors *modify the usual maintenance of a disorder*. Any biological, psychological or social factor could have this effect, but the most likely is the result of comorbidity, when the client is not only suffering from depression but has at least one other psychological disorder. Comorbid disorders can complicate the maintenance of depression, because the processes maintaining the other disorder can feed into depressive processes, and extend the ways in which it is perpetuated. In most cases, this will have implications for the therapeutic tasks needed to overcome depression; hence the link between this type of complication and task engagement within the working alliance.

Of the clients introduced in the book thus far, Angela had comorbid GAD, Chloe was traumatized (though she did not meet full criteria for PTSD), Daniel had OCD and social anxiety, and Frank had panic disorder, agoraphobia, social anxiety, GAD and height phobia. This suggests two key questions: (1) To what extent do other disorders complicate the maintenance of depression? (2) To what extent do other disorders need separate attention during treatment? These are substantial questions for therapists working with depression, because the majority of clients have comorbid disorders, and it is often implicit in treatment manuals how to approach them.

To begin reflecting on these questions, Figure 10.3 presents different types of *functional links* between comorbid disorders. Taking the simplest case of major depression (disorder A) and another disorder, such as GAD (disorder B), the figure represents four different scenarios. In the first scenario, the two disorders co-exist but do not interact. This means that B will not impede changes in A, which is potentially helpful for treatment; but neither will it benefit indirectly from improvements in A. B will not obstruct the treatment of A, but it will need separate treatment. In the second scenario, A influences B, but B does not influence A. For example, imagine that depressive rumination influences anxious worry, but not the converse. Depending on the degree of influence, a deterioration in rumination would

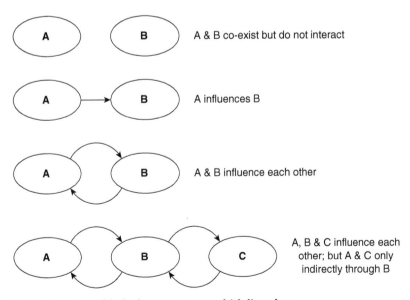

Figure 10.3   Functional links between comorbid disorders

make worry worse, and an improvement would make worry better. However, any changes in worry would not feedback into rumination. In this scenario, B will not impede the treatment of A, but it will fluctuate in response to changes in A, for better or worse. In the third scenario, A and B influence each other: they have a mutually maintaining effect, and depending on the degree and type of influence, they could impede or facilitate each other's treatment. If B improves when A improves, they are in a *sympathetic* relationship. If B worsens when A improves, they are in an *antagonistic* relationship. The fourth example is a more complex situation with three disorders and a combination of direct and indirect influences: A and B are mutually maintaining, as are B and C, whereas A and C are indirectly related through their links with B. As the number of disorders, or 'moving parts', increases there is a greater number of possible inter-relationships.

The functional links between comorbid disorders determine, to a great extent, how they need to be approached in treatment, and there are various strategies available. Our basic proposal is illustrated in Figure 10.4. The simplest type of comorbidity is when disorders co-exist but do not interact. In this scenario it is best to provide a *disorder-specific treatment*, for example, provide a course of therapy for depression, and when it is completed provide a separate course of treatment for the other disorder. There is a clear logic to this strategy, and for some time it was assumed this was how all treatment should proceed, with separate protocols for different disorders. In fact, nature is often kinder than this: a number of CBT evidence bases suggest that by treating one disorder successfully, other comorbid disorders tend to improve, even though they did not receive *direct* therapeutic attention.

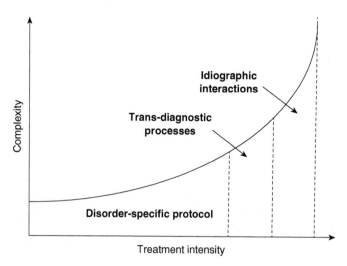

Figure 10.4   Therapeutic strategies for approaching comorbid presentations

How does this work? There are two potential explanations. One is that clients learn skills in a disorder-specific course of treatment that they then apply to their other problems. So even if two disorders co-exist and do not interact, CBT knowledge and skills can be applied beyond the parameters of the first disorder. Of course, this is what we want to encourage in any course of CBT: consolidation and generalization of the learning to tackle other problems and stay well in the future. The second explanation is that the first course of treatment has a *trans-diagnostic effect*: its effects span beyond the disorder that is directly targeted for change (Clark, 2009). Even within a disorder-specific treatment, cognitive and behavioural processes can be shared or functionally linked with other disorders. This fits with scenarios 2, 3 and 4 in Figure 10.3. Depending on the shared processes or functional links, a treatment entirely focused on one disorder could have a considerable impact on another, through trans-diagnostic effects. For these reasons, the treatment of comorbid presentations is not necessarily complex; disorder-specific treatments can still be effective and, on some occasions, may be sufficient. It depends on the client's learning and how far it is generalized. It also depends on the functional links between comorbid disorders; whether or not they share trans-diagnostic processes and are sympathetically linked.

The second treatment strategy is to provide a *trans-diagnostic therapy*. This seeks to take advantage of shared processes and functional links between disorders. In this scenario it is assumed, or known, that comorbid disorders share common psychological processes and/or are functionally linked in a mutually maintaining way. Complexity is likely to be higher in this scenario, because non-depression factors are influencing depression, and potentially altering how it is maintained. Rather than treat one disorder, in the hope that it has an indirect effect on the other, deliberately target the processes known to maintain both disorders. This will increase the likelihood of having a potent effect across different problems; it will also reduce the probability of needing separate, sequential courses of therapy with different protocols for different disorders. Of course, this strategy relies on having a clear model of what the trans-diagnostic processes are, and this will vary depending on the comorbidities that are present.

The final strategy is to provide a *bespoke treatment*. This uses a combination of trans-diagnostic and disorder-specific elements to target the unique relationships between an individual's disorders or problems. It is *idiographic*: highly specific to the individual case in question. Both the disorder-specific and trans-diagnostic approaches take *nomothetic* knowledge and apply it in an *idiographic* way; in other words, they take generalizable models of disorders, such as depression, GAD, OCD, etc., and seek to apply them to individual cases, with an appropriate level of individualization. In a stepped care system, it makes sense to try disorder-specific and trans-diagnostic approaches first, on the assumption they have a sufficiently high a priori probability of success. However, if disorder-specific and trans-diagnostic treatments have not been effective, it may be because those processes are not interacting in a normal or typical way in the case in question, i.e. there are unusual or atypical interactions at play that do not 'obey' the usual rules of how these problems are maintained.

As treatment progresses from disorder-specific to trans-diagnostic to bespoke, therapist competence also has to progress. Disorder-specific treatments need *competent* therapists who are responsive to client need and maintain good fidelity to treatment protocols. Trans-diagnostic treatments need *proficient* therapists who recognize shared maintenance processes across disorders and/or can target specific functional links. Bespoke treatments need *expert* therapists who can apply the principles of CBT in unusual or atypical situations where a protocol is not available. Alternatively, bespoke therapy can be offered by competent and proficient therapists receiving expert supervision. Bespoke therapy carries the greatest risk of therapeutic drift, hence why good supervision is essential.

In Chapters 11 and 12, we will explore how these principles are applied to the treatment of depression in the context of anxiety disorders, trauma and PTSD. These are the most common comorbidities of depression in clinical services, and we will explore how the complexity framework can support therapists to adjust treatment accordingly. Of course, there are a significant number of other comorbidities, including psychosis, mania, BDD (Body Dysmorphic Disorder), eating disorders, cognitive problems, personality problems, developmental problems and addictions: these are equally deserving of attention in terms of their relationship to depression. We realize it will be a disappointment to some readers that there are not separate chapters on these topics, particularly for those working in services where these are common presentations. This is the challenge of heterogeneity in major depression: it is a highly comorbid disorder and interacts in different ways with different problems. This would be an unfeasibly long book if it covered all possible comorbidities; instead we encourage readers to follow the same method and process that we lay out in Chapters 11 and 12, and apply these principles to the particular comorbidities presenting in your service.

Practitioner Tips: Working with Complex Cases

There are a number of guidance points to help CBT therapists work effectively with complex cases:

- Use exact terms when describing depressed clients and try not to conflate 'complex' with other features of depression such as severe, high-risk, recurrent or chronic. These features can create difficult personal and technical challenges, for clients and therapists, but they are not necessarily complicated or complex.

- Pay attention to biological, psychological and social factors that co-occur with depression. Presentations with several biopsychosocial factors can have 'multiple moving parts' that can cause therapy to become diffuse or unfocused. When multiple problems are present, it is helpful for care co-ordination to be held separately to the CBT.
- When multiple factors are present, provide a disorder-specific treatment in the first instance. Work with a *micro formulation* of the client's depression, that is, the cognitive and behavioural processes that perpetuate depressed moods. At the same time, keep a *macro awareness* of non-depression factors that could affect the client and the treatment.
- Complexity consists in biopsychosocial factors interacting to impede the *working alliance*. When this happens, pause and reflect on the way that the personal bond, or engagement with goals and tasks, is being blocked or frustrated. Try to understand the interaction of the factors that are having this effect, rather than assume it is a fixed attribute of the client.
- Complexity also consists in the maintenance of depression being extended or modified in some way, often through its interaction with comorbid disorders. Comorbidity does not prevent disorder-specific treatments from being effective, at least some of the time. When they are not effective, increase the focus on *trans-diagnostic processes* that could be maintaining several disorders.
- When disorder-specific and trans-diagnostic strategies have not been effective, it may be due to unusual or unstable interactions *between* a client's problems that are unique to that individual case. In this scenario, develop a bespoke formulation and treatment that attempts to understand and target case-level interactions.

11

Comorbid Anxiety Disorders

The main questions addressed in this chapter are: to what extent do anxiety disorders modify the maintenance of depression, and do they need separate attention during treatment? Approximately 50% of people with major depression have a comorbid anxiety disorder (Hirschfield, 2001; Kessler et al., 2015), but these are not necessarily *complications* as we have defined them in Chapter 10. This chapter explores three scenarios, one of comorbid depression with Generalized Anxiety Disorder (GAD), where the client (Angela, from Chapter 2) recovered from GAD without her anxiety disorder receiving direct attention. In this case, Angela's depression was *influenced* by anxious worry and other GAD-related phenomena, but disorder-specific treatment for depression was sufficient to treat both disorders. We explore the mechanisms through which treatment for depression can have indirect effects on GAD.

A disorder-specific strategy will not work in every case, particularly when there are multiple comorbidities, and in the second scenario, we reconsider Frank's treatment (Chapter 9) as a trans-diagnostic treatment that prioritized *shared maintenance processes* between several disorders: panic disorder, agoraphobia, social anxiety, GAD and height phobia. A combination of trans-diagnostic and disorder-specific processes resulted in a simpler and more efficient therapy than treating each disorder separately. In the final example, a bespoke formulation and therapy was developed to treat an unusual clinical presentation in which depressed mood was one of a number of unstable affective states, including OCD, hypomania and post-traumatic anger. This case begins to explore depression and anxiety in the context of other problems, such as trauma, which we will explore in more detail in Chapter 12. In this case, the relationship *between* the client's problems was highly specific to that individual, indicating an unusual set of maintenance processes. These three therapeutic strategies – *disorder-specific, trans-diagnostic, bespoke* – respond to increasing complexity, with maintenance processes that are modified in different ways through their interaction with comorbid anxiety.

Disorder-Specific Strategy

There is little doubt about the associations between depression, worry and GAD. From epidemiological studies, people with depression are eight times more likely to have GAD than people who are not depressed; and people with GAD are sixty-two times more likely to develop depression in the following 12 months, compared with people who do not have GAD (Hirschfield, 2001). Consequently, in epidemiological studies, approximately 15% of people with major depression have comorbid GAD. GAD is characterized by anxiety and excessive worry about a number of events or activities, occurring more days than not for at least 6 months. The individual has difficulty controlling their worries and typical symptoms include restlessness, being easily fatigued, difficulty concentrating, irritability, muscle tension and sleep disturbance. There can also be sweating, dry mouth, palpitations and urinary frequency.

Recall Angela, who we introduced in Chapter 2. She was suffering from a chronic, moderate depression with comorbid GAD that had been precipitated by problems in her marriage. She received a standard course of Beck's CBT for depression, and did not receive separate treatment for GAD. However, by the end of her treatment: (a) her anxiety levels had normalized, (b) she was worrying much less than before, (c) she had learned about the unhelpfulness of avoidance, (d) she had a more proactive orientation to solving problems, (e) she was more able to tolerate uncertainty, particularly regarding what other people thought of her. These changes suggest that Angela's GAD *had been* treated, through the indirect or trans-diagnostic effects of her depression treatment.

As we introduced in Chapter 10, we believe there are two potential explanations for improvements in 'non-treated' anxiety disorders: (1) clients apply the CBT skills they have learned with depression to their anxiety disorder; (2) treatment has a trans-diagnostic effect, depending on shared maintenance processes and/or specific *functional links* between the disorders. These are variants of the same underlying hypothesis that CBT can provoke *indirect change*: therapy impacts on problems that were not directly targeted. There is now compelling evidence from various CBT literatures that this is the case, with two caveats. Firstly, skill generalization depends on the learning and motivation of the client, and this varies greatly across clients. Secondly, the likelihood of a trans-diagnostic effect depends on the disorders in question, whether they share maintenance processes and/or have specific functional links (Ellard, Fairholme, Boisseau, Farchione & Barlow, 2010).

In the case of depression and GAD, we suspect there are several functional links, in other words *mutually maintaining* processes. On the one hand, this could be bad news because anxiety and worry might extend, and complicate, the maintenance of depression. On the other hand, it could be good news, because change in either disorder might have a 'virtuous' effect on the other. Improvements in worry will benefit depressed mood, and improvements in depressed mood will benefit worry – assuming they have a *sympathetic* relationship. We have speculated on the potential mechanisms in Angela's case, by considering the core maintenance processes of GAD, as proposed in the Laval model (Dugas, Gagnon, Ladouceur & Freeston, 1998), and reflected on how Angela's treatment could have indirectly impacted on them.

The Laval model of GAD proposes that there is an underlying intolerance of uncertainty that drives people to anticipate and try to control the future by worrying about it (*intolerance of uncertainty*). This results in *less* engagement in solving current problems, so worry can in fact be an avoidance of difficulties, rather than a way of facing them (*negative problem orientation*). However, people *feel as if* they are preventing danger, or at least preparing for it, so they tend to have positive beliefs about worry and appraise it as a helpful activity (*positive beliefs about worry*). People with GAD also generate hypothetical threats, that may or may not occur in the future, and then form an ambivalent relationship with them; sometimes they become highly engaged in the details of what could go wrong – which tends to be very distressing. On other occasions, they are motivated to suppress and escape from those thoughts, to obtain some relief from their fears (*cognitive avoidance*). A course of CBT for GAD seeks to increase tolerance of uncertainty, create more effective means of problem solving, reduce positive beliefs about worry and expose/habituate to hypothetical worries, rather than avoid them.

Table 11.1 lists the core features of GAD and the main components of the Laval treatment protocol. In the right hand column, we have speculated on those aspects of Angela's treatment that could have impacted, indirectly, on GAD processes. For each component of GAD, there is a potential *indirect effect* of activity scheduling, testing predictions, experimenting with thought suppression and exploring assumptions and beliefs. This is consistent with the hypothesis that the cognitive and behavioural changes needed to overcome depression are *sufficiently matched* to the changes needed to overcome GAD, so consequently, in Angela's case, the GAD improved and did not need separate treatment. We are not suggesting that there would have been no additional benefit in Angela receiving a full GAD protocol; on the contrary, it is possible that this would have been very helpful, and made the worry-related changes more explicit. However, this needs to be balanced with the therapeutic attention that was paid to Angela's other problems. Later in the chapter, we will demonstrate how the self-regulation model, compared with Beck's CBT, puts more emphasis on ruminative processes and their functional links with anxious worry.

To what extent did GAD *complicate* the maintenance of Angela's depression? In Angela's case, not very much; her worries generated a lot of negative predictions and these maintained a felt-sense of insecurity and pessimism, but worrying did not need separate attention during treatment, because Angela quickly learned that her predictions tended to be inaccurate and unhelpful. In relation to the disorder-specific strategy, this case demonstrates the potential value of *treating one disorder thoroughly*.

Table 11.1   Potential impacts of Angela's depression treatment on GAD

Core feature of GAD	GAD treatment protocol	Impact of depression treatment
Negative problem orientation (NPO)	*Problem-solving current difficulties* (a) Problem orientation and definition (b) Generation of alternative solutions (c) Decision making (d) Implementing solutions	*Activity scheduling* (a) Overcoming avoidance (b) Increasing assertiveness, e.g. phone-calls with solicitor and husband
Positive beliefs about worry (PBW)	*Re-evaluation of positive beliefs about worry* (a) Identify positive beliefs (b) Arguments for and against each belief (c) Tolerate uncertainty rather than try to control the future through worry	*Testing out predictions* (a) Predictions can be inaccurate, e.g. *'People will think I'm worthless if they know what I've been through'* – disconfirmed by disclosure to friends: *'My husband will hate me if I stand up to him'* – he was not as angry and dismissive as predicted (b) Thoughts are not facts (c) Predicting the future is not always possible or helpful
Cognitive avoidance (CA)	*Cognitive exposure* (a) Repeated exposure to worries about hypothetical situations, e.g. listen to worst fear on a tape loop	*Thought suppression experiments* (a) It makes things worse to put a lid on problems and push them out of mind
Intolerance of uncertainty (IU)	*Awareness training* (a) Differentiate worry about real and hypothetical problems (b) Recognize, accept and deal with uncertainty, rather than try to eliminate it	*Assumptions and beliefs* (a) Less belief in needing others' approval (b) Less worry about what other people think; more tolerant of not knowing what others think about her

Because Angela's depression was treated carefully and with good fidelity, this maximized the benefit to overcoming her depression *and* other non-targeted problems. If other disorders can benefit through indirect effects, those effects are more likely to occur when therapy is well organized and appropriately targeted.

We are not suggesting that a disorder-specific strategy is appropriate, or will be effective and sufficient, in all cases. We are suggesting that when it is adopted, it is best to *tether* to the agreed disorder, rather than oscillate attention between disorder A one session, then disorder B the next, and so on. This is one of the biggest traps in treating comorbid presentations: being caught between treating one disorder thoroughly and trying to give attention to all the client's problems. This is what can lead therapy to becoming diffuse and disorganized. It is not an easy balance to strike, particularly when the client's preferences, and personal situation, can change over time. In these scenarios, we try to remember the guidance in Figure 10.4: in most cases it is best tethering to one disorder to *find out* if a disorder-specific treatment can be effective. If it is not effective, or cannot be delivered, then clients need to step up to a trans-diagnostic or bespoke approach, either within the same course of therapy, to a different step within the service, or referred onto another service.

Tethering

The principle behind tethering is attempting to keep the therapeutic focus on an agreed target when comorbidity or multiple problems are present. The approach can be summarized as follows, and we have expressed these principles in a decision-tree format in Figure 11.1.

1. Tether to a primary target (A) and keep it the main priority, using an explicit *micro formulation*.
2. Monitor the influence of other factors on A, and A's effects on the other factors (*macro awareness*). If another factor (B) limits progress on A, give B time-limited therapeutic attention.
3. Attend only to those aspects of B that are limiting progress on A, and return the focus to A once those aspects of B have been resolved.
4. Review progress on A after a sustained dose of treatment has been delivered.
5. Only change the primary target:

    i. when A is resolved and other problems require further attention
    ii. if limited progress has been made on A, in spite of targeting it in a consistent way for a sustained period of time.

Trans-diagnostic Strategy

When multiple comorbidities are present, it is a priori less likely that a disorder-specific approach will be sufficient to treat the whole case. This does not mean that disorder-specific elements should be discarded. Indeed, the guidance in Figure 10.4

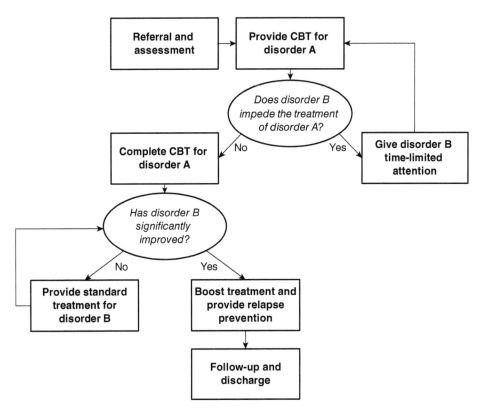

Figure 11.1   Decision tree for the disorder-specific treatment of comorbid depression and anxiety

can apply *within* a single course of treatment; a disorder-specific phase could reveal the need to focus the treatment in a different way. In addition to the fact that the client is likely to have multiple problems, the step up to a trans-diagnostic approach is characterized by three other differences. Firstly, trans-diagnostic effects are *intended*; they do not occur indirectly or accidentally, as in Table 11.1. Secondly, there is greater emphasis on *cognitive processes* and less on thought-content and beliefs, since it is processes that are often shared and linked across disorders. Thirdly, there is *less emphasis on diagnosis* and working within the parameters of a disorder-specific model (Barlow et al., 2017).

To illustrate these differences, we will reflect further on Frank's treatment (Chapter 9). As you will recall, Frank had received six courses of counselling, clinical psychology or psychotherapy, including a recent thirty-session course of CBT for panic and depression, so there had been plenty of opportunity for standard therapies to help him. He was affected by multiple anxiety comorbidities: panic disorder, agoraphobia, GAD, social anxiety disorder and height phobia. Notice what happens when we apply a macro strategy to formulating Frank's problems. Figure 11.2 maps out the potential comorbid relationships between his six diagnoses.

Figure 11.2 *looks* complicated. It certainly has multiple moving parts, but it is not obvious from visual inspection where one would begin treatment. On the assumption that there is an interaction between each comorbid pairing, there are fifteen comorbid relationships to consider. Within each of these relationships, there may be particular functional links, and these will vary from pairing to pairing. For example, if depression and GAD are functionally linked through disengagement/avoidance and rumination/worry, this would make (at least) two links within that comorbid relationship. Assuming two links within each pairing, the macro formulation would need to specify thirty maintenance processes to establish a comprehensive formulation.

We are not suggesting that these links do not exist; on the contrary, we believe that they do exist. But to work out what they are will be excessively time-consuming and confusing. It is not pragmatic or useful to do so, because it is not practical to deliver a

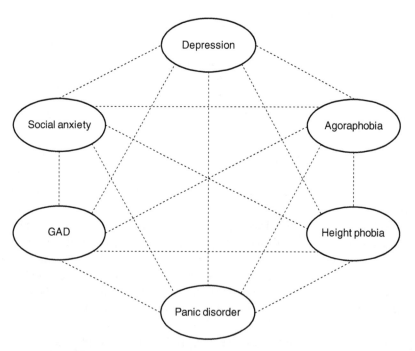

Figure 11.2   Potential interactions in a macro formulation of Frank's depression and comorbid anxiety disorders

course of treatment that targets thirty maintenance cycles. A comprehensive macro formulation, in this situation, could easily become an end in itself, with repeated cycles of conceptualization and minimal progress towards experimentation and change. In this situation, the complication would be the effect of the macro formulation on the working alliance, not the presence of multiple disorders *per se*. An alternative approach is to exploit the fact that depression and anxiety disorders are functionally linked through a number of trans-diagnostic processes. Rather than treat each individual anxiety disorder, target processes that are present *across* anxiety disorders.

Trans-diagnostic links between depression and anxiety

Figure 11.3 depicts a simplified version of the self-regulation model of depression, omitting the content level. Linked to each sub-system is a dashed figure outlining anxiety-based processes and structures. These are trans-diagnostic in the sense that they are not specific to any particular anxiety disorder; rather, they illustrate the *types*

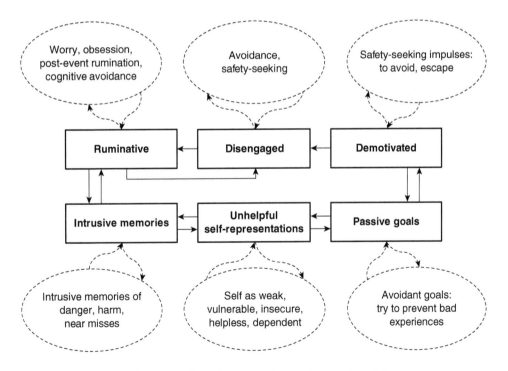

Figure 11.3   Trans-diagnostic links between depression and anxiety disorders

of processes and structures that are present across a range of anxiety disorders. When each of the depressive subsystems is considered, we can see various ways in which shared processes and functional links could manifest between depression and anxiety (Mansell, Harvey, Watkins & Shafran, 2009):

1. *Demotivated.* In anxious states, avoidant impulses produce urges to seek safety through avoidance and escape. Anxious people are motivated to prevent perceived threats, and this has the potential to interact with suppressed approach motivation.
2. *Disengaged.* Anxious avoidance and escape can be mutually maintaining with various forms of depressive disengagement: under-activity, social withdrawal, submissiveness, suicidality.
3. *Ruminative.* Unhelpful repetitive thinking is observed in several anxiety disorders: for example, worry (GAD, health anxiety, social anxiety), obsessional preoccupation (OCD, BDD), post-event rumination (social anxiety, PTSD). Anxiety disorders are also associated with thought suppression and cognitive avoidance.
4. *Intrusive memories.* People with anxiety disorders have increased access to memories of dangerous situations and perceived near misses. These can be intrusive and distressing, maintaining a felt-sense of insecurity and uncertainty (Speckens, Hackmann, Ehlers & Cuthbert, 2007).
5. *Unhelpful self-representations.* People with anxiety disorders sometimes represent themselves as weak, vulnerable, insecure, helpless or dependent. These can contribute to self-devaluation.
6. *Passive goals.* People with anxiety disorders form avoidant goals to try to prevent bad experiences, such as others rejecting them, becoming ill, causing harm, having a heart attack, and so on. Avoidant goals can contribute to the suppression of approach goals (Dickson & MacLeod, 2004).

In Frank's treatment, behavioural engagement was the primary change target throughout. The change process was nested within a structure of approach goals, incentivizing Frank towards the destination he desired, to become a painter/decorator. Behavioural engagement had the advantage of targeting *shared process* with behavioural avoidance that was present across all of Frank's anxiety disorders. This is illustrated in Figure 11.4. Compare the macro formulation in Figure 11.2 with the trans-diagnostic strategy in Figure 11.4: notice how much simpler the trans-diagnostic approach is. Rather than targeting thirty maintenance cycles, Frank's therapy mostly focused on two: behavioural disengagement and avoidance. Of course, the *objects* of Frank's avoidance varied over time, including being away from his house, fainting, people asking him what he had been doing, what his family would think, falling from steps, being unable to buy a coffee, being unable to manage college, and so on. In each case, there was a way of engaging behaviourally with the feared outcomes, and nesting approach behaviours within the structure of approach goals that had already been established.

As in the disorder-specific approach, when focusing on a trans-diagnostic target, it is important to remain 'macro aware' of potential interactions with other factors, just as Frank and his therapist did. Therapy was still *tethered* to behavioural engagement, but other factors, such as worry and self-critical rumination, were given time-limited attention to overcome their limiting effects, if and when they halted progress. Having received the attention they needed, this had a consolidating effect on Frank's learning, and treatment then returned to focus directly on behavioural engagement. Consequently, although Frank had six comorbid disorders, his treatment was *simple at the point of delivery*. It was not simplistic; it was carefully structured, targeted and supported. But his therapist avoided the trap of working from an overly complex macro formulation that could easily have resulted in a diffuse, confused or disorganized therapy.

To what extent did anxiety disorders *complicate* the maintenance of Frank's depression? In Frank's case, they extended it to some extent but in a generally predictable way; not in a way that was complicated to understand. Did they need separate attention during treatment? They needed some separate attention, but not very much, because by tethering to behavioural engagement, the therapy was able to target trans-diagnostic processes that were shared across disorders. Frank is a good example of a client who was difficult to treat, but not particularly complex. It was difficult, for both Frank and his therapist, to tolerate the slow process of change, and to support the developmental 'catch up' task, in terms of a second adolescence. But neither of these factors was *complex*, in terms of an impeded working alliance or unusual maintenance.

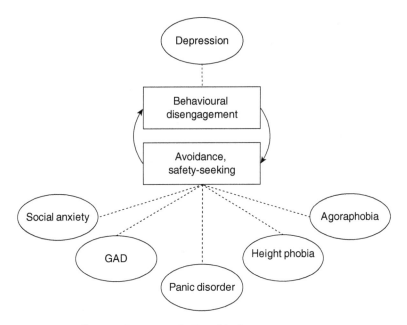

Figure 11.4   Trans-diagnostic targets in Frank's therapy

Bespoke Strategy

A bespoke treatment strategy develops a *micro formulation of the relationship between macro factors*. It is the option to explore when disorder-specific and trans-diagnostic approaches have been insufficient or ineffective. It is the highest intensity treatment option, because therapeutic expertise is needed to apply CBT principles in situations where there is no protocol, and/or the client's problems are at the edge of the evidence base. It is therefore difficult to standardize and benchmark bespoke treatments, and there is a risk of therapeutic drift. The need for good-quality supervision cannot be over-emphasized.

If problems A, B, C and D have not responded to disorder-specific or trans-diagnostic treatment, one explanation is that they are interacting in an antagonistic or unusual way. In these situations, the interactions between different factors are more complex than in Frank's case. They are *unpredictable* or *unstable*: targeting A has a deteriorating or unpredictable effect on B. What tends to result is an *oscillating focus* within treatment: some sessions are devoted to A, then there is a switch to B, then to C, then to D, then back to A, and so on. In this scenario it is very difficult to tether to a main target, because the clinical picture, and what is salient for the client, can change from one session to the next. A path to recovery is much harder to find, because whichever target is chosen it is difficult to effect change; other factors have a limiting effect, or deteriorate when the primary target improves. It can be confusing and dispiriting for both client and therapist in this situation. Therapists often become anxious and overwhelmed, which can reduce their reflective capacity, just when the need for supervision and reflective distance is most needed.

Under these conditions, it is essential to formulate the interactions *between* the client's problems, because it will otherwise be very difficult to find out what to target for change. The complication in this situation is not just the client's problems, it is the relationship between them that can modify normal maintenance processes and strain the working alliance. Consequently, bespoke therapy is finding a path through densely inter-woven difficulties in spite of cul-de-sacs, wrong turns and dead ends. A good case formulation is essential to map the territory, and therapists need to be tenacious, flexible and hopeful, viewing all setbacks as learning opportunities.

There are two main traps in this endeavour: (1) formulation becomes an end in itself, (2) therapy becomes complicated at the point of delivery. Clinical supervision is very important when working in this way, to offset the risks of excessive formulation and over-complicated treatment. Therapy should still be simple at the point of delivery, but deciding which simple task to undertake relies on a formulation of multiple factors affecting the case, some of which may be contextual (outside-in), and others intra-psychic (inside-out). Formulating and targeting the functional links *between* problems must be change-oriented, otherwise the therapy collapses into excessive formulation. In our experience, it takes a high level of therapeutic skill to balance support and change in these situations.

Case Illustration | Jeff

At the time of his referral to the Newcastle CBT Centre, Jeff was aged 48 and married with two daughters. He was a public service employee with a 20-year history of Obsessive Compulsive Disorder (OCD) with recurrent Major Depressive Episodes (MDE). Jeff had previously received three standard courses of CBT.

Jeff's previous courses of CBT

Treatment 1: CBT for Obsessive Compulsive Disorder (OCD). Jeff received fourteen sessions over a 4-month period. Due to unpredictable changes in mood and affect, it was difficult keeping the focus on OCD. During this treatment a psychiatric assessment resulted in a diagnosis of Bipolar II Disorder. Jeff disclosed his diagnosis to his employer, believing this was the right thing to do, and this initiated a lengthy process of occupational health assessment. The Bipolar diagnosis coincided with staffing changes in the service, and Jeff was offered a new therapist who specialized in the area of unstable mood.

Treatment 2: CBT for Bipolar Disorder (Meyer & Hautzinger, 2012). Jeff received fifty-three sessions over a 3-year period. The therapeutic dose reflected the severity of Jeff's depression, mood swings and occasional hypomanic episodes. Treatment was strongly affected by the occupational health process. Jeff was assessed by a number of medical practitioners, not all with psychiatric training. The stress and uncertainty provoked by these assessments interacted with Jeff's unstable moods and made it challenging to progress. Over an extended period there was a gradual improvement and stabilization of Jeff's mood. OCD was not the priority during this period, and it was not targeted explicitly within treatment.

Treatment 3: Consolidation of CBT for Bipolar Disorder. Jeff received a further twenty-three sessions over a 2-year period to consolidate progress and help him cope with the occupational health process. In the intervening period, his employer had reacted in a risk-averse way, moving him to a junior role within the organization. His manager informed him: 'your mental health problems mean you cannot talk

(Continued)

(Continued)

to the public'. This had a devastating effect on Jeff's self-esteem and shattered his assumptions about his employer's competence, loyalty and duty of care. It provoked extreme shock and anger, reactivated Jeff's OCD and led to further mood destabilization. The context of acute occupational stress was a complicating factor, because it increased uncertainty and made it difficult for Jeff to maintain a consistent treatment focus.

In spite of the benefits gained from these treatments, Jeff relapsed into severe depression (Beck Depression Inventory = 32), with occasional expansive moods, and his OCD had also worsened. He was preoccupied by anger with his employer and this was interfering with his functioning at work. Disorder-specific protocols had not had a lasting effect, so an alternative approach was adopted. Jeff was offered a new therapist and subsequently received forty-four sessions of CBT over a 2-year period. The strategy was firstly to map the non-depression factors that could be complicating his presentation, illustrated in Figure 11.5.

This revealed three social factors and three psychological factors. The therapist did not assume these were complicating Jeff's depression; rather there was a process of guided discovery to find out whether or not they were having a complicating effect. There was a potential healthcare factor concerning Jeff's repeated relapses that may have reduced his confidence in CBT or the service, and therefore his potential to form a working alliance. In fact, this was not the case. Jeff reported experiencing the benefits of the previous courses of CBT, but something stopped them having a sufficiently potent or lasting effect. There was a potential interpersonal factor following significant tensions between Jeff and his wife; however, they had managed to overcome these difficulties and they were no longer problematic. There was a clear and pronounced occupational factor that had a complicating effect during Jeff's previous treatments. Both his employer's behaviour, and the occupational health process, had a de-stabilizing effect on Jeff's moods; ironically, this was the problem the employer was seeking to assess and support. This regularly interfered with Jeff's readiness for treatment; the intensity of affect was so great as to reduce Jeff's capacity to reflect on his underlying problems, and made it difficult to maintain a consistent focus on therapeutic tasks. This resulted in Jeff needing a lot of support within the change process.

The three psychological factors were: OCD, hypomania and post-traumatic anger. Occupational stress over the previous 5 years had a traumatic impact on Jeff. He was not suffering from Post-Traumatic Stress Disorder (PTSD) but he continued to feel 'shocked and devastated' by his employer's actions. They had a profoundly disruptive impact on his self-identity, and Jeff felt extremely hurt and angry several years after the most stressful events had occurred. Jeff's work role had been a significant and self-defining aspect of his identity throughout his adult life.

Jeff's treatment can be summarized in four overlapping phases:

1. Mapping moods and affective states.
2. Using trans-diagnostic methods that can be applied in several mood-states.
3. Developing a micro formulation of the functional links between problems.
4. Applying disorder-specific components, staying aware of interactions with other problems.

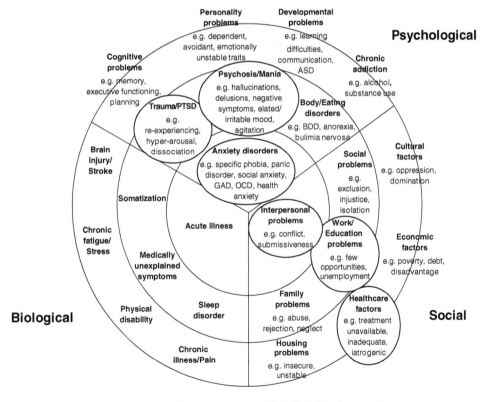

Figure 11.5 Biopsychosocial factors associated with Jeff's depression

Mapping moods and affective states

The first step was for Jeff and his therapist to understand the range of different mood and affective states that he experienced. Mood mapping is often a helpful strategy with clients who have unstable moods and/or oscillate between different affective and self-states. Treatment commenced with a macro-formulation strategy, so there was a risk of formulation becoming an end in itself. However, Jeff's affect and mood was so unstable, and unpredictable, that it would otherwise not have been possible to tether to any particular target. The initial map, shown in Figure 11.6, was very simple and it enabled Jeff to become more aware and reflective about his current mood-state. It encouraged him to *differentiate* his mental states, having recently viewed his moods and feelings simply as 'a complete mess'.

Jeff's task – which he could do at any point – was to *notice* which of the four main affective states were present. This created some helpful learning, because it was often the case that more than one mood-state was active at any point in time. This helped Jeff to understand why his mental and emotional life could be so confusing, depressing and at times terrifying. The mood map was a way of starting to make sense of the confusion. It also helped Jeff to understand the various diagnoses he had received, so they were grounded in his experience, not just professional communication and occupational health reports. In terms of the self-regulation model, mood mapping was encouraging *reflective processing*: paying attention to concrete experiences.

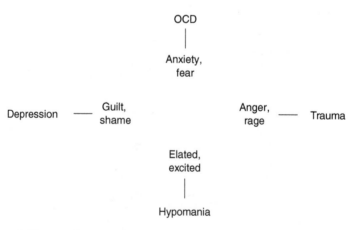

Figure 11.6   Jeff's mood map

Using trans-diagnostic methods that can be applied in several mood-states

Once Jeff was able to identify his current mood-state, the therapist helped him to learn two techniques to begin to self-regulate more effectively. It became apparent to his therapist how much of Jeff's distress was mediated through his memories and thought processes, with a lot of rumination, obsessional preoccupation and, at other times, exploring fantasies in his imagination. When Jeff was ruminative, his affect tended to become more intense and he was less reflective, so the therapist suggested a simple grounding technique to externalize his attention onto a physical object, whenever he noticed himself becoming ruminative or distressed. This was helpful to bring Jeff's attention back to the present moment, for example, when remembering upsetting events, it counteracted abstract processing when he was feeling down, and it helped him to reconnect with reality when becoming excited or hypomanic.

Like many clients with mixed anxiety/depression, Jeff had a tendency towards unhelpful repetitive thinking (URT) across different affective states. When depressed he was prone to self-critical rumination; when compulsive he would become mentally preoccupied and check his memory; when angry and upset he would replay memories and analyse them; when excited and hypomanic he would fantasize in various ways about things he had done or would like to do. In each of these states, Jeff's URT would be characterized by a range of unhelpful questions, such as: '*Will I ever recover from this? What if I act on these thoughts? Why should I have to suffer at their hands? Who else is going to take the fight to them? Why do I keep thinking like this? What if I can't change?*'

The model in Figure 11.7 was used to help Jeff understand the effects of unhelpful questions, and this increased his awareness of various ruminative mental loops and how unhelpful they were. Jeff recognized the feelings of distress and urges to analyse, understand or mentally explore; however, he had not previously realized how rarely he found the *answers* to his questions, and how they tended to maintain his upset and then lead to more unhelpful questioning.

This was an effective way of helping Jeff become more aware of his thought processes, with a technique he could apply at any time, and whatever his mental state. The main strategy was to *reflect on the question*: rather than trying to answer it. Jeff learned to ask whether it was a helpful question, and notice what effect it had in his mind. This is an extension of the method for counteracting depressive rumination that we introduced in Chapter 6. The same principle can be applied to questions that are observed in other types of URT. Again, it increases reflective processing, helping

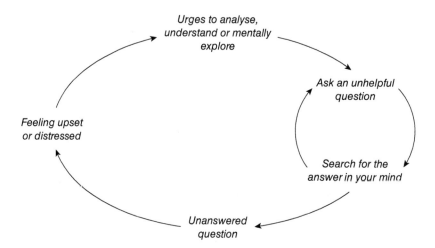

Figure 11.7   Trans-diagnostic model of unhelpful repetitive thinking (URT)

the client learn about unhelpful cognitive processes, at the same time acquiring new cognitive skills. Jeff's homework was to self-monitor his questions and write them down; then notice how they made him feel, whether he found an answer, and overall how helpful they were. This process gradually helped Jeff to 'run his head differently'; it helped him to develop a capacity for asking more helpful questions. It contributed to improved affect and self-regulation.

Developing a micro formulation of the functional links between problems

Gradually, Jeff became more aware of his moods and affective states. He was able to ground himself and notice when URT was taking over his mind. He found it difficult to counteract URT when it was present, but he recognized how unhelpful it was and almost always noticed when it was happening. The reflective process of paying attention to emotions, concrete experiences and cognitive processes enabled Jeff and his therapist to develop a better understanding of the ways his different affective states would feed off each other. The initial mood map was used as the starting point to build a better understanding of how Jeff's problems were functionally linked. As the formulation developed, it increased Jeff's mental freedom to decide how best to respond when his mind reacted in certain ways. The strategy was to accept and *not* try to control involuntary mental events, but rather encourage *mental agency* to develop a good self–mind relationship.

The final micro formulation is presented in Figure 11.8. It *appears* complex on first reading. There are multiple moving parts, and it can take some time to grasp the functional links between Jeff's problems. In summary, Jeff felt traumatized by the way his employer had treated him: he was deeply shocked and still emotionally upset by it several years after the most upsetting events. He did not have PTSD, but he had not fully accepted, processed or come to terms with what happened. Jeff would become very angry when he remembered what had happened, and this anger was still raw and unprocessed. Sometimes it would lead to urges for revenge and retaliation. Occasionally, Jeff would have violent images of how he could act on this. These were extremely upsetting for Jeff who was a conscientious, law-abiding citizen with a strong moral compass. They would activate obsessional concerns, and Jeff would feel a responsibility to do something to make sure he didn't act on these images.

A complication was the counter-tendency for Jeff's hypomanic mode to be activated by the violent images and impulses. He sometimes would become excited by

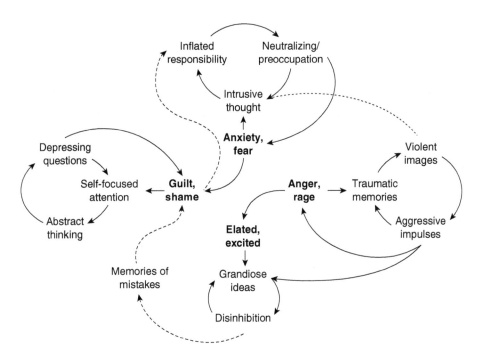

Figure 11.8   Micro formulation of the relationship between Jeff's problems

the idea of wreaking revenge on his bosses, and play it through in his mind as if it was a film and he was a movie star. When this happened, the therapist felt concerned about risk to others. Jeff was also concerned about this, because he had shameful memories of behaving inappropriately previously, when in a hypomanic state.

After careful assessment, all the evidence showed that Jeff had never been verbally or physically aggressive in his adult life, even when hypomanic. He was extremely law abiding and very concerned about right action; in fact, this was a core aspect of his self-identity, having a responsible position at work. When he had been inappropriate in the past, he had made unwise decisions about purchases, made promises to friends and colleagues that he was unable to keep, and disclosed personal information about family members. In his mind, these were terrible and shameful acts that fuelled his doubts about what he was capable of. Jeff's mood could become depressed after remembering these experiences; they would further inflate his sense of guilt and responsibility to prevent harm; hence, violent images could simultaneously trigger obsessions and hypomanic excitement, and either of these could lead to depressed mood, through different mental routes.

It took more than forty therapy sessions to build this formulation and use it to structure Jeff's treatment. What we want to emphasize is this: Jeff *understood* his formulation; he had helped to build it, piece by piece over several months. It was not given to him early in therapy like a completed jigsaw. It was the result of collaboration, experimentation and change. So although the final version has multiple moving parts, these were meaningful and helpful to Jeff, because he was one of its architects. This is one of the key pieces of guidance when creating a bespoke formulation and treatment: if something complicated needs to be understood, it needs to formulated *with* the client, and built up gradually with its various component parts. It also needs to inform experiments with change, so that it does not become an end in itself.

Applying disorder-specific components, staying aware of interactions with other problems

In Jeff's case, his depressed moods were mostly mediated by rumination and not behavioural disengagement. When Jeff was feeling down, the strategy was to encourage external attention, concrete processing and helpful questions. The question Jeff found most helpful was: *'What do I need right now?'* This would usually counteract rumination and help him to engage in adaptive actions. Jeff's hypomanic moods did not need any further direct treatment, only consolidation of his previous CBT: noticing hypomanic impulses when they were present, remembering unhelpful consequences of acting on them, keeping regular sleep patterns, and so on.

Jeff's OCD was treated with approximately ten sessions of Exposure and Response Prevention (ERP; National Collaborating Centre for Mental Health, 2005). Jeff learned to let violent thoughts be in his mind without suppressing them, analysing them or otherwise neutralizing them. What helped Jeff was to appraise them as 'the ghost under the bed'; an imaginary threat that is only given power if taken seriously. The only adjustment needed to standard ERP was Jeff monitoring for hypomanic impulses during the exposure, not to neutralize them, but to notice them.

Jeff's post-traumatic anger needed lots of opportunities to be remembered, expressed and validated, particular when there had been real unfairness in his workplace. By the time of Jeff's retirement from work, he had allowed a *lot* of anger and hurt to be felt and experienced, and over time this was accompanied by reduced rumination and a dissipation of the violent images. To Jeff's amazement, his manager made a public apology during his retirement lunch for how he had been treated, helping to provide further closure to that period of life. At the time of writing, Jeff has been stable and well for the past 2 years, with occasional mild anxiety and depressed moods that he has been able to self-regulate independently. His post-treatment Beck Depression Inventory score was 10.

To what extent did anxiety disorders *complicate* the maintenance of Jeff's depression? In Jeff's case, a great deal. For several sessions, Jeff and his therapist were bewildered trying to understand his different mood-states, obsessional fears and post-traumatic anger. When Jeff felt depressed, it manifested in a similar way to most depressed moods, but it rarely occurred in isolation. Jeff would oscillate between dejection, hurt, anger, fear and elation, sometimes in the same therapy session; a macro formulation of the interaction of these problems was essential for treatment to progress.

Did the other disorders need separate attention during treatment? In Jeff's case: yes. The main trans-diagnostic process was unhelpful repetitive thinking (URT); this provided a framework for Jeff to reflect on his mental state and guide his thinking towards concrete experiences and helpful questions. Within this framework, he needed specific help with obsessional preoccupation and post-traumatic rumination, so a combination of disorder-specific and trans-diagnostic elements was needed. Overall, the way that Jeff's problems interacted was complex, much more so than Angela or Frank. His therapist had to work hard not to allow the formulation to become an end in itself, but because it explained the *relationship between* Jeff's problems, and because Jeff was an equal partner in developing it, it ultimately had a simplifying effect on treatment, even though it had multiple moving parts.

Practitioner Tips: Working with Comorbid Depression and Anxiety

There are a number of guidance points to help CBT therapists work effectively with comorbid anxiety disorders:

- When treating comorbid presentations, the default option is to *treat one disorder well*. Therapy for comorbid depression and anxiety sometimes oscillates between disorders, resulting in neither receiving adequate attention. To counteract this, provide a disorder-specific treatment in the first instance. This could target depression, in the hope that it will have an indirect effect on the anxiety disorder; or it could target the anxiety disorder, in the hope that it will have an indirect effect on depression. It is therefore important know anxiety disorder models and protocols, not just models of depression.
- Tether to a primary target and try not to switch focus regularly to other problems. If other factors limit progress, give them time-limited attention and return the focus to the main target, when those aspects have been resolved. The more straightforward the formulation and intervention can be kept, the less likely therapy is to drift.
- Do not rush to provide bespoke therapy on observing 'multiple moving parts'. If it has not been possible to deliver a disorder-specific therapy, or it has not been effective, look for trans-diagnostic processes common to multiple disorders (e.g. URT, avoidance). Targeting common processes can provide effective interventions for the different disorders that they maintain.
- It can also be helpful to explore particular *functional links* between disorders, in other words, mutually maintaining cycles. If the formulation and targeting of links is accurate, this increases the likelihood of a positive effect on both disorders.
- A minority of cases will need an individualized formulation of the *interactions* between depression, anxiety disorders and other relevant biopsychosocial factors. These can be highly specific to the individual case and need to be targeted carefully for change. Therapy should still be simple at the point of delivery, and good quality supervision is essential to support and regulate this.
- If a bespoke formulation and therapy are required, take time to build the formulation in *full collaboration with the client*. Understanding the client's problems should not develop more quickly than the client's speed of learning. Therapists should retain a healthy scepticism of their own hypotheses, especially if they have a felt-sense of knowing better than the client.
- Remember: bespoke therapy does not constitute a departure from the commitment to evidence-based practice, but *adherence* to the underpinning evidence and principles of evidence-based practice in the treatment of complex and atypical presentations.

12

Post-Traumatic Depression

Introduction

Traumatic events are extremely stressful and can have shocking, painful, disturbing and upsetting effects that, for some individuals, persist for a long time afterwards. Trauma is partly defined by objective events and partly by subjective reactions. For example, news reports of natural disasters or terrorist attacks describe objective threats to life and wellbeing. Survivors of such events can be highly traumatized, and it is understandable when they are. However, many people survive near-death experiences without feeling significantly shocked or traumatized: they recover normal functioning quite quickly. When two people experience a similar objective threat, one can be left traumatized, while the other is relatively unaffected. From a psychological perspective, it is an individual's *subjective experience* (interpretation) that matters, not the objective danger. If an individual *feels* that there has been a subjective threat to their life, body, personal integrity or sanity – such as Jeff in Chapter 11 – this is the key factor in understanding the impact of that experience. Understandably, such experiences can have overwhelming physical, emotional and cognitive effects (Ehlers & Clark, 2000). They can compromise an individual's usual capacity to cope, during and afterwards, and this can lead to mental confusion when attempting to understand and come to terms with the experience.

Trauma can have a range of other psychological impacts and these depend, to some degree, on the nature of the events. In Type 1 trauma a single, sudden, unexpected event occurs, typically involving threat to life, for example, a car accident, rape, crime or natural disaster. This can provoke extreme distress and fear, for example, of death, annihilation or mutilation. Post-Traumatic Stress Disorder (PTSD) is the best-known psychological disorder following Type 1 trauma, but it is not the only post-traumatic problem; people can also be affected by adjustment disorders, depression and a range of anxiety disorders (McFarlane & Papay, 1992).

In Type 2 trauma, also called *complex trauma*, there are repeated experiences over an extended period, and these have a varied and often interpersonal basis, for example, physical, emotional and sexual abuse; childhood neglect and deprivation; betrayal of trust by primary caregivers; violation of self and moral values; victimization through exposure to violence or torture; combat and urban warfare; oppressive abuse of power, and so on. In severe cases, childhood trauma can lead to psychosis and disturbances in personality development, such as Dissociative Identity Disorder (DID). The various sequelae include problems with affect regulation, interpersonal difficulties, personality changes, a fragmented, broken or disrupted self-identity, and distorted concepts of others and the world. Not surprisingly, comorbidity with depression is very common (Korotana, Dobson, Pusch & Josephson, 2016). As we have described in previous chapters, a history of childhood trauma is strongly associated with recurrent and chronic depression, and also with heightened risk of relapse following treatment; hence the importance of understanding the relationship between trauma and depression, and knowing how to approach it in therapy.

In this chapter, we explain how the self-regulation model can be used to understand and treat post-traumatic depression, and we describe a number of clinical cases to illustrate this guidance. There are two main foci: (a) PTSD with comorbid depression; (b) depression in the context of developmental trauma. The model explains how disorder-specific treatments can be effective in the therapy of straightforward cases, with more complex cases needing careful targeting of trans-diagnostic links. We also include an example of bespoke treatment for a case of depression with developmental trauma, OCD and suicidality. We do not describe cases of traumatic psychosis or DID, but we explain how the proposed framework could be extended to work with more severe post-traumatic disturbances.

Self-Regulation Model of Post-Traumatic Depression

In Chapter 6, we proposed that many cases of depression can be successfully treated by receiving the core treatment components: *approach motivation, behavioural engagement* and *reflective processing*. We also suggested that, as cases become more difficult-to-treat or complex, it is likely that optional treatment components will be needed: *memory integration, self-organization* and *goal-organization*. Depression in the context of trauma is a good example of the need for the optional components. Figure 12.1 illustrates our proposals for how post-traumatic depression is precipitated and maintained, and it is primarily concerned with interactions between memory, self-identity and goal structures. Ruminative processing is also an important element. The model can be applied to any individual whose depression is precipitated in the context of trauma, whether or not they meet criteria for PTSD.

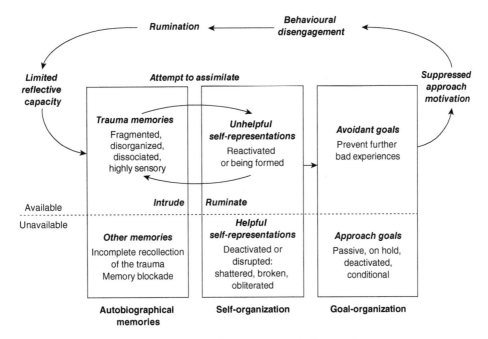

Figure 12.1   Self-regulation model of post-traumatic depression

The model proposes the following. In cases of post-traumatic depression, the initial shock provoked by the events, and/or the subsequent shock-wave, has a large perturbation on a person's self-identity. One or more of the following changes occur within self-organization:

a. *Unhelpful self-representations are reactivated.* This is common in people who have previously suffered from depression, or are in some way vulnerable to it. As we will explore later, it can also reactivate 'dormant' self-representations in people who have suffered previous trauma.
b. *New unhelpful self-representations start to form.* The individual begins to represent themselves in an unhelpful way, on the basis of the traumatic events and memories of them.
c. *Helpful self-representations are deactivated or disrupted.* For some people, disruption to their normal identity can be catastrophic, and this creates a subjective experience of being broken, shattered or obliterated. Helpful senses of self, that the individual normally relies on, are unavailable.

Unhelpful self-representations generate avoidance goals, so goal-organization becomes more oriented around avoidance and less around approach. Approach goals are put on hold and, as we have described in previous chapters, this suppresses approach impulses, increases avoidant impulses, and has corresponding effects on behavioural disengagement and ruminative processing. The depressed moods that result affect the autobiographical memory system in ways that we have already described: intrusions from prior distress, and a memory blockade of past positive events.

In the context of depressed mood, there is a strong likelihood of an individual experiencing some intrusions of the traumatic events (Mihailova & Jobson, 2018). In the case of comorbid PTSD, these will have a flashback quality that provokes re-experiencing and a felt-sense of current threat. However, it is unlikely that the trauma memories will be *fully* integrated into the autobiographical memory system, even if the individual is not suffering from PTSD. Memory integration is a *spectrum*, not an all-or-nothing process. If the memories are not fully processed at the time of the trauma, or soon after, they will tend to be incomplete and disorganized, and in some cases fragmented, dissociated and highly sensory in nature.

What usually develops is intermittent reflection on the memories and attempts to emotionally process them, make sense of them and *assimilate* them into memory (Speckens, Ehlers, Hackmann, Ruths & Clark, 2007). A variety of schematic knowledge is accessed trying to do this, including the world and others, but in post-traumatic depression, the process is hindered by *unhelpful self-representations* that are reactivated or formed during, or soon after, the traumatic events. These are activated during attempts to map the trauma memories onto self-identity; in other words, appraise which 'self' was present during the trauma, and/or how the self is changed by it. In a minority of cases, assimilation will be complete; intrusions will reduce, and unhelpful self-representations will be consolidated, thereby having a depressing effect on mood. What is more common is that assimilation is *partial*: incomplete and disorganized memories fail to map sufficiently onto self-identity. Hence, there are repeated attempts to make sense of what happened, but this process is frustrated by two factors: (a) memories of the events are incomplete; (b) helpful self-representations are deactivated and unavailable to support emotional processing. Instead, people try to map incomplete trauma memories onto unhelpful self-representations. There is a poor fit, and this results in repeating cycles of rumination and further intrusions (Michael, Halligan, Clark & Ehlers, 2007).

As depicted in Figure 12.1, the information that is needed to process the memories is unavailable and difficult to access. Because of this, attempts to process the memories result in cycles of rumination, with self-focused attention and abstract questions, for example, *'Why did this happen to me?'*, *'What have I done to deserve this?'* Rumination can also focus on trying to understand loss of self-identity: *'Why am I not me any more?'* Remember also that, during depression, there is reduced reflective capacity, so the individual may not have the resources needed to buffer these processing tasks in working memory. Hence, the process of understanding what happened, and coming to terms with the trauma, can be frustrating, distressing and overwhelming.

Not surprisingly, people sometimes resort to cognitive avoidance and attempt to suppress the memories, to have some respite from the distress. When ruminative processes are unproductive, trauma memories remain unprocessed, or only partially integrated, and the cycle of attempting assimilation recommences. The fundamental problem is the *unavailability* of the information and self-representations needed to integrate the trauma memories.

PTSD with Comorbid Depression

We will illustrate these processes with a number of case studies, starting with two clients who had PTSD with comorbid depression. Both of the cases received a disorder-specific course of CBT for PTSD, in the first instance. In the first case, treatment was sufficient to overcome both the PTSD and the depression; in the second case, the PTSD was successfully treated, but the depression needed separate attention.

Treatment for PTSD when depression is overcome

Case Illustration | Izzy: PTSD with comorbid depression

Izzy was a 35-year-old woman with no previous history of mental health problems. She was an innocent party in a fatal road accident. Travelling at around 50 miles per hour on a country road, the driver of an oncoming vehicle strayed some distance into Izzy's lane. Izzy was shocked to see the car coming towards her and she swerved to try to avoid it. The side of the cars collided, with Izzy's car spinning and coming to a halt several yards further down the road. She was deeply shocked but survived with minor injuries. Both cars turned over in the collision; the other driver was seriously injured and later died in hospital. In the following months, Izzy developed PTSD with moderate depression symptoms. Izzy knew rationally that she was not to blame for the accident, but several months afterwards she still felt guilty that she had survived and the other driver had not. She thought about the accident a great deal, ruminating about what would have happened if she had taken a different route that day, or had been driving more slowly. She also thought a lot about the young family of the man who had been killed. Izzy lost interest in some of her leisure pursuits and was much quieter and withdrawn with family and friends. She had continued driving as part of her work, but had become excessively cautious on the roads, sometimes driving dangerously slowly. She had also avoided the accident site.

Focusing on the depressive aspects of her presentation, Izzy was a very responsible person who was extremely concerned that her actions could have contributed to the accident. Her way of processing the event was to review all her actions that day to see if she had been negligent in any way, for example, her vision, the safety of her vehicle, the route she had taken, and so on. Although she was exonerated of any wrong-doing, she felt guilty witnessing the upset of the other driver's children at the inquest. This maintained a recurrent pattern of rumination and survivor guilt.

As depicted in Figure 12.2, we can understand Izzy's depression as a partial disruption of her usual self-representation as a *responsible adult* and *good citizen*. In the days after the accident, she started to feel blameworthy, even though she knew rationally that she was not negligent or to blame. Her memories of the accident were partial and selective; they also had a disorganized timeline and were very sensory in nature. When she had flashbacks she would sometimes try to push them out of mind, and other times she would try to remember what happened and process it, asking herself questions such as *'Why did it have to happen?'*, *'What could I have done to prevent it?'*, *'If only I had been driving more slowly – why was I going so fast?'*. Izzy's main strategy for processing the memories was to compare what happened with what she *wished* had happened, particularly that she had taken a different route that day (*counterfactual reasoning*). This was compounded by the fact that her memories of the accident were incomplete, so she was neither asking helpful questions, nor accessing the key pieces of information that would help her to answer them.

What developed was narrowed attention around certain memories, for example, the extremely loud noise made by her car scraping against the road: it had turned over following the impact of the crash. In Izzy's memory, this seemed to last for eternity, and the fact it lasted a long time told her she had been driving too fast. This *appraisal* of the memory maintained the unhelpful self-representation of being *blameworthy*.

Izzy received a standard course of trauma-focused CBT based on Ehlers and Clark's (2000) model of PTSD. Her treatment is a good example of disorder-specific therapy being sufficient to overcome both PTSD and depression. As part of the reliving process, Izzy visited the accident site and this helped her to remember more accurately where the cars had collided and where they had come to rest. In fact, it was a much shorter distance than she had remembered. This challenged her appraisal that she had been driving too fast, which started to weaken her felt-sense of being blameworthy. The major break-through, in terms of depressed mood, was the realization that, as she turned the previous corner before the cars collided, she had not known there was going to be an accident (Ehlers, Clark, Hackmann, McManus & Fennell, 2005). Of course, Izzy knew rationally that the accident was an unexpected shock, but months of ruminating, and the felt-sense of being to blame, had made her imagine that she knew beforehand the accident was going to happen, and so she could not come to terms with why she had not done more to prevent it. Once Izzy's memories of the accident

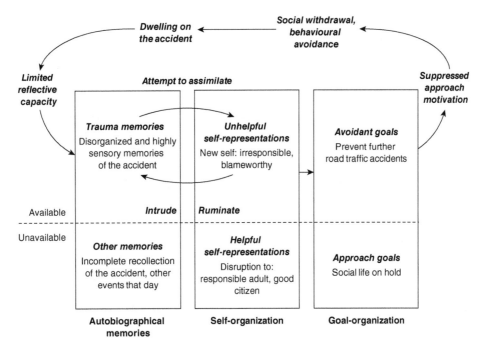

Figure 12.2   Memory, self-organization and goal structures maintaining Izzy's depression

were more complete and organized, and she was processing them in a more reflective, concrete and less ruminative way, there was a marked improvement in her mood that was sustained throughout the rest of therapy, and at follow up. Her sense of being a responsible adult and good citizen was restored, and her felt-sense of being in some way culpable started to dissipate.

Treatment for PTSD when depression is not overcome

In most cases of PTSD with comorbid depression, tethering treatment to the PTSD is likely to be the best therapeutic strategy, with time-limited attention given to depression, if and only if it interferes with the PTSD protocol. The exceptions to this are if the client's mood is severely depressed and they have insufficient energy, motivation or reflective capacity to manage trauma-focused treatment, or if their affect is so unstable that treatment would have a destabilizing effect. However, aside from these factors, tethering treatment to PTSD will not always be sufficient; sometimes comorbid depression will need separate attention. We will ground this exploration in a clinical case, Kyle, who received two courses of CBT: the first focused mainly on his PTSD, which achieved a good outcome, but with only partial amelioration of his depressed mood; the second treated the depression as the primary problem.

Case Illustration | Kyle: PTSD with comorbid depression

Kyle was a 42-year-old married man when he suffered a single-event trauma. He was out cycling in the countryside and suffered a random violent assault. Four men swerved towards him at speed, then stopped their car further ahead, got out of the car and walked towards him. Kyle, on seeing the parked car, came to a halt, feeling shocked, anxious and unable to escape. Without speaking to him, the men repeatedly kicked and punched him to the ground, amused by what they were doing. Kyle suffered bruising and multiple skull fractures. There was no theft, and in a matter of minutes the men returned to their car and drove off, leaving Kyle bleeding on the ground. In the following 10 minutes, several cars went past without stopping to help. Then a motorcyclist stopped and arranged for paramedic assistance and transport to the nearest A&E department. Kyle was in hospital for 3 days, had a minor operation 3 weeks later, resulting in two cranial metal plates. There was no brain damage or lasting effects on his cognitive functioning.

Kyle's sense of shock and confusion persisted during this period, feeling anxious and hyper-alert, mistrustful of others and experiencing intermittent flashbacks of the assault. The traumatic event shattered previous lifelong assumptions about personal security and the trustworthiness of others, and in the following months he developed PTSD. In spite of various primary care interventions, 6 years after the incident Kyle had developed chronic PTSD and persistent major depression. When referred to the Newcastle CBT Centre, he received an extended course of trauma-focused CBT with similar components to Izzy's therapy, as above, but more extensive work establishing a timeline, ten sessions reliving the index event, and several sessions experimenting with altered imagery. There was also extensive work overcoming social avoidance and dropping safety-seeking behaviours when with other people. Kyle's PTSD was successfully treated. His mood improved intermittently, but was prone to relapse. Kyle and his therapist attempted Behavioural Activation, to overcome social avoidance, and MBCT, to counteract rumination: both had a partial and unsustained effect.

Three years later, Kyle was re-referred because his depression had become chronic and severe. He had sustained the recovery from PTSD, but his depression remained a significant problem (PHQ-9 = 22). Working with Kyle helped us to learn that *post-traumatic depression is not necessarily maintained by traumatic memories*. Kyle's social withdrawal was very evident, with extreme wariness of other people, and his first course of CBT had tacitly assumed that this had its roots in the trauma memories, and some aspect of them was not fully integrated. However, Kyle's withdrawal did not have a post-traumatic quality, as if strangers could be unpredictably violent and therefore needed to be avoided. Rather, there appeared to be a deeper yearning for belonging and acceptance that was not reciprocated in Kyle's key relationships. He was no longer particularly frightened of strangers, though he had been prior to his PTSD treatment. Instead, he was wary of becoming too close to people who were already known to him. He also had regular bouts of angry rumination, the content of which centred on the lack of support he was receiving from his wife, friends and family.

The new course of treatment hypothesized that Kyle's depression was an *indirect* result of the assault: he had become depressed in response to lack of support from bystanders, family and friends in the aftermath of the incident. The main problem was not fear of assault; it was loneliness, dejection and anger in the face of lukewarm concern from others. Consequently, the primary formulation was based on Kyle becoming demotivated, disengaged and ruminative, as shown in Figure 12.3, rather than focusing on partially integrated trauma memories. The focus of the

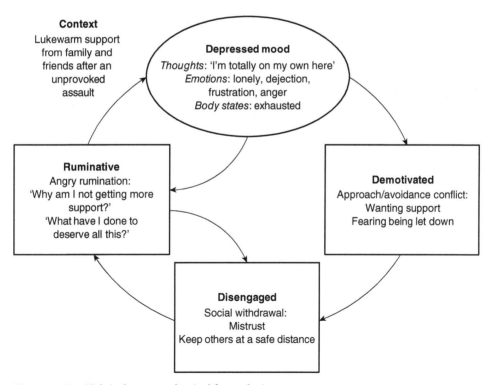

Figure 12.3　Kyle's downward spiral formulation

therapy began to consider two issues that could be underpinning his social disengagement and angry rumination: (a) the response of his wife, friends and family after the assault; (b) Kyle's pre-existing self-organization, including the impact of his early experiences.

Case Illustration | Kyle's early experiences and learning

Kyle's father died when he was very young. His mother remarried and her new husband had one son from a previous marriage. They had two children together. Kyle grew up with three half-siblings, sometimes feeling the odd one out, as if his presence was an inconvenience for his parents, who would have preferred a fresh start without children from their previous marriages. Kyle's basic needs were always met, and he was never abused or physically neglected, but he sometimes felt alone and disconnected from the rest of the family. He did not feel wholeheartedly accepted and loved, and as he reached middle childhood, he became increasingly aware of his parents' low expectations of him. They would sometimes say 'Kyle won't manage that', as if he wasn't intelligent or capable, which Kyle certainly was, for example he was doing very well at school.

Kyle sometimes felt that he was alone, unsupported and unfairly held back. These were painful feelings and it was difficult to tolerate and reflect on them. Kyle compensated by making a virtue out of a necessity, becoming very autonomous with strong opinions and a confident social presence in adolescence. He generated self-identities as *strong* and *independent*, distancing himself to some degree from his family, moving abroad to study, then starting a career in the armed forces. Kyle realized that his need for belonging, support and encouragement had not been fully met in his birth family, and he responded by projecting confidence, strength and independence to others, an approach encouraged in the armed forces. However, he did not always feel as confident as his external presentation.

Projecting strength and independence was a way of compensating for lack of support, but it did not signal Kyle's need for *mutually supportive relationships*. The un-met needs continued, and although Kyle functioned well as an adult with no mental health problems until the assault, he was carrying the pain of disconnection as a young person that had not been fully felt, accepted and reflected on. The assault and its aftermath activated this pain in a sudden and violent way, as if the whole world was now a war-zone, with a shattering of trust in human relationships. A lot of his metaphors had military connotations: depression was like being weighed down by chainmail; he felt imprisoned in a castle with the drawbridge up, isolated from other people. Post-assault, Kyle needed the support of others more than ever, but the effect of the trauma was to *reduce* his trust in other people, not increase it, and this created a depressing internal situation of keeping others at a safe distance, at the same time as suffering from their lack of emotional support. The less support Kyle received, the more wary of others he became, creating a virtual barricade and maintaining his representation of the world as a hostile, unfriendly, warzone. He visualized this as being a castle fortress on an island, his protective strategies fuelling his feelings of isolation.

Kyle's early life was not severely neglectful, abusive or traumatic, but there were emotionally painful experiences that were reactivated by the context of his assault. He already had *verbal access* to those childhood memories, but the traumatic situation reactivated painful *feelings and body states* that he had not previously experienced. Once these were identified as the roots of his mistrust, therapy could work with those memories, to emotionally process them and understand their impact on his development. Therapy encouraged Kyle to *feel* the pain of disconnection he felt as a child, while simultaneously seeking to rebuild interpersonal trust in his present life. Concurrent with remembering, feeling and soothing himself in the present, Kyle was encouraged to find out if he could *influence supportive relationships* that he needed and wanted in his life now. This became the rationale for behavioural engagement.

Kyle was encouraged to approach mistrust in a *differentiated* way, experimenting with very small increases in trust with particular people already known to him. This is reminiscent of the small steps taken by Frank, described in Chapter 9 – a key strategy when working with people with chronic and persistent depression. The goal was to find out whether this could bring about more understanding, recognition and support from others. It also created opportunities for disconfirmation, if others were less rejecting and dismissive than he feared.

These were big risks for Kyle, because he was opening himself up to more painful disconnection if others did not reciprocate. However, he had a huge amount to gain by increasing social connectedness if others did reciprocate. Over an 18-month period Kyle made a full recovery from depression, gradually increasing his trusting engagement with other people and exploring new employment possibilities (PHQ-9 = 1). The small increases in trust never backfired in a catastrophic way. The gradual and explicit nature of this process helped Kyle to learn who could be trusted with what, and who reciprocated his need for mutually supportive relationships. This led to some painful confirmations, for example, relationship limitations in his birth family. But it also led to new hope: there were other people who shared his values and recognized his qualities as a compassionate person. The process led Kyle to grow a different type of strength: based less on autonomy, and more on mutually supportive relationships.

Developmental Trauma

We want to extend the exploration of developmental factors, because childhood trauma, neglect and abuse are such key indicators of clients at greatest risk of recurrent and persistent depression (van der Kolk, 2005). One of the two cases we will discuss is Chloe, who we introduced in Chapters 5 and 6. Like Kyle, Chloe received a disorder-specific treatment in the first instance – tethering to her depression – and then needed additional help processing the trauma.

Unlike Kyle, Chloe did not have PTSD; however, she had been through a *traumatic process* and although her mood had improved significantly, it worsened when she remembered the traumatic events. Her PHQ-9 score had improved from 19 to 10 in the first batch of sessions but, as illustrated in Figure 12.4, she was now regularly experiencing intrusive thoughts and having short-term bouts of depression. The moods were not as intense or long-lasting as before, but they were interfering with her functioning at work and socially. The intrusions were not flashbacks

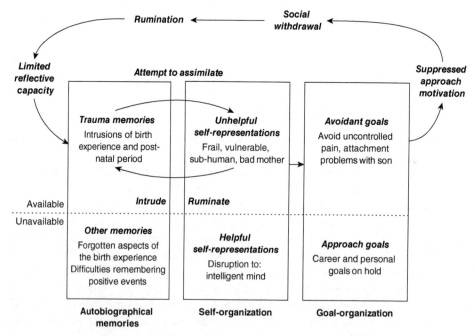

Figure 12.4 **Memory, self-organization and goal structures maintaining Chloe's depression**

but the memories were incomplete, disjointed and fragmented. When they came to mind she would make an effort to remember them clearly, to make sense of them and organize them. She was attempting to integrate the trauma memories, but having difficulty doing so. Chloe received an additional six sessions to help her emotionally process the trauma. There were three main targets for change: rumination, memory integration and self-organization.

1 Rumination

Chloe reflected on times when she thought about the trauma and paid attention to the questions she asked. Because the memories had a depressing effect, the questions tended to be abstract and self-blaming, such as: *'I'm mentally broken – so how come I'm still here?'*, *'Is my son really mine?'*, *'Did I bring all this on myself?'* By experimenting with these questions in session, Chloe quickly learned that they were unproductive and did not lead to helpful answers. We experimented with more concrete questions that had a better chance of accessing information she had forgotten, such as: *'What was the weather like the day my son was born?'*, *'Was my son born in the morning, afternoon or evening?'* To Chloe's surprise, these concrete questions, that appeared bland and unhelpful on first hearing, allowed her to access information that she had forgotten. The switch to a concrete processing mode enabled Chloe's memories to be accessed in a different way, making more information available to process the trauma.

2 Memory integration

Reliving the traumatic experience helped Chloe to access emotional hot spots and detailed information that had been unavailable up to that point. It was important to maintain a concrete processing mode with answerable questions, such as, *'What were my emotions when I felt out of control?'*, *'What happened when I was under the anaesthetic?'* Chloe had forgotten the way she felt treated by the medical staff and this helped her to remember and make sense of her emotional reactions. This was Chloe's feedback after the reliving process:

> Reliving helped me to remember all my emotions. I had remembered the fear but not the shame. When I remembered the fear, there was not much to work with – it seemed understandable to be afraid in these circumstances, and I couldn't move on from that. When I realized shame was the primary feeling I was able to unpick and acknowledge

the source of it, and store the experience alongside my prior healthcare and other experiences. I couldn't forgive myself, or understand my own reactions, until I could remember what had been the predominant driving emotion.

The reflective process of reliving enabled memory integration to take place. Chloe developed an accurate and complete timeline of events; she recognized the part her emotions had played in the situation; she was able to understand the actions of the healthcare staff. Although she did not agree with them, she came to accept they had not acted with the *intention* of undermining her or her intelligence. She found a way of *accommodating* what had happened and accepting it. She was also able to recognize how courageous she had been, on several occasions putting her son's health and wellbeing ahead of her own: these were not the actions of a bad or inadequate mother.

3 Self-organization

The process of memory integration helped to re-establish Chloe's identity as an 'intelligent mind', and deactivate her felt-sense of physical frailty and vulnerability. To achieve this, it was important to formulate the sources of the unhelpful self-representations that were activated during the traumatic process. One of these, 'bad mother', was a new self-representation that had gradually dissipated over the course of therapy. However, it was a further shock to Chloe to realize that her felt-senses of physical frailty and vulnerability were not new.

Case Illustration | Chloe's early experiences and learning

As a child, Chloe learned that her heart was 'flawed'. Significantly, there had been concerns whether she would survive her own birth, being born prematurely. It took a long time for her parents to accept that Chloe was going to live, and they spent years trying to conceive another child, in the hope that this would help them cope with losing Chloe. It is likely that in early development this led to Chloe internalizing that she was frail, delicate, unlikely to thrive, weak and so on. In middle childhood, having a heart defect became self-defining, to the point that she felt relieved when medical advice was against fixing it. We hypothesized that those early experiences led Chloe to internalize an unhelpful self-representation of being *physically frail*. Reflecting back on childhood, Chloe recognized that this was not an accurate depiction of her body and health. She was strong for her age, competent in physical tasks and often successful at sport; but she continued to have a *felt-sense of being frail*, in spite of the evidence to the contrary. Parental anxiety was as important as the heart condition, in terms of what Chloe learned and internalized.

As Chloe matured into adulthood, physical frailty became a much less prominent aspect of her self-identity; in fact, the area of physicality, body and appearance was of little day-to-day importance. Most of her early experiences helped Chloe to internalize helpful self-representations of being *intelligent*, *capable* and *responsible*, and her identity as an adult had become highly invested in being an *'intelligent mind'*. The early felt-sense of physical frailty had become deactivated to the point of being compartmentalized or dormant, and it was now rarely in Chloe's conscious awareness. It would be activated from time to time in specific situations involving ill-health, hospitals and doctors. Chloe certainly had an aversion to being a patient, associating it with pain, loss of control and vulnerability.

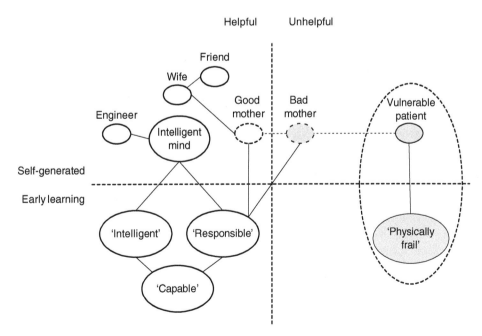

Figure 12.5   Chloe's hypothesized self-organization

Chloe's self-organization had mostly worked well for her, particularly in her education and career, but it masked a hidden susceptibility to emotional problems in the area of physicality, health and embodiment. Defining herself as a cognitive being became so pronounced that Chloe believed her mind could be put into any body, and she would be fully herself. Chloe's body had become *disconnected* from her mind; it was no longer integrated with other aspects of herself, and because the self-representation of physical frailty was compartmentalized and dormant, Chloe underestimated its capacity to threaten her wellbeing. As suggested in Figure 12.5, this self-representation was Chloe's hidden susceptibility to post-traumatic depression. We have circled it to represent its separateness and disconnection in her self-organization.

In relation to developmental trauma, and its link with depression, the key point is this: at no point did Chloe's adult trauma activate flashbacks of childhood experiences. It was not event-based memories of childhood illness that were reactivated. What was reactivated was a powerful somatic and emotional experience of *being* frail and vulnerable. This was a *non-verbal experience of being*; an internalized self-representation, rather than particular events. For this reason, the self-organization map was a critical part of Chloe's therapy, because it helped her to understand the role of her early health experiences in the post-traumatic depression. The pregnancy and birth process had reactivated a *dormant* and *disconnected* felt-sense of physical frailty and when this was reactivated, in a powerfully somatic and emotional way, it disrupted her felt-sense of being a respected intelligent mind. This combination was catastrophic for Chloe, leaving her feeling both physically and mentally broken. The process of mapping her self-organization helped Chloe to realize the role of her 'physically frail' self in the post-traumatic reaction. In Chloe's words:

> This realization has shifted from believing I was uninterested in my body, to realizing I do strongly identify with my body, but buried that identity because it is so painful and frightening – I don't trust my physical self because of its flaw.

With this formulation, it is understandable that Chloe became depressed. The depression-focused work from previous sessions, on approach motivation, behavioural engagement and reflective processing, had helped to restore her usual self-identity, to some degree. Her felt-sense of frailty and weakness had reduced, and her felt-sense of being an intelligent mind had mostly recovered. By the end of the additional six sessions, Chloe's PHQ-9 score had reduced to 5, and she was only occasionally having mild bouts of depression.

The additional benefit of mapping her self-organization was to increase *integration* among her different senses of self. Using the integrated approach, the aim is partly to return Chloe to more helpful representations of herself, but it is also to enable her to reflect on and make connections between different self-states. The self-state of being frail and vulnerable was extremely aversive for Chloe, and her emotions were considerably calmer and more pleasant when it was deactivated. But Chloe became more resilient, and more likely to stay well in the future, by allowing it *into* her self-identity; *be-friending* her body, rather than keeping it suppressed, separate, disconnected or dormant. Chloe summarized this very powerfully at the end of her treatment as *'waking up to the dormant self'* and *'trading ignorant bliss for greater resilience'*.

Case Illustration | Chloe's experience of integrating her dormant self

'I had the equivalent of a dead leg in my self-identity. I hadn't even realized it had gone dead, and then something forced me to notice it, and I realized it was there but I still didn't necessarily recognize it as belonging to me; then I know it's going to hurt to re-establish contact with it. When I did recognize it, I had to acknowledge that this painful disturbing thing is also fundamentally part of "me", which is a difficult experience, but at least it left me feeling whole. This painful part of me did not magically turn from unhelpful to helpful; it is still there, still negative, still active and still influencing how I feel about myself. Before I woke up to this, there were two branches inside me, one of which was dormant nearly all the time, but the branches are integrated now. I have incorporated this painful part into myself. I now have more negative influences on a day-to-day basis; but I've traded ignorant bliss for greater resilience.'

Bespoke formulation

We extend the discussion of developmental trauma by considering a more complex case, Mike, who needed a bespoke formulation and treatment. Mike was a 42-year-old psychological therapist and healthcare manager at the time he experienced a severe, first-onset depression. Unlike Izzy, Kyle and Chloe, Mike's depression was not precipitated by a traumatic (Type 1) event, nor was he suffering from PTSD. Several aspects of the self-regulation model of post-traumatic depression applied in Mike's case (see Figure 12.1), but they had to be adapted based on the particular way his difficulties were interacting. His pre-treatment PHQ-9 score was 20.

Case Illustration | Mike's downward spiral into depression

Over an extended period, Mike had experienced a gradual but significant increase in stress across various areas of his life. This included pressure in his work as a manager, maternal illness, conflict with neighbours and physical health problems for both himself and his wife. Mike had not noticed that the pressure was increasing and adversely affecting him; he began to behave more compulsively, particularly in his management role at work. Mike was a conscientious person who had a strong sense of responsibility and worked very hard for his clients, colleagues and employer. He had a history of obsessive–compulsive tendencies. He had received help for these some years ago, and they were generally not a problem.

There was a long period of heightened stress on the residential unit where Mike worked, which included elements of physical and psychological bullying, with some residents also using religious ideas to bully others. Mike started to become preoccupied by certain thoughts, of a religious nature, that he had heard on a radio programme. He was disturbed by the blasphemous content, which was very similar to things being said on the unit, and felt compelled to investigate further, researching the statements on the Internet. Within the course of a few days, Mike had become very distressed, not just by what he had heard, but because *he* had now said the words to colleagues, to find out their reaction. He also started to become preoccupied with his *reactions* to those thoughts, as if they demonstrated he was *bad* or *broken* and becoming mad or mentally ill. In Mike's words: *'only a broken mind would be engaging with thoughts and discussions like this'.*

Mike began to spiral into ruminative self-attack and obsessional preoccupation. He attacked himself vigorously on many levels – for 'breaking down' and being weak, for breaking bad and spoiling good things in his life. Although he also fought against these self attacks, this process felt physically terrifying, gutting, exhausting and out of control. His mood plummeted and he became severely depressed, feeling broken as a person and terrified he was losing his mind. The emotions were intolerable and within a few days Mike felt an urgency to find a way to stop them: he began to actively consider methods of suicide.

Because of the heightened risk to self, Mike's therapy commenced soon after this, by which time he was on sick leave and under the care of a consultant psychiatrist. Alliance formation might have been complicated by the fact Mike was a mental health professional, but he was open to receiving help, albeit with extreme scepticism that

CBT could be effective. By the time of the first session, Mike stated that he was '99% sure' he would not recover. His therapist accepted the 1% opportunity, which Mike later fed back was an important moment in building a working alliance and allowing some hope into the situation, however improbable it seemed at the time. Mike rejected the proposal to record his daily behaviour to explore whether he had become demotivated, disengaged and ruminative. Consequently, the therapist made the decision to build a bespoke formulation, noticing the unusual presentation and possible underlying complexity. In this respect, Mike's therapy was analogous to Jeff's treatment summarized in Chapter 11: there appeared to be an unusual combination of 'multiple moving parts' and it was unclear at the outset how to tether to a specific target.

Because Mike was ruminating compulsively, the therapist made the decision to focus on the functional links between OCD and depression, specifically self-attacking rumination and compulsive preoccupations. This was based on hypothesis A in Figure 12.6, which outlines possible macro formulations. Mike had already realized how unhelpful his ruminations had become, and he was also aware of the compulsive element. To the therapist's surprise, this proposal was met with extreme scepticism by Mike, who appeared unconvinced and communicated that it didn't adequately capture what he was experiencing. It reminded him of previous OCD-focused therapy, and also what his GP and therapist-friends had been saying over the previous few weeks. A few days later, Mike cancelled the next session.

Sensing that the working alliance was under threat, the therapist proposed a telephone appointment, to which Mike agreed. It was during this call that the therapist noticed how often Mike was using the word 'broken' to describe himself and his experience. The therapist wondered whether Mike was traumatized by his *current* experience, and with that in mind, he reflected back that feeling broken might suggest some kind of trauma, and asked whether Mike was feeling traumatized by what he was experiencing. This reminded Mike of a previous session when his therapist had asked about religious faith, in case it was relevant to the theistic content of his obsessions. Mike had previously disclosed that he had an unhappy time at boarding school which had put him off conventional religion, but that it did not feel relevant to his current experiences.

Attending to the *concrete experience* of brokenness was a significant turning point in the therapy. Mike had been describing feeling 'broken' to his GP and therapist-friends, all of whom reassured him he was not broken. Mike's therapist took a different approach, suggesting that perhaps something was broken or shattered, but it could be healed and out-grown. This conversation triggered powerful feelings within Mike that he had not expected to occur. He started to re-experience intense feelings from childhood, being aged 8 at boarding school (Novšak, Mandelj & Simonič, 2012).

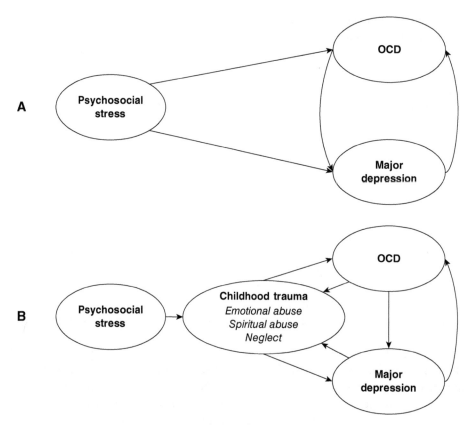

Figure 12.6   Alternative macro-formulations for Mike

Case Illustration | Mike's childhood trauma

Mike had previously reflected on his time at boarding school; he remembered how unhappy he had been, but did not believe it was linked to his current difficulties. As he disclosed more of what happened to him, his therapist became more convinced there could be a post-traumatic process driving his depression and OCD, reflected in hypothesis B in Figure 12.6.

Mike had been the victim of emotional and spiritual abuse: when first arriving at the boarding school he was groomed by two of his teachers, who were also priests, and made to feel special and superior to the others. After a short period of time, the teacher-priests began to threaten Mike as they did the other boys: there would be a severe beating for any boy who did not complete their homework perfectly and on time. Mike witnessed other boys being beaten in these circumstances, some with sexual overtones, and he was deeply shocked by what he saw. He felt terrified to avoid a beating, and put himself under immense pressure to perform perfectly, both in class and homework. Large amounts of work had to be completed, and Mike could remember the internal pressure and constant terror that if he made a mistake, at any moment he could be chosen for a beating, or worse. Mike described it as a time of imprisonment, humiliation and danger, never relaxing and never knowing if or when he would be unfairly punished. In Mike's words:

> I knew I had been unhappy and angry but I had never reconnected with feeling terrorized physically, psychologically and spiritually. It was all done 'in the name of God' and so I, and probably many others who went to such schools, know what it is to have 'the fear of God put into me'. As an adult I can see it was their version of God, hijacking my developing spirituality.

That period also coincided with Mike's parents' divorce; his father was not particularly available, having an extra-marital affair, and his mother was distressed and preoccupied with the situation, at times directing her marital anger at Mike. Mike was very alone and isolated, caught up in a distressing family situation, where his needs were not the priority, and an insecure, frightening and oppressive school situation. Mike lost all faith and belief in God. The teacher-priests abused their religious and educational authority for their own sadistic ends, and Mike was significantly traumatized by it. Tragically, no one in his family noticed. After 2 years, aged 10, Mike took matters into his own hands and found a way of 'escaping' the school, triggering a family argument and confronting his parents with their ignorance of what was happening, and their negligence in not paying more attention to him and his needs.

Within the therapy, Mike began to recognize the common patterns of isolation, terror and fear of punishment between his current feelings and his boarding school experiences. He recognized that a strong internal sense of responsibility had developed to avoid punishment: this had created an 'over-drive' mode, in which he would disattend to his needs and work urgently and excessively hard. As this explanation of his experiences made more sense, he was able to reappraise the obsessional thoughts in a less compulsive way, and he became less ruminative and self-attacking. He was able to decentre from intrusive thoughts and reappraise them as signs of internal stress and distress. His risk reduced, and he then disclosed how close he had been, just a few weeks before, to killing himself and making it appear like an accident.

One of the key elements in the treatment rationale was that Mike could overcome his felt-sense of brokenness and 'rebuild something bigger and freer'. Mike found it very helpful that the therapist validated his feeling of being broken, rather than challenge it or re-label it. It was then linked explicitly to the treatment goal for *post-traumatic growth*: to regain settled and helpful senses of self. This is a good example of balancing support and change, when the client is severely depressed. The full awfulness of the client's predicament has to be acknowledged and empathized with – it will strain the personal bond if the therapist tries to minimize it. However, the predicament needs to be linked *immediately* and *hopefully* to an *approach goal* that is rooted in the client's needs and desires. In simple terms: right now is awful for you; let's get working together to help you find a better place.

Self-organization

To understand the brokenness better, a self-organization map was developed, shown in Figure 12.7. Over several sessions, Mike recognized that he had internalized various unhelpful self-representations during his time at boarding school, such as *'bully, bad rebel, high performer, vulnerable/weak'*. The formulation that made most sense was hypothesis B in Figure 12.6: a gradual build-up of stress had activated Mike's sense of responsibility and 'over-drive' mode, particularly in his role as a manager. In a high-pressure healthcare context, with elements of management bullying, Mike's fears of making mistakes increased greatly, together with a felt-sense of responsibility to make sure things were done to a high standard. This created additional internal pressure and eventually there was a phase-shift out of his usual helpful self-representations of being caring, intelligent and hard-working, into a profound sense of being a bad person deserving of punishment.

We hypothesized that the suddenness and unpredictability of this shift was partly due to Mike's unhelpful selves being dormant and highly compartmentalized. He did not know they were there, and so did not recognize them when they were activated. This has echoes of Chloe's self-organization. Like Chloe, Mike could verbally report what had happened at boarding school, but he did not initially experience much distress doing so. He under-estimated its impact, because he could access the *facts* of what happened, but the *feelings* he experienced at that time were dissociated and disconnected from his awareness. It was the feelings that were reactivated and became overwhelming for Mike, leading to fear of punishment and self-loathing. The therapeutic strategy was to *integrate* the compartmentalized self-representations, so they were not disconnected and hidden from awareness. To do this, a range of self-compassionate exercises were developed, as a way of developing a kinder

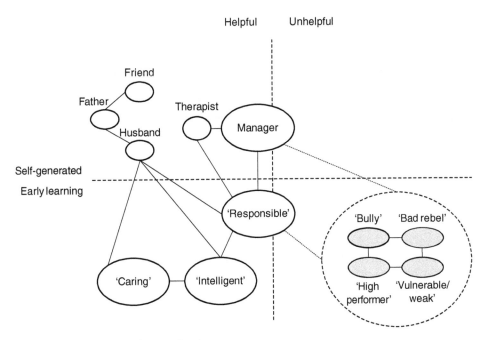

Figure 12.7   Mike's self-organization map

relationship with himself when his 'bad' or 'bully' self was active. Mike had experimented with self-compassion before, but this was the first time he had applied it in a whole-hearted, personal and affective way.

Mike made a full recovery, his PHQ-9 score reducing to zero after eighteen sessions of CBT, over a 9-month period. There were several key elements:

1. Developmental trauma grew into a credible and accurate formulation that gave Mike an alternative explanation for his experiences and helped to reduce his risk. It also updated his life-story, both in terms of his current experience and his time at boarding school.
2. Mike was encouraged to remember the *feelings and body states* he experienced at boarding school. No additional event-based memories came to mind, but for the first time Mike let himself remember what he *felt* at that time. This was painful and difficult at times, but it also had a healing and integrating effect.
3. Mike practised self-compassionate exercises as a way of counteracting his tendency for self-criticism and self-attack. He had previously used self-compassionate techniques and found them interesting. The difference this time was not just saying soothing things, but

bathing in compassion: being kind to himself, allowing a memory of being loved to affect his whole being, not just a mental image.

4. Mike used the self-organization map to help him notice that he can have different unhelpful senses of self, including: *bully*, *bad rebel*, *high performer*, *vulnerable/weak*, which can be triggered by different contexts and which can interact with each other. He has accepted these as self-states, rather than truths, and they are now more integrated with his other more helpful self-representations.

Complexity framework

In terms of the complexity framework, there were a number of biopsychosocial factors that could have impeded the working alliance, and needed to be overcome:

- There was a potential complication that Mike and his therapist worked in the same field; this could have made it difficult to form a personal bond, and build collaboration as different equals. Alternatively they could have become allied as two therapists, rather than client and therapist.
- At the outset of treatment, Mike was severely depressed and feeling hopeless about change; this left a very small window for therapeutic hope and an agreed goal.
- When hypothesis A was proposed, there was a potential disagreement about the formulation and tasks of treatment – the risk of a therapeutic rupture and client drop-out was high at that point.

Biopsychosocial factors also interacted to modify the usual maintenance of depression:

- Mike's depressive rumination (*self-attacking*) was functionally linked with his obsessional preoccupations (*compulsive over-drive*). Early in treatment this interaction was driving the over-valued idea that suicide could help to resolve Mike's internal predicament.
- At the outset of treatment Mike's childhood trauma was covert and had already been discounted as relevant to the current problems.
- Once the childhood trauma was identified, it had several elements that needed a compassionate response and sensitive formulation: emotional abuse, spiritual abuse, neglect.

Reflection

The cases described in this chapter illustrate a *spectrum* of post-traumatic depression from the relatively straightforward, in the case of Izzy, to the more complex, in the case of Mike. What characterizes each of the cases is the impact of unhelpful self-representations, such as: *blameworthy, isolated, unsupported, frail, vulnerable, bad, rebel, bully, weak*. These are self-devaluing, have a depressing effect on mood, and are maintained by a variety of processes, most prominently intrusive memories and rumination. Thinking in terms of spectrums, rather than diagnoses, there are two key dimensions to consider: one is how strongly *internalized* the representations are; the other is how *accessible* they are.

- *Izzy*. Her felt-sense of being *blameworthy* emerged from disruption to self-as-responsible. Being responsible was strongly internalized, but being blameworthy was not: consequently it was relatively easy for this to be overcome, once her usual sense of responsibility was restored. Within the time she had PTSD, Izzy was fully cognizant of feeling blameworthy.
- *Kyle*. His felt-sense of being *isolated* and *unsupported* was internalized to some degree in early life, however, mostly what was reactivated was autobiographical memories of times he had felt this way, rather than a felt-sense that he had always been an unlovable or unwanted person. These were painful, event-based memories rather than identities. Prior to the assault, Kyle could have verbally reported the facts of those events, but the trauma and depression brought back the feelings.
- *Chloe*. Her felt-sense of being *frail* and *vulnerable* was strongly internalized in early life, so when they were reactivated by the adult trauma, they created a felt-sense of *being* a frail and exposed person, rather than accessing memories of specific events. Prior to the birth trauma, Chloe was aware she disliked medical care and hospitals, and could verbally link that back to early experiences – but she had no awareness of physical frailty lying dormant as a self-identity.
- *Mike*. His felt-sense of being *bad, rebel, bully, weak* was also strongly internalized. These were self-identities, not just event-based memories. They were very compartmentalized, such that Mike had no awareness they were a covert part of his self-identity. Even when they were powerfully activated during his depression, Mike did not initially link them back to early traumatic experiences.

Many readers will have worked with clients whose difficulties are more complex again, where formative years have been characterized by sustained abuse and neglect. Those clients usually have even fewer helpful self-representations and less self-regulatory capacity. Their therapy needs longer preparatory phases to stabilize affect and, as far as possible, strengthen areas of resilience and functioning. However, the principle underpinning the cases in this chapter, and others you have encountered, remains the same: the choice of disorder-specific/trans-diagnostic/bespoke treatment is based on how the client's problems interact: whether they impede the working alliance and/or modify the usual maintenance of depression.

Practitioner Tips: Post-Traumatic Depression

- When a client is both traumatized and depressed, consider disorder-specific treatment in the first instance. Tether treatment to the agreed disorder, and monitor its effects on other problems, both through regular discussions with the client and use of appropriate psychometric measures.
- When depression is targeted, it is usually best to start with the core treatment components of approach motivation, behavioural engagement and reflective processing. Improvements in mood will help to support memory integration later in treatment.
- When disorder-specific therapy succeeds in treating the agreed target, but not other problems, switch the focus to other problems only once there is substantial improvement in the primary disorder. Beware of oscillating the focus too frequently during a single course of therapy, as this is likely to dilute its effectiveness.
- Postponing therapeutic tasks is not the same as avoiding them. It is better to form a treatment plan, with current and future tasks clearly differentiated, rather than work with whatever is currently salient.
- Even if your client does not have PTSD, be alert to the possibility of *intrusive* memories playing a pivotal role in post-traumatic depression, functioning as triggers to rumination as the individual seeks to assimilate them into autobiographical memory and self-identity.
- Post-traumatic depression is often maintained by unhelpful self-representations, rumination and partial memories of the trauma, but in some cases the *broader context* of the trauma, or its aftermath, is the trigger to a downward spiral of mood.
- Where there is evidence of marked identity-disruption in response to trauma, seek to formulate which helpful self-representations have been deactivated or disrupted, and which unhelpful representations have begun to form or have been reactivated.
- In cases of repeated or developmental trauma, dormant self-representations can be reactivated by current stress. These are likely to be non-verbal, highly somatic self-states, rather than flashbacks or event-based memories. Although they can be very distressing when they are activated, it is the fact they are *compartmentalized* that leaves the individual vulnerable to depression.
- The therapeutic aim in post-traumatic depression is *integration*: concrete reflection rather than rumination; attending to affect and body states; emotionally processing trauma memories; restoring helpful self-representations. In the case of developmental trauma, it is better to integrate unhelpful self-representations rather than suppress them back into a dormant state.

13

Integrated Approach:
Reflection and Synthesis

This chapter is a brief reflection and synthesis of the whole book, based on the aims set out in Chapter 1.

The Heterogeneity of Major Depression

One of the biggest challenges in treating major depression, and developing new treatments, is its heterogeneity. The case studies across the chapters have demonstrated how much variability there is, and some of the different ways in which treatment can be adjusted, based on individual need. Each chapter has focused on a specific issue, challenge or complexity factor. In clinical practice, clients present with *unique combinations* of these factors, and it is a challenge for therapists to maintain good fidelity to treatment components, while also being responsive to individual need.

This book is not a set of procedures that should be followed for all clients; on the contrary, it is *practitioner guidance* to support therapists to ask helpful questions, collaborate whole-heartedly with their clients, and make informed decisions about the treatment components and parameters that are indicated for each individual case. In following the guidance, you will need to draw on material from more than one chapter for any individual client. For example, the treatment of a client with highly recurrent depression, comorbid anxiety and a history of childhood neglect will be informed by Chapters 5 and 6, for the core components; Chapter 8, to adapt to a highly recurrent presentation; Chapter 11, to address comorbidity; Chapter 12, to consider potentially traumatic aspects of early experiences; and Chapter 4, to plan booster sessions and minimize the risk of relapse. This can be very satisfying work, particularly when it is done collaboratively with the client: but it is unlikely to be *easy* work; nor will it be obvious at the outset what each individual needs. Clients are in difficulties, sometimes complicated ones, and therapists need to enter into those difficulties, not to become depressed by them, but to understand what is maintaining them and find a path towards improvement.

This book is primarily for clients for whom standardized approaches have not been effective, or not had a lasting effect. In that situation, we have argued there is a need to adjust treatment on a case-by-case basis, *not* to lose fidelity and drift from the evidence base; rather, to apply the evidence base in a more *idiographic* way, more tailored to individual need. Hence our explicitness about the various treatment components; why they are the way they are, and when and how to apply them in practice. To individualize therapy in an evidence-based way, we believe there are (at least) twenty questions therapists need to be able to answer about their depressed clients, and we have listed them in Table 13.1. These cover the key domains of the *current depressive episode, early experiences, depression history, treatment history* and *potential complexity factors*. Therapists need to know the answers to these questions, in order that they can identify depression sub-types and, as far as possible, anticipate the particular challenges or complications that may occur during treatment.

Table 13.1 is not a structured interview in which therapists have to ask these exact questions; rather we are proposing that therapists find out the answers within the first two or three sessions with a new client, in order to tailor the treatment accordingly. Therapists who cannot answer these questions will, at best, be delivering a partial form of evidence-based practice. They may be adhering to an empirically supported protocol for depression, but the evidence base is much richer than that. One of the aims of the integrated approach is to *increase* evidence-based practice, by maximizing the connection between the phenomenology of each individual case and the specificity of the treatment parameters, components and processes most likely to be effective for them.

The answers to these questions will help to shape the *treatment parameters*, such as:

a. the treatment rationale
b. the balance of support and change
c. frequency of sessions
d. the therapeutic dose
e. initial goals and tasks
f. measures
g. treatment components (core/optional)
h. the length of treatment
i. disorder-specific, trans-diagnostic or bespoke approach
j. the need for care co-ordination

The art and science of CBT for depression is learning the relationships between contextual factors, client factors and the treatment parameters that are most likely to be beneficial for the case in question.

Table 13.1   Twenty questions therapists need to be able answer about their depressed clients

Domain	Question
Current depressive episode	1. Does the client meet criteria for major depression?
	2. How severe are their symptoms?
	3. Are the symptoms causing functional impairments (e.g. socially, work)?
	4. Is major life stress associated with the depressive episode?
	5. How long has the current episode lasted?
	6. Is the client currently receiving treatments for depression (psychological, medical, social), and if yes, what effect are they having?
	7. What is the client's current risk of self-harm or suicide?
Early experiences	8. Did the client experience trauma, abuse or neglect as a child?
	9. Did the client experience their first onset of major depression during adolescence (<18 years)?
Depression and treatment history	10. How many past major episodes has the client experienced?
	11. Does the client have a history of self-harm or suicide attempts?
	12. Has the client experienced trauma, abuse or neglect as an adult?
	13. Has the client experienced periods of wellness in their life when they were not depressed?
	14. Has the client received treatments for depression in the past (psychological, medical, social), and if yes, what effect did they have?
Potential complexity factors	15. Are there co-occurring biological or medical factors?
	16. Are there co-occurring psychological factors, including comorbidities?
	17. Are there co-occurring social factors?
	18. Are there factors that could impede forming a personal bond with a therapist?
	19. Are there factors that could impede engaging in therapeutic tasks?
	20. Is there anything unusual or atypical in the way the client's depression is maintained?

Contextual factors

Across the chapters, we have also observed heterogeneity in the contextual factors associated with different cases. There is an understandable temptation to simplify depression and try to reduce it to one or two key constructs, for example, attachment or loss. In our view, depression is bigger and messier than that. Our reflection on the various cases in this book suggests there are approximately nine types of inter-related contextual factors that can impact on an individual; to confer a vulnerability to depression, to precipitate a depressive episode, and/or to contribute to its mainte-nance: attachment problems (child or adult); loss, separation and adjustment; anxi-ety; trauma; neglect; abuse; oppression; major life events; punishing or unrewarding living circumstances.

In Table 13.2, we have cross-tabulated these factors with the individual cases in the book and what emerges is their *heterogeneity*. Most clients are affected, in some way, by more than one of these factors, and a number are affected by several. Each factor is present in some or most of the cases, but not all. Consequently, these types of factors tend to be moderately correlated with depression at a group level, but not necessarily present in all cases.

The main guidance is to stay open-minded about these various contextual influ-ences, rather than make narrow attributions about the causes of depression in particu-lar cases. To treat depression effectively, therapists need to be responsive to a broad range of phenomena: Table 13.2 can be a helpful framework for reflecting on individual cases, particularly when they are difficult to treat and/or complex.

The Heterogeneity of CBT

As we outlined in Chapter 1, CBT therapies for depression can have a range of benefi-cial effects, and these vary partly as a function of the client, and partly as a function of the type of CBT they receive. They include: reality orientation, activation, prob-lem solving, engagement, acceptance, self-compassion, mindfulness, mental freedom. Different types of CBT tend to emphasize certain effects over others, for example, Beck's CBT emphasizes realistic and functional thinking; BA emphasizes the activation of rewarding behaviours, and so on. What seems most likely, though as yet unproven, is that these therapies provoke the biggest changes in the processes they *directly* target. However, as in Figure 1.3, we believe each type of CBT can, in principle, *indirectly* provoke changes across the spectrum, even those that are not their primary concern. For example, Rumination-Focused CBT (RFCBT) could have a mindful effect, through increasing attention onto concrete experiences; Compassion Focused Therapy (CFT)

Table 13.2 Contextual factors associated with cases of major depression

	Attachment problems	Loss/ Separation/ Adjustment	Anxiety	Trauma	Neglect	Abuse	Oppression	Major life events	Punishing/ Unrewarding circumstances
Angela	X	X	X		X	X	X		X
Bob		X	X				X	X	
Chloe	X		X	X			X	X	
Daniel	X	X	X		X	X	X		X
Evelyn	X				X				
Frank	X	X	X						X
Gemma	X	X			X	X	X		
Jeff			X	X			X	X	
Izzy			X	X					
Kyle	X		X	X	X		X		
Mike			X	X	X	X	X	X	X

could have a reality-orienting effect, because clients develop more functional beliefs about the developmental causes of their problems; BA could have a self-compassionate effect, because scheduling enjoyable activities could be experienced as an act of kindness to oneself, and so on.

If this is true – and it is an 'if' – one way forward is to research and develop *prescriptive factors*, that is, pre-treatment client characteristics that could be measured and used to allocate clients to a specific type of CBT, or perhaps to a different therapeutic modality. Matching client need to therapy type could lead to much greater effectiveness. At this point in time, the field does not know a great deal about *treatment specificity*, in other words, the unique effects of particular CBT therapies, as opposed to general effects across models of CBT. With some exceptions, the field also does not know a great deal about the particular client groups that are most likely to benefit from specific approaches. There are, of course, notable exceptions that we have already mentioned; for example, a behavioural focus with severe depression, and a full MBCT protocol with clients who have suffered childhood trauma. But the general principle still holds: we are a long way from knowing what is most likely to work for whom.

Of course, a prescriptive approach would have cost implications for training and supervision, assuming that CBT therapists would need to train in each model. Alternatively, if such an approach was adopted at a service-wide level, then the need for a range of therapies to be available could be supported by strategic management of the skill mix across the workforce. If the prescription hypothesis were to be shown to hold true, this would suggest that short-term additional training costs would be more than balanced by long-term efficiency gains. Prescription is also underpinned by the tacit assumption that specific effects are bigger than common effects across CBT therapies. The idea behind prescription assumes an advantage for one approach over another, under certain conditions, and if shared variance is large, and unique variance is small, the bonus effect in prescribing might be less than we would like it to be.

Integrated approach

The prescription hypothesis would allocate clients to an established therapy as their first treatment. The integrated approach is intended for non-responders to those therapies, and it is seeking an alternative way of maximizing effectiveness. Rather than clients receiving a particular type of CBT, the emphasis is on finding out the particular ways in which depression is maintained at the individual case level. The model specifies a range of different interactions within self-regulatory processes, and these interactions determine which treatment components are delivered. As a general rule, all depressed clients need help with *approach motivation*, *behavioural engagement* and *reflective processing*; difficult-to-treat and complex cases are additionally likely to need help with *memory integration*, *self-organization* and *goal-organization*.

We believe that 'unsticking the grid-lock' of self-dysregulation can have a number of emergent therapeutic effects, such as becoming more engaged, accepting, mindful, self-compassionate and integrated. Using the integrated approach, there is no *prior* commitment to one of these types over any other. Therapists do not need to ask: 'is my client more likely to respond to this type of CBT or that type'; they need to ask: 'what is maintaining this particular client's depression?'.

From discussions with our clients, the main emergent effects are as follows though, of course, any particular case will experience these to different degrees and in different ways:

- *Engaged*. Clients become more absorbed in their actions and connect with other people in a more direct and assertive way. They are more centred in their experiences and less in abstract ideas.
- *Accepting*. Clients spend less time wishing for a better past, or trying to over-control their future. Instead, they are more focused on satisfying needs and paying attention to deeper desires, in the present moment.
- *Mindful*. Clients are more aware of internal and external experiences, and pay attention in a flexible way, sometimes internally, sometimes externally. They have a capacity to decentre when they need it.
- *Self-compassionate*. Clients are more aware of the need to have a good-enough relationship with their self; they are more likely than before to act out of kindness to their self.
- *Integrated*. Clients are more aware of different aspects of their self-identity, of what defines them and what is 'core' in terms of their priorities, needs and desires.

Next Steps

Is the integrated approach complete? No! It has taken a lot of development to get this far, but there are still a lot of hypotheses to be tested and clinical processes to be developed. Psychotherapy integration will have a long arc. In our view, depression is too heterogeneous and prone to complexity for there to be new therapies that will be suddenly be more effective than what is already established. Instead, there are opportunities for marginal gains, pooling learning, and inspiring more therapists to roll up their sleeves and grapple with how best to respond to the individual needs of their clients. At this point in the field's development, we believe the strategy to integrate and organize what is already known is a good way of taking a significant step forward.

The cases in this book all had good clinical outcomes. As we mentioned in Chapter 1, they were not a random sample of clients from our caseloads. They all received a full course of treatment and were willing to be included in the book so, of course, clients fitting those criteria are likely to have better than average outcomes. However, we did not select the most successful cases; the criterion was who could best illustrate a particular issue, not who had the best outcome. The main purpose of this book is practitioner guidance; it is not reporting a controlled test of the treatment's efficacy. However, we believe – as practice-based evidence – the cases demonstrate that this approach can work, and does work with difficult-to-treat and complex cases. Of course, there is a lot more empirical work to do to test the various proposals we have outlined. With that in mind, we will finish with two proposals that we believe would advance evidence-based practice and practice-based evidence in the field.

1 Treatment research needs to reduce heterogeneity to make new discoveries

There has been a lot of diversification in the field of CBT for depression, but the gains in terms of efficacy and increased potency have been quite modest. One of the reasons is that large-scale RCTs test and report average effects of treatments applied to heterogeneous clinical groups, with a broad range of contextual influences. When one considers the interaction of multiple contextual factors, multiple client factors and multiple treatment components, perhaps we should not be too surprised that it is difficult to make a significant advance in treatment potency, because the same standardized treatment has to have an efficacious effect in clients who differ so much from each other, and are affected by such a diverse range of external influences. We have represented this situation in Figure 13.1: the number of possible interactions is so large, and nonlinear, it will be difficult (a) to deliver a treatment that operates effectively under all possible conditions, (b) to understand how the treatment works when it is effective.

The difficult science is establishing which treatment components, and their interactions, are effective with which client parameters, and their interactions, varying as a function of a broad range of contextual factors, and their interactions. In one sense, this book has been written to help therapists deal with this situation on a case-by-case basis, and the strategy has been to organize general knowledge (*nomothetic*) and apply it sensitively to the needs of individual cases (*idiographic*). This is one possibility for treatment research going forward: rather than reporting average effects across large heterogeneous groups, treat successive single cases by adjusting therapy parameters in the way that is indicated for that individual, then aggregate the effect size across multiple cases.

Another possibility is constraining the heterogeneity of client factors and contextual factors, to try to optimize therapy under more defined conditions, for example, only treat certain sub-types or comorbidities: CBT for depression with comorbid PTSD, or CBT for depression in survivors of childhood neglect, and so on. If contextual, and

Contextual factors	X	Client factors	X	Treatment components
Attachment problems (child or adult)		Severity		Risk assessment
		Risk		Clinical assessment
Loss, separation and adjustment		Recurrence		Alliance building
Anxiety		Chronicity		Treatment rationale
Trauma		Age of first-onset		Approach motivation
Neglect		Childhood adversity		Behavioural engagement
Abuse		Comorbidity		Reflective processing
Oppression		Biological factors		Memory integration
Major life events		Social factors		Self-organization
Unrewarding living circumstances		Treatment history		Goal organization
				Staying well

Figure 13.1   The heterogeneity problem in depression treatment research

client factors are both allowed to vary freely, heterogeneity will be so great we will be consigned to average effects with a natural ceiling on progress; treatments will be potent for certain context–client interactions, and inert for others – they will cancel each other out to reproduce treatments with similar average effects to past treatments. In the next phase of treatment research, contexts and clients need to be more constrained and homogenous, and we need greater specificity in the treatment components that are applied under different conditions, for example, finding out if different patterns of self-regulation correspond to different depressive sub-types.

2 Prioritize clients at highest risk of lifetime difficulties with depression

As we were writing this book, one of the most common pieces of feedback was the apparent 'luxury' of having clients registered with our service for several months, and sometimes years. It might also appear luxurious, or perhaps inefficient, to be providing such large numbers of therapy sessions: the majority of cases in the book received over forty.

We empathize fully with readers based in services with more restrictive parameters; that will make it difficult to implement some of the guidance.

Nevertheless, when one considers that depression is now the leading source of disability worldwide, there are serious health-economic questions about the cost–benefit ratio of providing high-intensity therapies for clients carrying the greatest risk of lifetime difficulties. As we outlined in Chapter 7, a fully strategic health service would identify clients at high risk as early as possible in the lifespan, or as early as possible in their progression to high-risk status.

In the case of major depression, many of the high-risk people are adolescents aged 13–18, whose depression is not self-correcting and not responding to evidence-based treatment. They are also people who have experienced childhood trauma, abuse and neglect. They are also people who have experienced a second or third major episode, who are now at considerably greater risk of having more. It is our belief that investing in high-intensity treatments earlier in the progression of the disorder would produce both a large health benefit and a long-term saving in resources. We urge healthcare commissioners and service managers to consider innovative models of care that will take a long-term and developmental view of the need to provide high-intensity therapies for people at greatest risk of recurrent, chronic and complex depression.

References

Bandura, A. (1977). Self-efficacy: Toward a unifying theory of behavioral change. *Psychological Review, 84*(2), 191–215.

Barber, J.P., & DeRubeis, R.J. (1989). On second thought: Where the action is in cognitive therapy for depression. *Cognitive Therapy and Research, 13*(5), 441–457.

Barlow, D.H., Farchione, T.J., Sauer-Zavala, S., Ellard, K.K., Murray Latin, H., Bentley, K.H., Bullis, J.R., Boettcher, H.T., & Cassiello-Robbins, C. (2017). *Unified Protocol for Transdiagnostic Treatment of Emotional Disorders: Therapist Guide* (2nd ed.). Oxford: Oxford University Press.

Barnhofer, T., Brennan, K., Crane, C., Duggan, D., & Williams, J.M.G. (2014). A comparison of vulnerability factors in patients with persistent and remitting lifetime symptom course of depression. *Journal of Affective Disorders*, Jan, 155–161.

Barton, S., Armstrong, P., Freeston, M., & Twaddle, V. (2008). Early intervention for adults at high risk of recurrent/chronic depression: Cognitive model and clinical case series. *Behavioural and Cognitive Psychotherapy, 36*(03), 263–282.

Beck, A.T. (1972). *Depression: Causes and treatment.* Philadelphia, PA: University of Pennsylvania Press.

Beck, A.T. (1976). *Cognitive therapy and the emotional disorders.* Madison, CT: International Universities Press, Inc. [New York: Penguin Books, 1979].

Beck, A.T., Rush, A.J., Shaw, B.F., & Emery, G. (1979). *Cognitive therapy of depression: A treatment manual.* New York: Guilford Press.

Beck, A.T., Steer, R.A., & Brown, G.K. (1996). *Manual for the Beck Depression Inventory–II.* San Antonio, TX: Psychological Corporation.

Beck, A.T., Steer, R.A., & Garbin, M.G. (1988). Psychometric properties of the Beck Depression Inventory: Twenty-five years of evaluation. *Clinical Psychology Review, 8*(1), 77–100.

Beck, A.T., Ward, C.H., Mendelson, M., Mock, J., & Erbaugh, J. (1961). An inventory for measuring depression. *Archives of General Psychiatry, 4*, 561–571.

Beck, J.S. (2011). *Cognitive behavior therapy: Basics and beyond* (2nd ed.). New York: Guilford Press.

Beevers, C.G., Wenzlaff, R.M., Hayes, A.M., & Scott, W.D. (1999). Depression and the ironic effects of thought suppression: Therapeutic strategies for improving mental control. *Clinical Psychology: Science and Practice*, 6, 133–148.

Bondolfi, G., Jermann, F., Van der Linden, M., Gex-Fabry, M., Bizzini, L., Weber Rouget, B., Myers-Arrazola, L., Gonzalez, C., Segal, Z., Aubry, J-M., & Bertschy, G. (2010). Depression relapse prophylaxis with Mindfulness-Based Cognitive Therapy: Replication and extension in the Swiss health care system. *Journal of Affective Disorders*, 122(3), 224–231.

Brewin, C. (2006). Understanding cognitive behaviour therapy: A retrieval competition account. *Behaviour, Research and Therapy*, 44(6), 765–784.

Brewin, C.R., Reynolds, M., & Tata, P. (1999). Autobiographical memory processes and the course of depression. *Journal of Abnormal Psychology*, 108(3), 511.

Carver, C.S., & Scheier, M.F. (1999). *On the self-regulation of behaviour*. Cambridge: CUP.

Clark, D.A. (2009). Cognitive behavioral therapy for anxiety and depression: Possibilities and limitations of a transdiagnostic perspective. *Cognitive Behaviour Therapy*, 38(supp1), 29–34.

Clark, D.A., Beck, A.T., & Alford, B. (1999). *Scientific foundations of cognitive theory and therapy of depression*. New York: Wiley.

Clark, D.M. (2011). Implementing NICE guidelines for the psychological treatment of depression and anxiety disorders: The IAPT experience. *International Review of Psychiatry*, 23(4), 318–327.

Coffman, S., Martell, C.R., Dimidjian, S., Gallop, R., & Hollon, S.D. (2007). Extreme non-response in cognitive therapy: Can behavioural activation succeed where cognitive therapy fails? *Journal of Consulting and Clinical Psychology*, 75(4), 531–541.

Conway, M.A. (2005). Memory and the self. *Journal of Memory and Language*, 53, 594–628.

Conway, M.A., & Pleydell-Pearce, C.W. (2000). The construction of autobiographical memories in the self-memory system. *Psychological Review*, 107(2), 261–288.

Cooper, A.A., & Conklin, L.R. (2015). Dropout from individual psychotherapy for major depression: A meta-analysis of randomized clinical trials. *Clinical Psychology Review*, 40, 57–65.

Coughlan, K., Tata, P., & MacLeod, A.K. (2016). Personal goals, well-being and deliberate self-harm. *Cognitive Therapy and Research*, 1–10.

Cristea, I.A., Huibers, M.J.H., David, D., Hollon, S.D., Andersson, G., & Cuijpers, P. (2015). The effects of cognitive behavior therapy for adult depression on dysfunctional thinking: A meta-analysis. *Clinical Psychology Review*, 42, 62–71.

Crocetti, E. (2017). Identity formation in adolescence: The dynamic of forming and consolidating identity commitments. *Child Development Perspectives*, 11, 145–150.

Cuijpers, P., Hollon, S.D., van Straten, A., Bockting, C., Berking, M., & Andersson, G. (2013). Does cognitive behaviour therapy have an enduring effect that is superior to keeping patients on continuation pharmacotherapy? A meta-analysis. *BMJ Open*. 3:e002542.

Cuijpers, P., Karyotaki, E., Weitz, E., Andersson, G., Hollon, S.D., & Straten, A. (2014). The effects of psychotherapies for major depression in adults on remission, recovery and improvement: A meta-analysis. *Journal of Affective Disorders, 159*, 118–26.

Cuijpers, P., van Straten, A-M., Schuurmans, J., van Oppen, P., Hollon, S.D., & Andersson, G. (2010). Psychotherapy for chronic major depression and dysthymia: A meta-analysis. *Clinical Psychology Review, 30*(1), 51–62.

Curry, J.F., & Wells, K.C. (2005). Striving for effectiveness in the treatment of adolescent depression: Cognitive behavior therapy for multisite community intervention. *Cognitive Behavioural Practice, 12*(2), 177–185.

DeRubeis, R.J., Cohen, Z.D., Forand, N.R., Fournier, J.C., Gelfand, L.A., & Lorenzo-Luaces, L. (2014). The Personalized Advantage Index: Translating research on prediction into individualized treatment recommendations. A demonstration. *PloS ONE, 9*(1).

DeRubeis, R.J., Hollon, S.D., Amsterdam, J.D., Shelton, R.C., Young, P.R., Salomon, R.M., et al. (2005). Cognitive therapy versus medications in the treatment of moderate to severe depression. *Archives of General Psychiatry, 62*, 409–416.

Dickson, J.M., & MacLeod, A.K. (2004). Approach and avoidance goals and plans: Their relationship to anxiety and depression. *Cognitive Therapy and Research, 28*: 415. https://doi.org/10.1023/B:COTR.0000031809.20488.ee.

Dickson, J.M., Moberly, N.J., & Kinderman, P. (2011). Depressed people are not less motivated by personal goals but are more pessimistic about attaining them. *Journal of Abnormal Psychology, 120*(4), 975–980.

Dickson, J.M., Moberly, N.J., O'Dea, C., & Field, M. (2016). Goal fluency, pessimism and disengagement in depression. *PLoS ONE 11*(11), e0166259.

Dimidjian, S., Hollon, S.D., Dobson, K.S., Schmaling, K.B., et al. (2006). Randomized trial of behavioural activation, cognitive therapy, and antidepressant medication in the acute treatment of adults with major depression. *Journal of Consulting and Clinical Psychology, 74*, 658–670.

Dobson, K., Hollon, S., Dimidjian, S., Schmaling, K., Kohlenberg, R., Gallop, R., Rizvi, S., Gollan, J., Dunner, D., & Jacobson, N. (2008). Randomised trial of behavioural activation, cognitive therapy, and anti-depressant medication in the prevention of relapse and recurrence in major depression. *Journal of Consulting and Clinical Psychology, 76*, 468–477.

Driessen, E., & Hollon, S.D. (2010). Cognitive behavioral therapy for mood disorders: efficacy, moderators and mediators. *Psychiatr. Clin. North Am., 33*(3), 537–555.

Dugas, M.J., Gagnon, F., Ladouceur, R., & Freeston, M.H. (1998). Generalized Anxiety Disorder: A preliminary test of a conceptual model. *Behaviour Research and Therapy, 36*(2), 215–226.

Dykman, B.M. (1998). Integrating cognitive and motivational factors in depression: Initial tests of a goal-orientation approach. *Journal of Personality and Social Psychology, 74*(1), 139–158.

Ehlers, A., & Clark, D.M. (2000). A cognitive model of Posttraumatic Stress Disorder. *Behaviour Research and Therapy, 38*, 319–345.

Ehlers, A., Clark, D.M., Hackmann, A., McManus, F., & Fennell, M. (2005). Cognitive therapy for PTSD: Development and evaluation. *Behaviour Research and Therapy, 43*, 413–431.

Ekers, D., Webster, L., Van Straten, A., Cuijpers, P., Richards, D., & Gilbody, S. (2014). Behavioural activation for depression: An update of meta-analysis of effectiveness and sub group analysis. *PLoS ONE, 9*(6), e100100.

Elkin, I., Shea, M.T., Watkins, J.T., et al. (1989). Treatment of Depression Collaborative Research Program: General effectiveness of treatments. *Archives of General Psychiatry, 46*(11), 971–982.

Ellard, K.K., Fairholme, C.P., Boisseau, C.L., Farchione, T.J., & Barlow, D.H. (2010). Unified protocol for the transdiagnostic treatment of emotional disorders: Protocol development and initial outcome data. *Cognitive and Behavioral Practice, 17*(1), 88–101, ISSN 1077–7229. https://doi.org/10.1016/j.cbpra.2009.06.002.

Ferster, C.B. (1973). A functional analysis of depression. *American Psychologist, 28*, 857–870.

Forand, N.R., & DeRubeis, R.J. (2014). Extreme response style and symptom return after depression treatment: The role of positive extreme responding. *Journal of Consulting and Clinical Psychology, 82*(3), 500–509.

Garcia-Toro, M., Rubio, J.M., Gili, M., Roca, M., et al. (2013). Persistence of chronic major depression: A national prospective study. *Journal of Affective Disorders, 151*(1), 306–312.

Garland, A. (2015). Cognitive behavioural case formulation for complex and recurrent depression. In N. Tarrier & J. Johnson (Eds.), *Case formulation in cognitive behaviour therapy: The treatment of challenging and complex cases* (pp. 119–142). Hove: Routledge.

Gilbert, P. (2000). Varieties of submissive behaviour: Their evolution and role in depression. In L. Sloman & P. Gilbert (Eds.), *Subordination and defeat: An evolutionary approach to mood disorders and their therapy* (pp. 3–46). New York: Lawrence Erlbaum Associates.

Gilbert, P. (2009). *Overcoming depression: A self-help guide using cognitive behavioral techniques* (3rd ed.). London: Constable and Robinson.

Gilbert, P., Baldwin, M.W., Irons, C., Baccus, J.R., & Palmer, M. (2006). Self-criticism and self-warmth: An imagery study exploring their relation to depression. *Journal of Cognitive Psychotherapy, 20*, 183–200.

Gilbert, P., & Procter, S. (2006). Compassionate mind training for people with high shame and self-criticism: Overview and pilot study of a group therapy approach. *Clinical Psychology & Psychotherapy, 13*, 353–379.

Girard, J.M., Cohn, J.F., Mahoor, M.H., Mavadati, S.M., Hammal, Z., & Rosenwald, D.P. (2014). Nonverbal social withdrawal in depression: Evidence from manual and automatic analyses. *Image and Vision Computing, 32*(10), 641–647.

Goddard, E., Wingrove, J., & Moran, P. (2015). The impact of comorbid personality difficulties on response to IAPT. *Behaviour Research and Therapy, 73*, 1–7.

Godfrin., K.A., & van Heeringen, C. (2010). The effects of mindfulness-based cognitive therapy on recurrence of depressive episodes, mental health and quality of life: A randomized controlled study. *Behaviour Research and Therapy, 48*, 738–746.

Goodyer, I.M., Dubicka, B., Wilkinson, P., Kelvin, R., & Roberts, C. (2008). A randomised controlled trial of cognitive behaviour therapy in adolescents with major depression treated by selective serotonin reuptake inhibitors: The ADAPT trial. *Health Technology Assessment, 12*(14), iii–iv, ix–60.

Goodyer, I.M., Reynolds, S., Barrett, B., Byford, S., et al. (2017). Cognitive behavioural therapy and short-term psychoanalytical psychotherapy versus a brief psychosocial intervention in adolescents with unipolar major depressive disorder (IMPACT): A multicentre, pragmatic, observer-blind, randomised controlled superiority trial. *The Lancet Psychiatry, 4*(2), 109–119.

Gortner, E.T., Gollan, J.K., Dobson, K.S., & Jacobson, N.S. (1998). Cognitive-behavioural treatment for depression: Relapse prevention. *Journal of Consulting and Clinical Psychology, 66*, 377–384.

Griffith, J.W., Claes, S., Hompes, T., Vrieze, E., Vermote, S., Debeer, E., & Hermans, D. (2016). Effects of childhood abuse on overgeneral autobiographical memory in current major depressive disorder. *Cognitive Therapy and Research, 40*(6), 774–782.

Hadley, S.A., & MacLeod, A.K. (2010). Conditional goal-setting, personal goals and hopelessness about the future. *Cognition and Emotion, 24*(7), 1191–1198.

Hamilton, M. (1960). A rating scale for depression. *Journal of Neurology, Neurosurgery & Psychiatry, 23*, 56–62.

Hamilton, M. (1967). Development of a rating scale for primary depressive illness. *British Journal of Social and Clinical Psychology, 6*, 278–229.

Handley, T.E., Kay-Lambkin, F.J., Baker, A.L., Lewin, T.J., Kelly, B.J., Inder, K.J., Attia, J.R., & Kavanagh, D.J. (2016). Investigation of a suicide ideation risk profile in people with co-occurring depression and substance use disorder. *Journal of Nervous & Mental Disease, 204*(11), 820–826.

Hardy, G.E., Barkham, M., Shapiro, D.A., Stiles, W.B., Rees, A., & Reynolds, S. (1995). Impact of cluster C personality disorders on outcome of contrasting brief psychotherapies for depression. *Journal of Consulting and Clinical Psychology, 63*(6), 997–1004.

Hargus, E., Crane, C., Barnhofer, T., & Williams, J.M.G. (2010). Effects of mindfulness on meta-awareness and specificity of describing prodromal symptoms in suicidal depression. *Emotion, 10*(1), 34.

Harkness, K.L., Bruce, A.E., & Lumley, M.N. (2006). The role of childhood abuse and neglect in the sensitization to stressful life events in adolescent depression. *Journal of Abnormal Psychology, 115*(4), 730–741.

Hawton, K., Comabella, C.C., Haw, C., & Saunders, K. (2013). Risk factors for suicide in individuals with depression: A systematic review. *Journal of Affective Disorders, 147*(1), 17–28.

Hayes, A.M., Yasinski, C., Barnes, J.B., & Bockting, C. (2015). Network destabilization and transition in depression: New methods for studying the dynamics of therapeutic change. In E. Koster, C. Bockting & R. De Raedt (Eds.), *Psychological interventions for depression: A roadmap to stable remission*, special issue of Clinical Psychology Review, *41*, 27–39.

Hayes, S.C. (2004). Acceptance and Commitment Therapy and the new behavior therapies: Mindfulness, acceptance and relationship. In S.C. Hayes, V.M. Follette & M. Linehan (Eds.), *Mindfulness and acceptance: Expanding the cognitive behavioral tradition* (pp. 1–29). New York: Guilford.

Hirschfield, R.M.A. (2001). The comorbidity of major depression and anxiety disorders: Recognition and management in primary care. *Primary Care Companion. Journal of Clinical Psychiatry, 3*(6), 244–254.

Hollon, S.D. (2001). Behavioural activation treatment for depression: A commentary. *Clinical Psychology: Science and Practice, 8*, 271–274.

Hollon, S.D., Jarrett, R.B., Nierenberg, A.A., Thase, M.E., Trivedi, M., & Rush, A.J. (2005). Psychotherapy and medication in the treatment of adult and geriatric depression: Which monotherapy or combined treatment? *Journal of Clinical Psychiatry, 66*(4), 455–468.

Holtzel, L., Harter, M., Reese, C., & Kriston, L. (2011). Risk factors for chronic depression: A systematic review. *Journal of Affective Disorders, 129*(1–3), 1–13.

Hughes, C., Herron, S., & Younge, J. (2014). *Cognitive behavioural therapy for mild to moderate depression and anxiety: A guide to low-intensity interventions.* London: Open University Press.

Huibers, M.J.H., Cohen, Z.D., Lemmens, L.J.H.M., Arntz, A., Peeters, F.P.M.L., Cuijpers, P., & DeRubeis, R.J. (2015). Predicting optimal outcomes in cognitive therapy or interpersonal psychotherapy for depressed individuals using the Personalized Advantage Index approach. *PloS ONE, 10*(11).

Improving Access to Psychological Therapies (IAPT) Executive Summary (November 2016). *NHS Digital*, ISBN 978-1-78386-946-6.

Jacobson, N.S., Dobson, K.S., Truax, P.A., Addis, M.E., Koerner, K., Gollan, J.K., Gortner, E., & Prince, S.E. (1996). A component analysis of cognitive-behavioural treatment for depression. *Journal of Consulting and Clinical Psychology, 64*, 295–304.

James, I.A., & Barton, S.B. (2004). Changing core beliefs with the continuum technique. *Behavioural and Cognitive Psychotherapy, 32*, 431–442.

James, I.A., Reichelt, F.K., Freeston, M.H., & Barton, S.B. (2007). Schemas as memories: Implications for treatment. *International Journal of Cognitive Psychotherapy, 21*, 51–57.

Jarrett, R.B., & Thase, M.E. (2010). Comparative efficacy and durability of continuation phase cognitive therapy for preventing recurrent depression: Design of a double-blinded, fluoxetine- and pill placebo-controlled, randomized trial with 2-year follow-up. *Contemporary Clinical Trials, 31*(4), 355–377.

Jarrett, R.B., Basco, M.R., Risser, R., Ramanan, J., Marwill, M., Kraft, D., & Rush, A.J. (1998). Is there a role for continuation phase cognitive therapy for depressed outpatients? *Journal of Consulting and Clinical Psychology, 66,* 1036–1040.

Jarrett, R.B., Eaves, G.G., Granneman, B.D., & Rush, A.J. (1991). Clinical, cognitive, and demographic predictors of response to cognitive therapy for depression: A preliminary report. *Psychiatry Research, 37*(3), 245–260.

Jarrett, R.B., Kraft, D., Doyle, J., Foster, B.M., Eaves, G.G., & Silver, P.C. (2001). Preventing recurrent depression using cognitive therapy with and without a continuation phase: A randomized clinical trial. *Archives of General Psychiatry, 58*(4), 381–388.

Jonsson, U., Bohman, H., von Knorring, L., Olsson, G., Paaren, A., & von Knorring, A-L. (2011). Mental health outcome of long-term and episodic adolescent depression: 15-year follow-up of a community sample. *Journal of Affective Disorders, 130*(3), 395–404.

Joyce, P.R., McKenzie, J.M., Carter, J.D., Rae, A.M., Luty, S.E., Frampton, C.M., & Mulder, R.T. (2007). Temperament, character and personality disorders as predictors of response to interpersonal psychotherapy and cognitive-behavioral therapy for depression. *British Journal of Psychiatry, 190*(6), 503–508.

Kanter, J., Busch, A.M., & Rusch, L.C. (2009). *Behavioural activation: Distinctive features.* Hove: Routledge.

Kennerley, H., Kirk, J., & Westbrook, D. (2016). *An Introduction to Cognitive Behaviour Therapy: skills and applications* (3rd ed.). London: Sage.

Kessler, R.C., & Bromet, E.J. (2013). The epidemiology of depression across cultures. *Annual Review of Public Health, 34,* 119–138.

Kessler, R.C., Sampson, N.A., Berglund, P., … Wilcox, M.A. (2015). Anxious and non-anxious major depressive disorder in the World Health Organization World Mental Health Surveys. *Epidemiology and Psychiatric Sciences, 24*(3), 210–226.

Klein, J.B., Jacobs, R.H., & Reinecke, M.A. (2007). Cognitive-behavioral therapy for adolescent depression: A meta-analytic investigation of changes in effect-size estimates. *Journal of the American Academy of Child and Adolescent Psychiatry, 46*(11), 1403–1413.

Klimstra, T.A., Hale III, W.W., Raaijmakers, Q.A.W., Branje, S.J.T., & Meeus, W.H.J. (2010). Identity formation in adolescence: Change or stability? *Journal of Youth and Adolescence, 39*(2), 150–162.

Koppe, K., & Rothermund, K. (2017). Let it go: Depression facilitates disengagement from unattainable goals. *Journal of Behavior Therapy and Experimental Psychiatry, 54,* 278–284.

Korotana, L.M., Dobson, K.S., Pusch, D., & Josephson, T. (2016). A review of primary care interventions to improve health outcomes in adult survivors of adverse childhood experiences. *Clinical Psychology Review, 46,* 59–90.

Kroenke, K., & Spitzer, R.L. (2002). The PHQ-9: A new depression diagnostic and severity measure. *Psychiatric Annals, 32*(9), 509–515.

Kupfer, D.J. (1991). Long-term treatment of depression. *Journal of Clinical Psychiatry, 52*(Suppl), 28–34.

Kuyken, W., Byford, S., Taylor, R.S., Watkins, E., Holden, E., White, K., et al. (2008). Mindfulness-Based Cognitive Therapy to prevent relapse in recurrent depression. *Journal of Consulting and Clinical Psychology, 76*, 966–978.

Lee, A., & Hankin, B.L. (2009). Insecure attachment, dysfunctional attitudes, and low self-esteem predicting prospective symptoms of depression and anxiety during adolescence. *Journal of Clinical Child & Adolescent Psychology, 38*(2), 219–231.

Lcjuez, C.W., Hopko, D.R., LePage, J.P., Hopko, S.D., & McNeil, D.W. (2001). A brief behavioural activation treatment for depression. *Cognitive and Behavioural Practice, 8*, 164–175.

Lewinsohn, P.M. (1974). A behavioural approach to depression. In R.M. Friedman & M.M. Katz (Eds.), *The psychology of depression: Contemporary theory and research* (pp. 157–185). New York: Wiley.

Lewinsohn, P.M., Allen, N.B., Seeley, J.R., & Gotlib, I.H. (1999). First onset versus recurrence of depression: Differential processes of psychosocial risk. *Journal of Abnormal Psychology, 108*, 483–489.

Lewinsohn, P.M., Joiner, T.E., Jr., & Rohde, P. (2001). Evaluation of cognitive diathesis-stress models in predicting major depressive disorder in adolescents. *Journal of Abnormal Psychology, 110*(2), 203–215.

Lewinsohn, P.M., Rohde, P., Seeley, J.R., Klein, D.N., & Gotlib, I.H. (2000). Natural course of adolescent major depressive disorder in a community sample: Predictors of recurrence in young adults. *American Journal of Psychiatry, 157*(10), 1584–1591.

Lorenzo-Luaces, L., Driessen, E., DeRubeis, R.J., Van, H.L., Keefe, J.R., Hendriksen, M., & Dekker, J. (2016). Moderation of the alliance-outcome association by prior depressive episodes: Differential effects in cognitive-behavioral therapy and short-term psychodynamic supportive psychotherapy. *Behavior Therapy, 48*(5), 581–595. doi: 10.1016/j.beth.2016.11.011.

Lorenzo-Luaces, L., German, R.E., & DeRubeis, R.J. (2015). It's complicated: The relation between cognitive change procedures, cognitive change, and symptom change in cognitive therapy for depression. *Clinical Psychology Review, 41*, 3–15.

Lyubormirsky, S., & Nolen-Hoeksema, S. (1995). Effects of self-focused rumination on negative thinking and interpersonal problem-solving. *Journal of Personality and Social Psychology, 69*, 176–190.

Ma, H.S., & Teasdale, J.D. (2004). Mindfulness-Based Cognitive Therapy for depression: Replication and exploration of differential relapse prevention effects. *Journal of Consulting and Clinical Psychology, 72*(1), 31–40.

Maier, S.F., & Seligman, M.E. (2016). Learned helplessness at fifty: Insights from neuro-science. *Psychological Review, 123*(4), 349.

Mansell, W., Harvey, A., Watkins, E & Shafran, R. (2009). Conceptual foundations of the transdiagnostic approach to CBT. *Journal of Cognitive Psychotherapy, 23*(1), 6–19.

March, J., Silva, S., Petrycki, S., et al. (2004). Fluoxetine, cognitive-behavioral therapy, and their combination for adolescents with depression: Treatment for Adolescents with Depression Study (TADS) randomized controlled trial. *JAMA, 292*(7), 807–820.

Martell, C.R., Addis, M.E., & Jacobson, N.S. (2001). *Depression in context: Strategies for guided action.* New York: W.W. Norton.

Martell, C.R., Dimidjian, S., & Herman-Dunn, R. (2010). *Behavioral activation for depression: A clinician's guide.* New York: Guilford Press.

Martin, D.J., Garske, J.P., & Davis, M.K. (2000). Relation of the therapeutic alliance with outcome and other variables: A meta-analytic review. *Journal of Consulting & Clinical Psychology, 68*, 438–450.

Maslow, A.H. (1943). A theory of human motivation. *Psychological Review, 50*(4), 370–396.

Maslow, A.H. (1954). *Motivation and personality.* New York: Harper and Row.

McCullough, J.P., Jr. (2003). Treatment for chronic depression: Cognitive behavioral analysis system of psychotherapy (CBASP). *Journal of Psychotherapy Integration, 13*(3–4), 241–263.

McFarlane, A.C., & Papay, P. (1992). Multiple diagnoses in Posttraumatic Stress Disorder in the victims of a natural disaster. *Journal of Nervous and Mental Disease, 180*(8), 498–504.

McGlinchey, J.B., & Dobson, K.S. (2003). Treatment integrity concerns in cognitive therapy for depression. *Journal of Cognitive Psychotherapy: An International Quarterly, 17*, 299–317.

Meyer, T.D., & Hautzinger, M. (2012). Cognitive behaviour therapy and supportive therapy for bipolar disorders: Relapse rates for treatment period and 2-year follow-up. *Psychological Medicine, 42*, 1429–1439.

Michael, T., Halligan, S.L., Clark, D.M. and Ehlers, A. (2007). Rumination in Posttraumatic Stress Disorder. *Depression and Anxiety, 24*, 307–317.

Mihailova, S., & Jobson, L. (2018). Association between intrusive negative auto-biographical memories and depression: A meta-analytic investigation. *Clinical Psychology and Psychotherapy*, 1–16.

Miranda, J., & Persons, J.B. (1988). Dysfunctional thoughts are mood-state dependent. *Journal of Abnormal Psychology, 97*, 76–79.

Moore, R.C. & Garland, A. (2003). *Cognitive therapy for chronic and persistent depression.* New York: Wiley.

National Collaborating Centre for Mental Health (2005). *Obsessive–compulsive disorder: Core interventions in the treatment of obsessive–compulsive disorder and body dysmorphic disorder* (Clinical guideline CG31). British Psychological Society & Royal College of Psychiatrists. www.nice.org.uk/CG031.

NICE (National Institute for Health and Care Excellence) (2009). *Depression in adults: Recognition and management.* Clinical guideline CG90. nice.org.uk/guidance/cg90.

NICE (National Institute for Health and Care Excellence) (2017). *Depression in adults: Treatment and management.* NICE guideline: draft for consultation, July 2017.

Nolen-Hoeksema, S. (1991). Responses to depression and their effects on the duration of depressive episodes. *Journal of Abnormal Psychology, 100,* 569–582.

Novšak, R., Mandelj, T.R., & Simonič, B. (2012). Therapeutic implications of religious-related emotional abuse. *Journal of Aggression, Maltreatment & Trauma, 21*(1), 31–44. DOI: 10.1080/10926771.2011.627914.

Ottenbreit, N.D., Dobson, K.S., & Quigley, L. (2014). An examination of avoidance in major depression in comparison to social anxiety disorder. *Behaviour Research and Therapy, 56,* 82–90.

Papworth, M., Marrinan, T., & Martin, B., with Keegan, D., & Chaddock, A. (2013). *Low intensity cognitive-behaviour therapy: A practitioner's guide.* London: Sage.

Pavlov, I.P. (1902). *The work of the digestive glands.* London: Griffin.

Piet, J., & Hougaard, E. (2011). The effect of mindfulness-based cognitive therapy for prevention of relapse in recurrent major depressive disorder: A systematic review and meta-analysis. *Clinical Psychology Review, 31,* 1032–1040.

Porter, E., Chambless, D.L., McCarthy, K.S., DeRubeis, R.J., Sharpless, B.A., Barrett, M.S., & Barber, J.P. (2017). Psychometric properties of the reconstructed Hamilton Depression and Anxiety Scales. *The Journal of Nervous and Mental Disease, 205*(8): 656–664. DOI: 10.1097/NMD.0000000000000666.

Post, R.M. (1992). Transduction of psychosocial stress into the neurobiology of recurrent affective disorder. *American Journal of Psychiatry, 149,* 999–1010.

Praharso, N.F., Tear, M.J., & Cruwys, T. (2017). Stressful life transitions and wellbeing: A comparison of the stress buffering hypothesis and the social identity model of identity change. *Psychiatry Research, 247,* 265–275.

Raes, F., Dewulf, D., Van Heeringen, C., & Williams, J.M.G. (2009). Mindfulness and reduced cognitive reactivity to sad mood: Evidence from a correlational study and a non-randomized waiting list controlled study. *Behaviour Research and Therapy, 47*(7), 623–627.

Reinecke, M.A., Ryan, N.E., & DuBois, D.L. (1998). Cognitive–behavioral therapy of depression and depressive symptoms during adolescence: A review and meta-analysis. *Journal of the American Academy of Child and Adolescent Psychiatry, 37,* 26–34.

Richards, D.A., Ekers, D., McMillan, D., Taylor, R.S., Byford, S., Warren, F.C., Barrett, B., Farrand, P.A., Gilbody, S., Kuyken, W., O'Mahen, H., Watkins, E.R., Wright, K.A., Hollon, S.D., Reed, N., Rhodes, S., Fletcher, E., & Finning, K. (2016). Cost and Outcome of BehaviouRal Activation versus Cognitive Behavioural Therapy for Depression (COBRA): A randomised, controlled, non-inferiority trial. *Lancet, 388,* 871–880.

Rimes, K.A., & Watkins, E. (2005). The effects of self-focused rumination on global negative self-judgements in depression. *Behaviour Research and Therapy, 43,* 1673–1681.

Riso, L.P., & Newman, C.F. (2003). Cognitive therapy for chronic depression. *Journal of Clinical Psychology, 59*(8), 817–831.

Rittel, H.W.J., & Webber, M.M. (1973). Dilemmas in a general theory of planning. *Policy Sciences, 4,* 155–169.

Rohde, P., Lewinsohn, P.M., & Seeley, J.R. (1990). Are people changed by the experience of having an episode of depression? A further test of the scar hypothesis. *Journal of Abnormal Psychology, 99,* 264–271.

Roth, A. and Pilling, S. (2007). *The competences required to deliver effective cognitive behavioural therapy for people with depression and with anxiety disorders.* London: Department of Health.

Segal, Z.V., Bieling, P., Young, T., MacQueen, G., Cooke, R., Martin, L., Bloch, R., & Levitan, R.D. (2010). Antidepressant monotherapy vs sequential pharmacotherapy and mindfulness-based cognitive therapy, or placebo, for relapse prophylaxis in recurrent depression. *Archives of General Psychiatry, 67*(12), 1256–1264.

Segal, Z.V., Kennedy, S., Gemar, M., Hood, K., Pedersen, R., & Buis, T. (2006). Cognitive reactivity to sad mood provocation and the prediction of depressive relapse. *Archives of General Psychiatry, 63,* 749–755.

Segal, Z.V., Williams, J.M.G., & Teasdale, J.D. (2012). *Mindfulness-Based Cognitive Therapy for depression* (2nd ed.). New York: Guilford Press.

Seligman, M.E.P. (1975). *Helplessness: on depression, development, and death.* San Francisco: W.H. Freeman.

Shahar, B., Britton, W.B., Sbarra, D.A., Figueredo, A.J., & Bootzin, R.R. (2010). Mechanisms of change in mindfulness-based cognitive therapy for depression: Preliminary evidence from a randomized controlled trial. *International Journal of Cognitive Therapy, 3*(4), 402–418.

Shea, M.T., Pilkonis, P.A., Beckham, E., Collins, J.F., Elkin, B., Sotsky, S.M., & Docherty, J.P. (1990). Personality disorders and treatment outcome in the NIMH Treatment of Depression Collaborative Research Program. *American Journal of Psychiatry, 147*(6), 711–718.

Sherdell, L., Waugh, C.E., & Gotlib, I.H. (2012). Anticipatory pleasure predicts motivation for reward in major depression. *Journal of Abnormal Psychology, 121*(1), 51–60.

Skinner, B.F. (1938). *The behavior of organisms.* New York: Appleton–Century–Crofts.

Sotksy, S.M., Glass, D.R., Shea, M.T., et al. (1991). Patient predictors of response to psychotherapy and pharmacotherapy: Findings in the NIMH Treatment of Depression Collaborative Research Program. *American Journal of Psychiatry, 148*(8), 997–1008.

Speckens, A.E.M., Ehlers, A., Hackmann, A., Ruths, F.A., & Clark, D.M. (2007). Intrusive memories and rumination in patients with post-traumatic stress disorder: A phenomenological comparison. *Memory, 15*(3), 249–257. DOI: 10.1080/0965821 0701256449.

Speckens, A.E.M., Hackmann, A., Ehlers, A. & Cuthbert, B. (2007). Intrusive images and memories of earlier adverse events in patients with obsessive compulsive disorder. *Journal of Behavior Therapy and Experimental Psychiatry, 38*(4), 411–422. ISSN 0005-7916, https://doi.org/10.1016/j.jbtep.2007.09.004.

Spitzer, R.L., Williams, J.B., Gibbon, M., & First, M.B. (1992). The structured clinical interview for DSM-III-R (SCID): I: History, rationale, and description. *Archives of General Psychiatry, 49*(8), 624–629.

Starr, S., & Moulds, M.L. (2006). The role of negative interpretations of intrusive memories in depression. *Journal of Affective Disorders, 93*, 125–132.

Tang, T.Z., & DeRubeis, R.J. (1999). Sudden gains and critical sessions in cognitive-behavioral therapy for depression. *Journal of Consulting and Clinical Psychology, 67*, 894–904.

Tang, T.Z., DeRubeis, R.J., Beberman, R., & Thu, P. (2005). Cognitive changes, critical sessions, and sudden gains in cognitive-behavioral therapy for depression. *Journal of Consulting and Clinical Psychology, 73*, 168–72.

Tarrier, N., & Johnson, J. (Eds.) (2015). *Case formulation in cognitive behaviour therapy: The treatment of challenging and complex cases* (2nd ed.). Hove: Routledge.

Teasdale, J.D. (1988). Cognitive vulnerability to persistent depression. *Journal of Cognition and Emotion, 2*, 247–274.

Teasdale, J.D. (1997). Assessing cognitive mediation of relapse prevention in recurrent mood disorders. *Clinical Psychology & Psychotherapy, 4*(3), 145–156.

Teasdale, J.D. (1999). Emotional processing, three modes of mind and the prevention of relapse in depression. *Behaviour Research and Therapy*, July.

Teasdale, J.D., & Barnard, P.J. (1993). *Affect, cognition and change: re-modelling depressive thought*. Hove: Lawrence Erlbaum Associates.

Teasdale, J.D., Segal, Z.V., and Williams, J.M.G. (1995). How does cognitive therapy prevent depressive relapse and why should attentional control (mindfulness) training help? *Behaviour Research and Therapy, 33*, 25–40.

Teasdale, J.D., Segal, Z.V., Williams, J.M., Ridgeway, V.A., Soulsby, J.M., & Lau, M.A. (2000). Prevention of relapse/recurrence in major depression by mindfulness-based cognitive therapy. *Journal of Consulting and Clinical Psychology, 68*, 615–623.

Teasdale, J.D., Scott, J., Moore, R.G., Hayhurst, H., Pope, M., & Paykel, E.S. (2001). How does cognitive therapy prevent relapse in residual depression? Evidence from a controlled trial. *Journal of Consulting and Clinical Psychology, 69*, 347–357.

Thapar, A., Collinshaw, S., Pine, D.S., & Thapar, A.K. (2012). Depression in adolescence. *The Lancet, 379*(9820), 1056–1067.

Thomsen, D.K., Pillemer, D.B., & Ivcevic, Z. (2011). Life story chapters, specific memories and the reminiscence bump. *Memory, 19*, 267–279. DOI: 10.1080/09658211.2011.558513.

Thorndike, E.L. (1898). Animal intelligence: An experimental study of the associative processes in animals. *Psychological Monographs: General and Applied, 2*(4), i–109.

Treadway, M.T., Bossaller, N.A., Shelton, R.C., & Zald, D.H. (2012). Effort-based decision-making in major depressive disorder: A translational model of motivational anhedonia. *Journal of Abnormal Psychology, 121*(3), 553–558.

Treatment for Adolescents with Depression Study Team (2005). The Treatment for Adolescents with Depression Study (TADS): Demographic and clinical characteristics. *Journal of the American Academy of Child and Adolescent Psychiatry, 44*(1), 28–40.

Trew, J. (2011). Exploring the roles of approach and avoidance in depression: An integrative model. *Clinical Psychology Review, 31*(7), 1156–1168.

van der Kolk, B.A. (2005). Developmental trauma disorder: Toward a rational diagnosis for children with complex trauma histories. *Psychiatric Annals, 35*(5): 401–408. https://doi.org/10.3928/00485713-20050501-06.

Vittengl, J.R., Clark, L.A., Dunn, T.W., & Jarrett, R.B. (2007). Reducing relapse and recurrence in unipolar depression: A comparative meta-analysis of cognitive-behavioural therapy's effects. *Journal of Consulting and Clinical Psychology, 75*(3), 475–488.

Waller, G., & Turner, H. (2016). Therapist drift redux: Why well-meaning clinicians fail to deliver evidence-based therapy, and how to get back on track. *Behaviour Research and Therapy, 77*, 129–137.

Wampold, B.E. (2001). *The great psychotherapy debate: Models, methods and findings.* Mahwah, NJ: Lawrence Erlbaum.

Wampold, B.E., Minami, T., Baskin, T.W., & Callen Tierney, S. (2002). A meta-(re) analysis of the effects of cognitive therapy versus 'other therapies' for depression. *Journal of Affective Disorders, 68*(2–3), 159–165.

Watkins, E.R., & Moberly, N.J. (2009). Concreteness training reduces dysphoria: A pilot proof-of-principle study. *Behaviour, Research & Therapy, 47*(1), 48–53.

Watkins, E.R., Mullan, E., Wingrove, J., Rimes, K., Steiner, H., Bathurst, N., Eastman, R., & Scott, J. (2011). Rumination-focused cognitive–behavioural therapy for residual depression: phase II randomised controlled trial. *British Journal of Psychiatry, 199*, 317–322.

Watkins, E., Scott, J., Wingrove, J., Rimes, K., Bathurst, N., Steiner, H., Kennell-Webb, S., Moulds, M., & Malliaris, Y. (2007). Rumination-focused cognitive behaviour therapy for residual depression: A case series. *Behaviour Research and Therapy, 45*(9), 2144–2154.

Watkins, E., & Teasdale, J.D. (2001). Rumination and overgeneral memory in depression: Effects of self-focus and analytic thinking. *Journal of Abnormal Psychology, 110*, 353–357.

Watson, D., Clark, L.A., & Tellegan, A. (1988). Development and validation of brief measures of positive and negative affect: The PANAS scales. *Journal of Personality and Social Psychology, 54*(6), 1063–1070.

Webb, C.A., DeRubeis, R.J., Dimidjian, S., Hollon, S.D., Amsterdam, J.D., & Shelton, R.C. (2012). Predictors of patient cognitive therapy skills and symptom change in two randomized clinical trials: The role of therapist adherence and the therapeutic alliance. *Journal of Consulting and Clinical Psychology, 80(3)*, 373–381.

Williams, J.M.G. (1996). Depression and the specificity of autobiographical memory. In D.C. Rubin (Ed.), *Remembering our past: Studies in autobiographical memory* (pp. 244–270). Cambridge: CUP.

Williams, J.M.G., Crane, C., Barnhofer, T., Brennan, K., et al. (2014). Mindfulness-Based Cognitive Therapy for preventing relapse in recurrent depression: A randomized dismantling trial. *Journal of Consulting and Clinical Psychology, 82*(2), 275–286.

Williamson, D.E., Birmaher, B., Frank, E., Anderson, B.P., Matty, M.K., & Kupfer, D.J. (1998). Nature of life events and difficulties in depressed adolescents. *Journal of the American Academy of Child & Adolescent Psychiatry, 37*(10), 1049–1057.

World Health Organization (1992). *The ICD-10 Classification of Mental and Behavioural Disorders: Clinical descriptions and diagnostic guidelines.* Geneva: World Health Organization.

World Health Organization (2017). Depression and other common mental disorders: Global health estimates. WHO/MSD/MER/2017.2.

Yang, X., Hang, J., Zhu, C., Wang, Y., Cheung, E.F.C., Chan, R.C.K., & Xie, G. (2014). Motivational deficits in effort-based decision making in individuals with subsyndromal depression, first-episode and remitted depression patients. *Psychiatry Research, 220*(3), 874–82. doi: 10.1016/j.psychres.2014.08.056.

Zettle, R.D. (2007). *ACT for depression: A clinician's guide to using acceptance and commitment therapy in treating depression.* Oakland, CA: New Harbinger Publications.

Zisook, S., Lesser, I., Stewart, J.W., Wisniewski, S.R., Balasubramani, G.K., Fava, M., Gilmer, W.S., et al. (2007). Effect of age at onset on the course of major depressive disorder. *American Journal of Psychiatry, 164*(10), 1539–1546.

Index

Note: page numbers in italics refer to terms in figures and those in bold to terms in tables.